THE FIRST ENGLIS

THE FIRST ENGLISH EMPIRE

POWER AND IDENTITIES IN THE BRITISH ISLES 1093–1343

R. R. DAVIES

The Ford Lectures
Delivered in the University of Oxford
in Hilary Term 1998

OXFORD
UNIVERSITY PRESS

OXFORD
UNIVERSITY PRESS

Great Clarendon Street, Oxford OX2 6DP

Oxford University Press is a department of the University of Oxford.
It furthers the University's objective of excellence in research, scholarship,
and education by publishing worldwide in

Oxford New York

Athens Auckland Bangkok Bogotá Buenos Aires Cape Town
Chennai Dar es Salaam Delhi Florence Hong Kong Istanbul Karachi
Kolkata Kuala Lumpur Madrid Melbourne Mexico City Mumbai Nairobi
Paris São Paulo Shanghai Singapore Taipei Tokyo Toronto Warsaw

with associated companies in Berlin Ibadan

Published in the United States
By Oxford University Press Inc., New York

First published 2000
First published in paperback 2002

British Library Cataloguing in Publication Data

Data available

Library of Congress Cataloging in Publication Data

Davies, R. R.
The First English Empire: Power and Identities in the British Isles 1093–1343 / R. R. Davies.
p. cm. — (The Ford lectures ; 1998)
Includes bibliographical references and index.
1. Great Britain—History—Medieval period, 1066–1485. 2. National characteristics,
English—History—To 1500. 3. Great Britain—History, Military—1066–1485. 4.
Imperialism—History—To 1500. I. Title. II. Series.
DA175.D335 2000 942–dc21 00–037500

ISBN 0–19–820849–9 (hbk)
ISBN 0–19–925724–8 (pbk)

1 3 5 7 9 10 8 6 4 2

Typeset by Graphicraft Limited, Hong Kong
Printed in Great Britain
on acid-free paper by
T. J. International Ltd,
Padstow, Cornwall

Preface

When I was honoured by the invitation to deliver the Ford Lectures at the University of Oxford in Hilary term 1998, the electors kindly indicated that thereafter the series would bear the title of the James Ford Lectures in British, rather than English, history. (Not that the previous title had stood in the way of some very distinguished lectures on the histories of Ireland, Scotland, and Wales!) This change of title seemed an appropriate pretext for me to use the occasion to explore further some of the historiographical issues that have preoccupied me for some time—notably the challenges, opportunities, and insights to be gained from approaching the histories of Britain and Ireland in the Middle Ages comparatively and, in some degree, integrally. Such an approach, it should be emphasized, lays no claim to displace existing historiographical patterns, notably the deeply entrenched habit of writing the histories of the four countries of the British Isles within national frameworks; rather does it set out to complement and possibly enrich such traditions.

The chapters in this book represent substantially the lectures as they were delivered. The exception is Chapter 3, which was prepared as a lecture but not delivered, out of respect for the stamina and patience of my audience. In preparing the lectures for publication, I have occasionally augmented the argument and the detail. But the major departure is, of course, a substantial body of annotations. The footnotes are meant not only to try to validate and exemplify the arguments and claims of the text but, more important, to draw attention to the excellent corpus of primary and secondary literature which is now available for the comparative study of the medieval British Isles.

Public lectures impose severe constraints on the lecturer. Not only must he operate within the bounds of the allotted hour; but he must also sharpen the focus of his arguments and the vividness of his chosen examples if he is to retain the attention of his audience. He must also paint with a very broad brush and do so possibly in a cavalier fashion, especially if his canvas is as large and complex as the one I have selected. I acknowledge that these constraints have shaped, and possibly distorted, some of my arguments. The chapters of this book are thereby a series of exploratory and interpretative essays; they lay no claim to being a rounded and definitive history of the medieval British Isles (whatever that might be). I console myself with Proust's observation that what stand as 'Conclusions' for the author should serve as 'Incitements' to the reader. I should also perhaps add that, as should become obvious, I am as concerned (if indeed not more so) with perceptions, images, and attitudes as with what are sometimes called the realities of material power. *Mentalités* are not an adjunct to the study of past societies; they are central to it.

So much by way of apologia. Thanks can be briefer, but are more important. First, to the electors of the Ford Lectures for their invitation, however alarming such invitations appear when they first arrive. Second, to the body of scholars of the histories of England, Ireland, Scotland, and Wales, and of the British Isles generally, on whose work an interpretative book such as this is founded. My debt to them is by no means exhausted by the acknowledgements in the footnotes, since their conclusions have by now entered into my very way of thinking about the medieval past of the British Isles. Third, to two of those scholars—Robin Frame and Keith Stringer—who have gone the extra mile by reading the typescript of the book and providing that mixture of comment, criticism, and encouragement which every author needs. I owe both an immense debt for what is only the latest kindness over a prolonged period of academic companionship. Fourth, to Stephanie Jenkins who has borne my handwriting and an avalanche of revisions to her beautifully typed text with equanimity. Fifth, to Alastair Dunn and Brock Holden who greatly relieved me of some of the chores of bibliographical checking and preparing an index. Finally, to Ruth Parr and her colleagues at Oxford University Press; they, like their predecessors, are truly the author's friend.

Words and terms come laden with different connotations to different people. I should therefore make it clear that I use the term British Isles in the sense of the definition given by the *Oxford English Dictionary*: 'a geographical term for the islands comprising Great Britain and Ireland with all their offshore islands including the Isle of Man and the Channel Islands'.

R. R. D.

October 1999

Contents

Maps

Abbreviations

Anglo-Scottish Relations	*Anglo-Scottish Relations 1174–1328*, ed. E. L. G. Stones (Oxford, 1970)
Anderson, *Scottish Annals*	*Scottish Annals from English Chroniclers A.D. 500 to 1286*, ed. A. O. Anderson (1908)
Anderson, *Early Sources*	*Early Sources of Scottish History 500–1286*, ed. A. O. Anderson, 2 vols. (Edinburgh, 1922)
Berry, *Statutes*	*Statutes and Ordinances, and Acts of the Parliament of Ireland. King John to Henry V*, ed. H. F. Berry (Dublin, 1910)
Brut	*Brut y Tywysogyon or The Chronicle of the Princes. Peniarth MS 20 version*, ed. and trans. Thomas Jones (Cardiff, 1941–52)
Brut (RBH)	*Brut y Tywysogyon or The Chronicle of the Princes. Red Book of Hergest version*, ed. and trans. Thomas Jones (Cardiff, 1955)
CDI	*Calendar of Documents relating to Ireland 1171–1307*, ed. H. S. Sweetman, 5 vols. (1875–86)
Davies, *Conquest*	R. R. Davies, *Conquest, Coexistence and Change. Wales 1063–1415* (Oxford, 1987), reissued in paperback as *The Age of Conquest. Wales 1063–1415* (Oxford, 1991)
Davies, *Domination and Conquest*	R. R. Davies, *Domination and Conquest. The Experience of Ireland, Scotland and Wales 1100–1300* (Cambridge, 1990)
Duncan, *Scotland*	A. A. M. Duncan, *Scotland. The Making of the Kingdom* (Edinburgh, 1975)
Foedera	*Foedera, Conventiones, Litterae*, ed. T. Rymer, 4 vols. in 7 parts (1816–69)
Gerald of Wales, *Opera*	*Giraldi Cambrensis Opera*, ed. J. S. Brewer et al., 8 vols. (Rolls Series, 1861–91). The Description and Itinerary of Wales are quoted by book and chapter to ease cross-references to modern translations
Gerald of Wales, *Expugnatio Hibernica*	Giraldus Cambrensis, *Expugnatio Hibernica: The Conquest of Ireland*, ed. and trans. A. B. Scott and F. X. Martin (Dublin, 1978)

HRB	*The Historia Regum Britannie of Geoffrey of Monmouth, I. Bern, Bürgerbibliothek, MS 568*, ed. N. Wright (Cambridge, 1984)
Lloyd, *Wales*	J. E. Lloyd, *A History of Wales from the Earliest Times to the Edwardian Conquest*, 2 vols. (3rd edn., 1939)
NHI, II	*A New History of Ireland, vol. II. Medieval Ireland 1169–1534*, ed. A. Cosgrove (Oxford, 1981)
Otway-Ruthven, *Medieval Ireland*	A. J. Otway-Ruthven, *A History of Medieval Ireland* (1968)
PRO	The Public Record Office, London
R.R.S.	*Regesta Regum Scottorum*. 1. *The Acts of Malcolm IV*, ed. G. W. S. Barrow (Edinburgh, 1960); 2. *The Acts of William I*, ed. G. W. S. Barrow (Edinburgh, 1971)
R.S.	Rolls Series
Song	*The Song of Dermot and the Earl*, ed. G. H. Orpen (Dublin, 1892)
William of Malmesbury *GR*	William of Malmesbury, *Gesta Regum Anglorum. The History of the English Kings*, ed. and trans. R. A. B. Mynors, R. M. Thomson, and M. Winterbottom, 2 vols. (Oxford 1998–9). All references are to vol. 1.

INTRODUCTION

Two contemporary images of the history of medieval England may serve to introduce the central theme of this book. The first is to be found in the earliest manuscript of *Flores Historiarum* (*Flowers of Histories*), composed originally at the abbey of St Albans around 1250 and subsequently continued at Westminster. The *Flores* belongs to a common genre of medieval historical writing, an abbreviated universal chronicle from the Creation to the present. Though it starts with Adam and then grafts the story of the Trojans to its narrative line, its focus becomes increasingly and overwhelmingly English. The book was a remarkable success. In terms of the surviving manuscripts and of its use by subsequent compilers, 'no English chronicler,' concluded its Victorian editor, 'has been so popular'. But it is the nine framed illustrations which accompany the manuscript which call for particular attention here. Eight of them depict the coronation of the successive kings of England (with the exception of Harold) from Edward the Confessor to John; in the late thirteenth century an illustration of Edward I's coronation was added. The one earlier king who was deemed to merit this illustrative memorial was King Arthur. In other words, King Arthur had been assigned a cardinal, one might even say primary, place in the canonical version of English history.[1]

He occupies the same position in the second image, this time in stained glass rather than on parchment. The glass was originally designed for the library at All Souls College, Oxford, founded by Henry Chichele, archbishop of Canterbury, in 1438. It was subsequently relocated in the west and north windows of the antechapel. The gallery of saints and kings represented in the glass is an illuminating exercise in the historical memory of the Lancastrian dynasty. Eight of the kings so memorialized were of pre-Conquest vintage, their distinction lying apparently either in their sanctity (Aethelbert, Oswald, Edmund, Edward the Martyr, and Edward the Confessor) or in their contribution to the making of England (Alfred, Athelstan, Edgar, and, possibly,

[1] The manuscript (Manchester Chetham Library MS 6712) is described in N. J. Morgan, *Early Gothic Manuscripts. Vol. 2, 1250–85* (1985), 50–2, with illustrations nos. 6–8. The text is edited by H. R. Luard, *Flores Historiarum* (3 vols., Rolls Series, 1890): his comment is at p. ix. The view of Arthur in English historical circles in the early twelfth century, before Geoffrey of Monmouth's *Historia* (see below pp. 139–41) launched him on to the international stage, is well represented in William of Malmesbury's famous deflating comment: 'This Arthur is the hero of many wild tales among the Britons even in our own day.' William of Malmesbury, *GR*, 26–7.

Cnut). The later kings are, with the anomalous and puzzling exception of Edward II (probably an error for Edward III) the lineal representatives of the Lancastrian dynasty—John of Gaunt, king of Spain, Henry IV, Henry V, and Henry VI himself. The intervening Norman and Angevin kings were not deemed worthy of a place. That left room for two others. One was Constantine, allotted a space, one assumes, for his imperial and Christian status but doubtless reinforced by the myth, which Geoffrey of Monmouth had promoted, about his British—or, as the official guide has it, English—mother. The other was King Arthur. When the glass was finally reset in 1879 it was King Arthur who was given the honour of sharing the lower window over the north door with the twin founders of All Souls College—Archbishop Henry Chichele and King Henry VI. There is a nice irony that in a college established by the leaders of the English Church and State, the founders should nowadays share their glory with Arthur, a figure who—whatever else he was or was not—was most certainly not English.[2]

These two images raise several issues. One is the way in which the English at an early date—certainly by the end of the twelfth century—had appropriated the figure of King Arthur into what was in effect the authorized version of the history of England and of the English monarchy. This was in part the appropriation of the tales of a world-conquering hero, whose exploits were too wondrous to be reserved for the defeated Britons. But it was much more. It was part of the attempt to graft the early, pre-Saxon history of Britain on to the story of the advance and triumph of the English, and one which ultimately served and furthered an essentially English historical mythology.[3]

But the historical mythology so developed had, consciously or not, a further significance. It constructed an agenda for the past, and thereby in effect for the present, which effectively sidestepped, or indeed consigned to an oubliette, the question of the relationship between England and the rest of the British Isles. It was the making of England and the unbroken continuity of English history which commanded attention and required explanation. The rest of the British Isles was, literally and metaphorically, peripheral to this central concern. This essentially Anglocentric approach has been in effect the dominant historiographical tradition in England from at least the twelfth to the twentieth centuries.[4] Furthermore it has been, and remains, the determining paradigm in historical writing about the British Isles generally. So it is that it is not only

[2] F. E. Hutchinson, *Medieval Glass at All Souls College* (1949).

[3] See the outstanding study by R. William Leckie Jr., *The Passage of Dominion. Geoffrey of Monmouth and the Periodization of Insular History in the Twelfth Century* (Toronto, 1981).

[4] Rees Davies, *The Matter of Britain and the Matter of England. An Inaugural Lecture* (Oxford, 1996).

the history of England but likewise the histories of Ireland, Scotland, and Wales which have largely gone their separate ways, and plotted their development along their own individual trajectories. Why this should be so is in itself a matter of considerable significance, both for our understanding of the past and for our perception of the present, and indeed the future. After all, England was, and is, of Britain and the British Isles. Equally the histories of the rest of the British Isles have been substantially shaped by what is its dominant country and people, England and the English. Exploring the relationship between England and the British Isles, and equally exploring why that relationship did not develop, substantively or historiographically, into an integrative one, are the major themes of this book. The period with which it deals—the 250 years from 1093 to 1343—is, it will be argued, a critical one in the shaping of that relationship. But ultimately it is but one chapter in a long and unfinished story, the problem that is the British Isles.

I

THE HIGH KINGSHIP OF THE BRITISH ISLES

1066, so we have long been told, is the one date which every schoolboy knows. It depends, of course, where the boy goes to school. The annalist who was memorializing events in west Wales considered the Norman victory as worthy of no more than a long sentence; in Ireland the battle of Hastings was either unknown to, or overlooked by, the scribe (quite probably at Lismore) who was composing his annals, known to us as the Annals of Inisfallen. 1093 was altogether a different matter for both scribes; now *that* was indeed an *annus mirabilis*, or rather *annus horribilis*, for both scribes and for the same reasons. Two events dominated the year: the first, around May, was the death in an ambush or a battle of Rhys ap Tewdwr, king of Deheubarth or south Wales; the second was the slaughter in November of Malcolm 'Canmore', king of the Picts and the Scots, and his eldest son, Edward, followed soon thereafter by the death from grief of Malcolm's wife, Margaret, sister of Edgar Aetheling and a future saint.[1] In the litany of deaths and murders which constitute the staple diet of Welsh and Irish annalists, such a cull of the mighty was not of itself remarkable. But the events of 1093 were seen as different. First, the deaths were not caused by family strife or by inter-dynastic native rivalry; the perpetrators in both cases were identified as 'the French', or as we would term them the Normans. Secondly, contemporaries quickly recognized that both events were transforming the map of political power in Britain. It was no wonder that the Welsh translator of the west Wales annals should add the suitably apocalyptic gloss: 'And then fell the kingdom of the Britons.' It was a view shared by English observers at Worcester: 'from that day kings ceased to bear rule in Wales.'[2]

Chronologies are the temporal structures we erect to impose order on the worlds of memories we have constructed. By that token the annalists of

[1] *Brut*, *s.a.* 1066, 1093; *Annals of Inisfallen*, ed. and trans. S. MacAirt (Dublin, 1951), *s.a.* 1066, 1093.

[2] *Brut*, *s.a.* 1093; *Annals of Ulster*, ed. and trans. W. M. Hennessy and B. MacCarthy, 4 vols. (Dublin, 1887–1901), *s.a.* 1093; *The Chronicle of John of Worcester*, ed. R. R. Darlington and P. McGurk (Oxford, 1995–   ), III, 64–5.

western Britain and Ireland were surely right to focus on 1093 in particular and the 1090s in general as a period of seismic importance. It was then that the Norman advance and settlement which had so transformed the face of most of midland and southern England since Hastings spilt over uncontrollably and apparently irresistibly into outer Britain; it was then that the English domination of Britain and, eventually, Ireland resumed a momentum which was not to be exhausted until the early fourteenth century. The prospect of a high kingship of the British Isles was coming into view, albeit now under the initiative of an acquisitive Norman dynasty and its aristocracy.

Contemporaries were not in doubt; nor should historians be.[3] In north Wales the Anglo-Normans harried the Llŷn peninsula in the far west, established what is still an impressive foothold at Aberlleiniog in Anglesey, and installed a Norman nominee, Hervé, in the see of Bangor as early as 1092 (the first bishop in Wales known for certain to have received consecration in England). In mid and south-west Wales they poured into Ceredigion and Dyfed in the wake of the death of Rhys ap Tewdwr, established castles at Cardigan and Pembroke, and in the words of the native chronicler 'seized all the lands of the Britons'. In the south, William Rufus posted himself at Gloucester and supervised and rewarded his barons as they and their followers carved out lordships, manors, and settlements for themselves in the coastal plains and rich river valleys of the area.[4] It is the response of the Welsh themselves which registers most clearly that a political and indeed cultural meltdown was taking place. A series of revolts from 1094 to 1098 directed against what contemporaries called 'the unbearable tyranny, injustice, oppression and violence of the French' indicated an awareness that the world was being turned upside down. It seemed to be only a matter of time, a short time, before the whole of Wales was firmly in the Anglo-Norman orbit.[5]

Much the same was happening, albeit less bloodily, in north Britain and at much the same time. The later years of Rufus's reign were critical in the assertion of Anglo-Norman, and specifically royal, control over the unshired area of what we know as England north of the Ribble in the west and the Tees in the east. It was a process which accelerated at a galloping pace during Henry I's reign. Were we to look for chronological markers for it, we could do

[3] The basic narrative, with references, is established in Lloyd, *Wales*, II, chs. xi–xii. For a more recent account, Davies, *Conquest*, ch. 2.

[4] *Brut*, *s.a.* 1093; *Episcopal Acts and Cognate Documents relating to Welsh Dioceses 1060–1272* (Cardiff, 1948–53), I, 108–14. Cf. the comments of Frank Barlow, *William Rufus* (1983), 323–4: 'The king's involvement in "the conquest of Wales" cannot be doubted . . . Wales was his to give, even if not his to conquer.'

[5] *Brut*, *s.a.* 1094; *Brut (RBH)*, *s.a.* 1098. See also M. Lapidge, 'The Welsh-Latin Poetry of Sulien's Family', *Studia Celtica* 8–9 (1973–4), 68–106 for a remarkable late eleventh-century response to the coming of the Normans.

worse than take the forty or so years which separate Rufus's seizure of Cumbria and the establishment of a castle-borough and English settlers at Carlisle in 1092 from the creation of a diocese of Carlisle (filled by an Englishman, Aethelwulf) in 1133. It is a process which has too often been sidelined in the history books because it lies chronologically and geographically beyond Domesday Book and thereby beyond the ken of much English historiography.[6] During the same period the northern kingdom—or perhaps more accurately kingship—of the Scots was brought into a client status *vis-à-vis* England. 1093 was again a significant date in that process. It was in that year, according to John of Worcester, that William Rufus deliberately snubbed Malcolm III at Gloucester when the king of Scots resisted pressure to plead his case in the English royal court and to accept the judgement of the English barons. Malcolm's view was that he was obliged to answer the king of England only on the frontier of the two countries and by judgement of the leading men of both countries. If the report is correct, it shows that the issue which was to haunt Anglo-Scottish relations throughout the Middle Ages and indeed beyond had already been brutally identified—were the two kingships of equal status or did the English kingship already entertain ambitions for the supremacy of the whole of Britain?[7]

Malcolm III's death at the hand of Robert Mowbray's forces in November 1093 allowed the English king to answer that question, for the time being, in his own favour. By 1097 Malcolm's son Edgar had been installed as king with Rufus's help; as Geoffrey Barrow has said, 'he was clearly the dependent client or vassal of the Norman kings of England.' For the next generation or so the kings of Scots were at the very least politically, socially, and culturally beholden to the kings of England.[8] Contemporaries had little doubt what was

[6] See, in general, G. W. S. Barrow, 'The Pattern of Lordship and Feudal Settlement in Cumbria', *Journal of Medieval History* I (1975), 117–38; W. E. Kapelle, *The Norman Conquest of the North: The Region and its Transformation 1000–1135* (1979); H. Summerson, *Medieval Carlisle: The City and its Borders from the Late Eleventh to the Mid-sixteenth Century* (Cumberland and Westmoreland Antiquarian Society, Extra Series XXV, 1993); C. Phythian-Adams, *Land of the Cumbrians. A Study of British Provincial Origins* (1996), esp. ch. 2; Richard Lomas, *North-east England in the Middle Ages* (Edinburgh, 1992).

[7] For a narrative account, see Duncan, *Scotland*, ch. 6. The passage from John of Worcester is translated in Anderson, *Scottish Annals*, 110.

[8] G. W. S. Barrow, *Kingship and Unity. Scotland 1000–1306* (1981), 31–2. This was also the view of Geoffrey Gaimar when he came to write his History of the English around 1140: 'William had set Edgar up in his kingdom, In free service and without tribute. He granted him freely sixty shillings a day when he came to court and to his heirs . . . in proof that the king was his lord' (Gaimar, *L'Estoire des Engleis*, ed. A. Bell (Anglo-Norman Text Society, 1960), lines 6180–94). The Anglo-Saxon chronicler already took the view in 1086 that William I had 'reduced Scotland to subjection by his strength'. The dependence of the Scottish monarchy on Anglo-Norman aid was likewise eloquently expressed in the speech which Ailred of Rievaulx put into the mouth of Robert Bruce in his account of the events of 1138: Anderson, *Scottish Annals*, 192–5.

afoot: that is why the Scots, in one of the few attempts to stem the tide, insisted in 1094 that the new king should agree that 'he should never again introduce into Scotland either English or Normans or allow them to give him military service.' In saying as much they were acknowledging that the kingdom of the Scots—at least in the south and the eastern lowlands—was being brought within the ambit of Anglo-Norman power and within reach of the territorial ambitions of the Anglo-Norman baronage and its followers. What is sometimes known, rather euphemistically and misleadingly, as the introduction of feudalism to Scotland is part of that process. Submission, dependence, and influence can take a whole variety of forms, social and tenurial as well as political and military. It is forty years since Professor Archie Duncan commented provocatively that 'it is doubtful if we can sustain for much longer the thesis that there was no Norman Conquest of Scotland.'[9] It rather depends how we define a conquest; but in other respects it is time that his doubts were reactivated. There seemed to be no limit to the reach of the Norman kings' influence. Even the earl of Orkney, according to William of Malmesbury, 'though by hereditary right subject to the king of Norwegians, so regarded [Henry I's] esteem that he sent him frequent presents'.[10]

If Wales and Scotland and much of what we know as northern England were being brought within the ambit of the power of the king and barons (and Church) of England—be it directly or indirectly or through a mixture of both methods—why not Ireland? Why not indeed? Boasts to that effect were the common currency of the political rhetoric of the period. Had not the Anglo-Saxon chronicler bragged that if William the Conqueror had lived but two years longer 'he would have conquered Ireland by his prudence and without any weapons'?[11] William Rufus was altogether a more boastful character than his father and thought in grander terms: on seeing, or believing that he saw, the mountains of Ireland from the Welsh coast he is alleged to have claimed that he would build a pontoon bridge of ships to go over to conquer it.

[9] For the texts on the 1094 rising, Anderson, *Scottish Annals*, 117–18 incl. footnotes; for A. A. M. Duncan's comment, 'The Earliest Scottish Charters', *Scottish History Review* 37 (1958), 103–35 at p. 135. The appropriateness of the comment is not substantially altered by the revised consideration of the charters in Joseph Donnelly, 'The Earliest Scottish Charters?', *Scottish Historical Review* 68 (1989), 1–22. See generally G. W. S. Barrow, *The Anglo-Norman Era in Scottish History* (Oxford, 1980).

[10] William of Malmesbury, *GR*, 740–1. Likewise, according to the *Chronicon regum Mannie et Insularum*, ed. G. Broderick (Belfast, 1979), 10, the son of Godred Crovan (d.1095), king of Man, took up residence at Henry I's court; whilst Fergus of Galloway may have married one of Henry I's illegitimate daughters: R. D. Oram in *Galloway. Land and Lordship* (Edinburgh, 1991), ed. R. D. Oram and G. P. Stell, 119.

[11] *Anglo-Saxon Chronicle*, *s.a.* 1086. See B. T. Hudson, 'William the Conqueror and Ireland', *Irish Historical Studies* 29 (1994–5), 145–58 for a major reassessment of the relations of early Norman kings with the Irish.

Henry I had other and tastier fish to fry than the Irish; he was also in the habit of getting his way without using brute force. So it was in Ireland, according to William of Malmesbury again: the king of Munster and his successors were allegedly so terrified of Henry that 'they would write nothing but what would please him and do nothing but what he commanded.'[12] In short, all of Britain and indeed possibly Britain and Ireland seemed to dance, more or less, to the tune of the kings of England by the early twelfth century. That was not just the view of English royal braggarts; others were of the same opinion. It was as 'the prince of the Normans and king of the Saxons and Britons [i.e. the Welsh] and Scots' that William the Conqueror was memorialized by the Welsh annalist. As for Henry I, he was 'king of England and Wales and all the island beside'; Henry 'the Great', 'the man who had subdued under his authority all the island of Britain and its mighty ones'.[13] The Welsh may be given to exaggeration and eloquence at the drop of a hat—or a pen; but we would do well to take note of the awe in which they now stood of the king of England. It was a view likewise shared by well-placed English commentators, such as the author of the Anglo-Saxon Chronicle or, in the later twelfth century, Walter Map.[14]

King of England or of the English, maybe; but also potentially the ruler of Britain, but not so in style or title or even, other than exceptionally, in propaganda and rhetoric. Why that was so—and indeed formally remained so until James VI and I floated the idea of calling himself 'King of Great Britain' on 20 October 1604—is the central issue of this book. It is, surely, a question which needs to be asked in terms both of power and of ideology. At the level of ideology and memory the Anglo-Saxons had bequeathed a rich inheritance to their Norman successors in terms of pretensions to mastery of the *orbis Britanniae*.[15] Even if we discount (at least for the moment) some of the more grandiloquent titles which the kings of tenth-century Wessex-England gave themselves, and discount likewise some of the liturgy and rhetoric of their imperial pretensions, we are still surely left with an overkingship which—especially from Athelstan to Edgar—was truly formidable in the range of its

[12] Gerald of Wales, *Opera*, 109 (*Itinerarium Kambrie*, II, c. 1); William of Malmesbury, *GR*, 738–9.

[13] *Brut*, *s.a.* 1087, 1116 (p. 42), 1157 (p. 59).

[14] *Anglo-Saxon Chronicle*, *s.a.* 1087; Walter Map, *De Nugis Curialium. Courtiers' Trifles*, ed. and trans. M. R. James, C. N. L. Brooke, R. A. B. Mynors (Oxford, 1983), 436–7, 472–3 ('King Henry was king of England, duke of Normandy, "consul" of Maine, and lord of Scotland, Galloway and the whole of the English island'). Gerald of Wales (*Opera*, VI, 79, 103, 106, 121) was likewise of the opinion that during Henry I's reign English power in effect prevailed throughout Wales; so was Roger Howden (*Chronica*, ed. W. Stubbs, 4 vols. (R.S. 1868–71), IV, 104). The archbishop of York, unsurprisingly, advanced the view in 1126 that 'Scotland was part of the realm of England': Hugh the Chantor, *The History of the Church of York 1066–1127*, ed. C. Johnson (1961), 126.

[15] See below, Ch. 2.

power and its claims.[16] And the claim was to nothing less than to the rulership of the whole of Britain, with Ireland also occasionally thrown in for good measure.[17] It looked, at least on an optimistic reading, as if the other rulers of Britain by the 970s had accepted, or been forced to accept, the effective hegemony of the rulers of England. What remained to be determined was what form this federative overkingship would take. Would it, like Irish high-kingship, be punitive and occasionally tribute-gathering but otherwise more potent in the realm of ideology and myth than in terms of practical power? Or would its *superioritas*—what political sociologists call extensive power—be converted into something more precise and regular? And, crucially, what would it be called?

Such questions were, understandably, shelved in the 120 years which separate Edgar's coronation at Bath in 973 from the starting date of the present discussion, 1093. They were shelved maybe, but assuredly not altogether forgotten. Take Edward the Confessor, for example: it was as king of the whole of Britain (*rex totius Britanniae*) that he was invariably styled in all his charters emanating from Winchester; king of the English he might be in his biography, but the biographer assumed—as Walter Map did later—that he was ruler of Britain and that Britain was the name of the land he ruled.[18] It may well be that the Normans had more realistic and pressing business on their agenda than grand dreams about the hegemony of Britain; but that remarkable group of early twelfth-century historians who instructed them in, and constructed for them, a continuous history of the English did not allow them to forget British pipedreams.[19] John of Worcester, for example, reminded them of Edward the Elder, 'that most invincible king of the English who had ruled with

[16] For Athelstan, see especially Michael Wood, 'The Making of King Aethelstan's Empire: an English Charlemagne', in *Ideal and Reality in Frankish and Anglo-Saxon Society. Studies presented to J. M. Wallace-Hadrill*, ed. P. Wormald et al. (Oxford, 1983) and David Dumville, 'Aethelstan, First King of England' in idem, *Wessex and England from Alfred to Edgar* (Woodbridge, 1992), 141–71.

[17] For claims that Ireland was part of Britain or at least of the *imperium* of the pre-Conquest, and thereby post-Conquest, kings, see, for example, *The Chronicle of Aethelweard*, ed. A. Campbell (Oxford, 1962), 53; D. Bethell, 'English Monks and Irish Reform in the Eleventh and Twelfth Centuries', *Historical Studies* 8 (1971), 111–35, esp. pp. 129–30; M. T. Flanagan, *Irish Society, Anglo-Norman Settlers, Angevin Kingship. Interactions in Ireland in the Late Twelfth Century* (Oxford, 1989), 44–9.

[18] F. Barlow, *Edward the Confessor* (1970), 135–7; *The Life of King Edward*, ed. and trans. F. Barlow (2nd edn., Oxford, 1992), 18, 20; Walter Map, *De Nugis Curialium* (as in n. 14), 192–3.

[19] See the seminal essay by James Campbell, 'Some Twelfth-Century Views of the Anglo-Saxon Past', *Peritia* 3 (1984), 131–50, republished in *Essays in Anglo-Saxon History* (1986). Also J. Gillingham, 'Henry of Huntingdon and the Twelfth-Century Revival of the English Nation', in *Concepts of National Identity in the Middle Ages*, ed. S. Forde, L. Johnson, and A. V. Murray (Leeds, 1995), 75–101.

the greatest glory over all the inhabitants of Britain whether English, Scots, Cumbrians, Danes or Welsh'.[20] But it was King Edgar above all who provided the historical prototype of what a ruler of Britain had been and could yet be: he ruled nothing less than the whole of Britain (*totam Britanniam*); his prowess in securing the submission of eight under-kings (including those of Scots, Cumbrians, and Welsh) to him at Chester flourished into the evocative legends of these under-kings rowing their over-king on the Dee.[21] But it was Gaimar, in his French verse in the 1130s, who perhaps best captured the all-British achievement of Edgar and did so for a lay audience: 'he held the land as an emperor. . . . He alone ruled over all the kings. And over the Scots and the Welsh. Never since Arthur had any king such power.'[22]

'Never since Arthur': clearly the memories and dreams of an imperial Britain were still tickling literary and historical fancies in the 1120s and 1130s; indeed, as we shall see, they continued to do so throughout the Middle Ages. Norman kings and barons were made of stuff too stern and realistic to surrender to such reveries; they measured empires in terms of power. But even in such crude materialist terms, the prospect of a single, albeit loose-limbed, unit of power—an empire of the British Isles, if you will, just as historians speak by way of shorthand of a Norman or Angevin empire—seemed to be very much on the cards from the 1090s onwards, and particularly so during Henry I's reign. What, then, became of the prospect?

Part of the answer is that such federative empires, in medieval as in modern times, are particularly vulnerable to political frailty at the centre. King Stephen's reign quickly showed that. Indeed, his reign was far more important in the history of Britain as a whole and in the balance of power within it than is perhaps fully recognized by those who divide its events neatly along the perforations of subsequent national boundaries and national histories. The network of clientships, protectorates, submissions, and alliances whereby Rufus and Henry I had begun to assert effective overlordship of most of the outer zones of Britain began to unravel; the apparently invincible momentum of

[20] *The Chronicle of John of Worcester* (as cited above, n. 2), II, 384–5, cf. 354–5.

[21] Edgar's reputation as a pan-British ruler was a contemporary one: *Regularis Concordia*, ed. T. Symons (1953), 1. It is interesting to note that Edgar's place in English mythology was later compared by Roger Howden (*Chronica* (as cited above, n. 14), I, 64) to that of Arthur among the Britons—a very perceptive analogy. The story of the rowing incident at Chester appears in the *Anglo-Saxon Chronicle s.a.* 973 and had been further elaborated by the twelfth century, e.g. William of Malmesbury, *GR*, 238–41. For modern assessment of Edgar as 'the most imperial of the late Anglo-Saxon rulers', see J. Campbell, *Essays in Anglo-Saxon History* (1986), 217, and N. Banton, 'Monastic Reform and the Unification of Tenth-century England', *Studies in Church History* 18 (1982), 71–85.

[22] Gaimar, *L'Estoire des Engleis*, ll. 3561–7. For comment see esp. J. Gillingham, 'Gaimar, the Prose *Brut* and the Making of English History', in *L'histoire et les nouveaux publics dans l'Europe médiévale*, ed. J.-P. Genet (Paris, 1997), 165–76.

the Norman military machine, and with it the onward march of English settlement, was halted and even spectacularly reversed in different parts of Wales; even more strikingly, a whole tract of Cumbria and Northumbria north of the rivers Ribble and Tees—the very area which it had been part of the achievement of the forty years before 1135 to bring under Anglo-Norman control, if not fully within the structure of the English state—was lost to the kings of Scots who built or rebuilt castles at Carlisle, Warkworth, Tulketh near Preston, and possibly Bamburgh, Appleby, and Lancaster; struck coins at Carlisle, Bamburgh, and Corbridge; persuaded many of the barons and monasteries of the area to accept the *fait accompli* of Scottish control, and even schemed to bring the bishopric of Durham under their power.[23] The map of power in Britain seemed to be in the process of being redrawn radically. The outrage with which contemporary chronicles responded to what they termed the barbarism of the Scots, Gallovidians, and Welsh is surely to be explained in part by the shock of the Anglo-Normans on realizing that their economic and cultural superiority and civility as well as their military dominance were being challenged for the first time in three generations.[24] Empire-builders are distressed by challenges to their right to build their empires.

What happened in the secular world was replicated—indeed even more significantly and irreversibly so—in the world of ecclesiastical politics. It was among churchmen, as we shall see, that the ideas of an all-Britain, indeed an all-British Isles, unit of authority were most fondly cherished in the early twelfth century.[25] It was in this sphere that they were now both ideologically and organizationally challenged. Canterbury's pretensions to primatial authority over Ireland were finally scuppered at the synod of Kells in 1152 with the establishment of four archbishoprics in Ireland; plans, already being promoted in the 1120s, for metropolitan status for St Andrews over the Scottish Church did not meet with success but the papacy increasingly treated Scotland as an autonomous ecclesiastical unit (a position which was eventually and very

[23] See, most recently, David Crouch, 'The March and the Welsh Kings', and Geoffrey Barrow, 'The Scots and the North of England', in *The Anarchy of King Stephen's Reign*, ed. Edmund King (Oxford, 1994), 255–89, 231–53; Geoffrey Barrow, 'The Kings of Scotland and Durham', in *Anglo-Norman Durham 1093–1193*, ed. D. Rollason, M. Harvey, and M. Prestwich (Woodbridge, 1994), 311–23; K. J. Stringer, 'North-East England and Scotland in the Middle Ages', *Innes Review* 44 (1993), 88–99; idem, 'State-Building in Twelfth-Century Britain: David I, King of Scots and Northern England', in *Government, Religion and Society in Northern England 1000–1700* (Gloucester, 1997), 40–62; Ian Blanchard, 'Lothian and Beyond: the Economy of the "English empire" of David I' in *Progress and Problems in Medieval England. Essays in Honour of Edward Miller* (Cambridge, 1996), 23–46.

[24] J. Gillingham, 'Conquering the Barbarians: War and Chivalry in Twelfth-century Britain', *Haskins Society Journal* 4 (1993), 57–84; Matthew Strickland, *War and Chivalry. The Conduct and Perception of War in England and Normandy 1066–1217* (Cambridge, 1996), ch. 11.

[25] See below, pp. 37–9.

belatedly confirmed in 1192); even Wales came within an ace in 1140 of securing its own archbishopric and indeed technically may have succeeded in its ambitions.[26] The pan-Britannic vision and propaganda of Lanfranc, Anselm, and their successors was contracting into an *ecclesia anglicana*. In short, it was not just within England or as between England and Normandy that the template of political and ecclesiastical power and authority was being radically recast by the events of Stephen's reign; the same was true of the British Isles as a whole. It was a reminder that a high kingship of Britain or the British Isles built outwards from an English heartland on the basis of power and settlement could rapidly contract into its English shell when political crosswinds blew. Stephen's reign had shown as much; the experience was to be repeated in the closing months of John's reign and again in the 1250s and 1260s.

Nor should we lose sight of the fact that control or power over the outer zones of the British Isles was, literally, of peripheral importance to the rulers and the great majority of the aristocracy of England. Their primary ambitions lay in England and in northern France. This had been so under the Norman rulers; it was so again to an even greater degree after the accession of Henry II in 1154. Britain was now part of an Angevin empire whose centre of gravity lay on the Loire rather than on the Thames and whose pressure points were located in Toulouse or the Vexin rather than in the Cheviots or Glamorgan. Henry II showed as much by leading no expedition into Wales after 1165 and by declining to take up an open papal invitation, subsequently reinforced by an appeal from an Irish king, to extend his power to include Ireland in his dominions, until the private-enterprise activities of some of his English barons galvanized him into action, more to control their ambitions than to conquer Ireland. Richard I, as one might expect, showed even less regard for notions of overlordship of the British Isles; Scotland after all is small beer for those whose hearts are set on European power and global glory. Within five months of his father's death, Richard allowed the Scots to pay for the cancellation of the Treaty of Falaise of 1174 which had formalized their client status *vis-à-vis* the king and Church of England for the last fifteen years; in 1194 Richard even toyed with the idea of selling the earldom of Northumberland (while reserving his right to the key castles) to the king of Scots for 15,000 marks.[27] Kings

[26] D. Bethell, 'English Monks' (as in n. 17); M. T. Flanagan, *Irish Society* (as in n. 17), esp. 36–41 (Ireland); M. Brett, *The English Church under Henry I* (1975), 14–28; Duncan, *Scotland*, 257–61; A. D. M. Barrell, 'The Background to *Cum Universi*: Scoto-papal Relations, 1159–1192', *Innes Review* 46 (1995), 116–38 (Scotland); J. Conway Davies, *Episcopal Acts* (as in n. 4), I, 192–208; Henry, Archdeacon of Huntingdon, *Historia Anglorum*, ed. and trans. D. Greenway (Oxford, 1996), 18–19 and n. 25; Lesley Johnson and Alexander Bell, 'The Anglo-Norman Description of England', in *Anglo-Norman Anniversary Studies*, ed. Ian Short (Anglo-Norman Text Society, 1993), 11–47 at ll. 197–201 (Wales).

[27] *Anglo-Scottish Relations*, 12–17; Anderson, *Scottish Annals*, 311–14 (from Roger Howden's Chronicle).

who indulge in such auctions can hardly be said to place the overlordship of the British Isles high on their agenda.

But Richard I's financial pranks should not mislead us in this respect. The Angevin kings still assumed—as indeed did their Norman and even some of their Anglo-Saxon predecessors—that they had a natural right, in respect of power and mythology, to the overlordship of Britain and, after 1170, of Ireland also. They quickly showed that their overwhelming power and resources put them in a league of their own within the islands and that they were, or could be, as much over-kings and emperors within them as Edgar or Arthur were believed to have been. Overlordship or high kingship—it cannot be too strongly emphasized—is not the same as unitary, exclusive, direct kingship; it does not demand the sort of recurrent and intrusive power such as the king of England exercised within England itself; it even tolerated other sources of authority so long as they acknowledged their ultimate dependence on its overriding lordship. What form such high kingship took and how effective it could be in terms of its own ambitions can perhaps be best illustrated from the events of a single year, 1175.

In May 1175 Henry II returned to England, anxious to put his British house in order after the trauma of the last two years. On 29 June at Gloucester he met a delegation of Welsh leaders, headed by the Lord Rhys, ruler of Deheubarth (native south-west Wales) and possibly Henry II's justiciar there, who had doubtless been summoned to meet him. The occasion was a public reaffirmation of their submission to the king and, in some cases, of public reconciliation with him for past offences. Henry also took the opportunity to secure a public oath from the major Marcher barons, including the earl of Gloucester and William Braose, that they were obliged to support any future royal action against the Welsh. It was, all in all, a very public display close to the borders of Wales of the king's ultimate supremacy over Wales, be it under native or Anglo-Norman rule.[28] The next such display was much more theatrical and altogether far more momentous. The date was 10 August; the venue, the church of St Peter's at York; the audience, the chief men of the English kingdom. Thither came William, king of Scots, his bishops, abbots, earls, barons, and knights, and the freeholders of his land, as the contemporary source says, 'from the greatest even to the least', to swear fealty and/or do homage to Henry II. This was, of course, the public act of submission of the Scottish political and territorial community which Henry exacted in return for releasing the captured king of Scots from his prison. He now insisted that

[28] [Roger of Howden], *Gesta Regis Henrici Secundi*, ed. W. Stubbs, 2 vols. (R.S., 1867), I, 92; *Brut*, *s.a.* 1175 (pp. 70–1). The discussion of this meeting in Lloyd, *Wales*, II, 544–5 is rather incomplete. Cf. Davies, *Conquest*, 222, 290–1.

the hugely demeaning agreement (the so-called Treaty of Falaise), which was the price of that release, not only be sealed by William and his brother at the ceremony but also be publicly read out before the assembled political nations of England and Scotland. This was indeed, as one contemporary observer noted, 'the heavy yoke of domination and servitude'.[29] Two small but crucial drafting features of that agreement indicate, diplomatically as it were, the scale of the humiliation: Scotland was recurrently referred to as a land (*terra*), not as a kingdom (*regnum*), thereby anticipating by over a century Edward I's vocabulary of demotion, while the premier-league status of Henry II's title as 'the lord king' (*dominus rex*) stood in pointed superiority to that of William, merely 'king of the Scots' (*rex Scottorum*). Not for the last time in the history of imperial domination, the victor was deploying his control of language and his drafting of the documents of submission to delineate the contours and obligations of power on his own terms.[30] Furthermore, the regular visits (at least eight in ten years) which the king of Scots made to the king of England's court from 1176 to 1188—by Henry II's command, albeit masquerading as invitations, and occasionally accompanied by a large delegation of the leading ecclesiastical and lay magnates from Scotland—made it abundantly clear to all, at the most public venues, that the king of Scots was indeed beholden and subject to the king of England.

From York Henry II travelled south and on 6 October held a great council at Windsor. It was there, in the presence of the archbishops of Canterbury, Dublin, and Tuam, that he concluded the so-called Treaty of Windsor with the representatives of Rory O'Connor, king of Connacht in north-west Ireland. All that we need to note here, very briefly, is the assumptions that Henry II makes in the treaty: he assumes that Ireland is part of his dominions and that it is his right to determine the distribution of power within it, as Irish high-kings had occasionally done so in the past; he takes it for granted that the most powerful Irish ruler of the day, the king of Connacht, is a king 'under him' (*sub eo*) but only 'as long as he serves him faithfully'; he assumes that his position as ultimate high-king entitles him to a regular tribute from the peoples of Ireland which his under-king (for that is what he is) is expected to collect on his behalf.[31]

[29] The major texts for the submission of 1175 are conveniently assembled in Anderson, *Scottish Annals*, 258–63; Anderson, *Early Sources of Scottish History*, II, 292–3; *Anglo-Scottish Relations*, 2–11. For the phrase 'heavy yoke of domination and servitude', see Melrose chronicle as quoted in Anderson, *Early Sources*, II, 322.

[30] *Terra* (land) is also the word consistently used by Roger Howden, *Gesta Henrici Secundi*, I, 95–6. Stones's translation (*Anglo-Scottish Relations*, 3–11) obscures the significance of the references to '*terra*' and '*dominus rex*'.

[31] M. T. Flanagan, *Irish Society* (as in n. 17), ch. 7 and pp. 312–13 (for the text). It is worth quoting the very different perception of the agreement recorded by an Irish annalist: 'Cadla Ua

These three occasions in 1175 are highly revealing episodes of the choreography of power in the British Isles in the late twelfth century. Historians have, arguably, been too obsessed with the 'constitutional' and 'feudal' significance of such occasions, too anxious to measure the calculus of power in terms of conquest and castles. Power is no less impressive, arguably indeed more so, when expressed in theatrical display and social obeisance. By that token Henry II was, and believed himself to be, master of the British Isles. Our reluctance to concede him that mastery is shaped in part by the convenience of vacuum-sealed boxes of national historiography, in part by our assumption that power has to be direct, immediate, and regular, the sort of power that was already the norm in lowland England. But in the Angevin empire as a whole—as in earlier and later empires, including those of our own day—the format and density of power ranged across a whole gamut of authority.[32] Henry II could on occasion address a writ to 'the French, English and Scots of the whole of England and Scotland' as if they were all equally and directly his subjects; he might refer, as he did in his second charter to the city of Dublin, to the whole land (*totam terram*) of England, Normandy, Wales, and Ireland as if he regarded it as a single unit.[33] But for the most part he was too busy with the practicalities and problems of power to be concerned with its labels or with a theoretical analysis of its nature. He knew that he was in effect high king of the British Isles. So did his contemporaries. Gerald of Wales was no apologist for the Angevins nor an uncritical admirer of Henry II; but he stood in awe of his achievements in the British Isles. He had, he said, subdued Ireland and triumphed over Scotland; his rule extended from the Channel to the Orkneys; he had—and these are pregnant words—'included the whole island of Britain in one monarchy'.[34] In other words, he was in all but title over-king of Britain and lord of Ireland.

Other Angevin kings came close to emulating Henry II's achievements in this respect, none more so than King John. He already demonstrated early in his reign his appreciation of how his power within the British Isles could be

Dubthaig [i.e. the archbishop of Tuam] came out of England from the sea of the Empress, having with him the peace of Ireland, and the kingship thereof, both Foreigner and Gael, to Ruaidrí Ua Conchobair [Rory O'Connor]; and to every provincial king his province from the king of Ireland and their tributes to Ruaidrí' (*Annals of Tigernach*, trans. Whitley Stokes, 2 vols. (Llanerch Reprints, 1993), *s.a.* 1175 (p. 293).

[32] Cf. J. Le Patourel, *The Norman Empire* (Oxford, 1976), 320–5. For a revealing modern discussion, Michael Mann, *The Sources of Social Power*. Vol. 1. *A History of power from the beginning to A.D. 1760* (Cambridge, 1986).

[33] G. W. S. Barrow, 'A Writ of Henry II for Dumfermline Abbey', *Scottish Historical Review* 36 (1957), 138–43; *Historical and Municipal Documents of Ireland, 1172–1320*, ed. J. T. Gilbert (R.S., 1870), 2.

[34] Gerald of Wales, *Opera*, VIII, 156–7.

theatrically stage-managed for the benefit of a hand-picked audience. 'On a great hill' outside Lincoln on 21 November 1200, 'in the sight of all the people, William, king of Scots became the man of John king of England for his right.' The limited nature of the homage (in respect of the king of Scots' lands in England) was well recognized by those in the know; but it was the physical act of homage and the resplendent assembly which remained—and was meant to remain—in the memories of those present. The audience included ten English archbishops and bishops, nine English earls, and a distinguished gathering of 'the barons of England and Normandy'. Even more striking was the presence of the archbishop of Dublin, the bishops of St Andrews, Llandaff, Bangor, and Meath, the earl of Dunbar, the prince of Galloway, the 'kings of south Wales', and 'many others from the kingdom of Scotland'. It was, and was meant to be, a demonstration of power and one witnessed by key persons from distant parts of the British Isles.[35]

John displayed the reality as well as the pomp of this power over the British Isles recurrently throughout his reign, but never more so than in the years 1209–12.[36] In a whirlwind series of campaigns across those years he brought the king of Scots and the most powerful princes of Wales utterly to their knees, and in the last English royal expedition to Ireland for almost 200 years he terrorized and cajoled many of the native Irish kings and the Anglo-Norman barons there into total submission; his political schemes even embraced the princelings of the outer limits of the British Isles—the king of Man, the prince of Galloway, the lord of the Isles, and the earl of Orkney.[37] It was an awesome display of the military might and diplomatic reach of the English crown within the British Isles. The London author of the *Leges Anglorum*, compiled in John's reign, certainly thought in extravagant pan-British terms: he peppered his text with references to the kingdom of Britain and to the monarchy and

[35] Roger of Howden, *Chronica* (as cited n. 14), IV, 141–2. Other accounts of this fascinating episode are conveniently assembled in Anderson, *Scottish Annals*, 232–5. The episode was intensively used by English propagandists in their historical polemics of the 1290s, e.g. *Edward I and the Throne of Scotland 1290–1296. An Edition of the Record Sources for the Great Cause*, ed. E. L. G. Stones and G. G. Simpson, 2 vols. (Oxford, 1978), II, 306.

[36] For a general consideration of the significance of John's reign and policies for the British Isles, see briefly Davies, *Domination and Conquest*, 79–82 and the secondary discussions cited there, and, more recently, the essays by A. A. M. Duncan, Seán Duffy and Ifor Rowlands in *King John. New Interpretations*, ed. S. D. Church (Woodbridge, 1999).

[37] Anderson, *Early Sources of Scottish History*, II, 365 n. 1, 387–8, 391; K. J. Stringer, *Earl David of Huntingdon. A Study in Anglo-Scottish History* (Edinburgh, 1985), 46; idem, 'Periphery and Core in Thirteenth-Century Scotland: Alan son of Roland, Lord of Galloway and Constable of Scotland', in *Medieval Scotland, Crown, Lordship and Community. Essays presented to G. W. S. Barrow*, ed. A. Grant and K. J. Stringer (Edinburgh, 1993), 82–114; R. Andrew McDonald, *The Kingdom of the Isles. Scotland's Western Seaboard c.1100–c.1336* (East Linton, 1997), 87–8.

crown of the same; he even proclaimed that empire (*imperium*) was a more appropriate word than kingdom (*regnum*) for such an assemblage of power.[38] Historians understandably preoccupied with the serious, indeed fatal, setbacks that John experienced in France and England should take due note of how contemporaries, unencumbered by hindsight, rated his achievement in the British Isles. 'There is now no one in Ireland, Scotland and Wales who does not obey the command of the king of England; that, as is well known, is more than any of his ancestors had achieved.'[39]

Like so many political tributes, the comment of the Barnwell chronicle proved short-lived and premature. But even in defeat the shadow of John's power in Britain and Ireland lay over events. Magna Carta is, and has been seen as, a quintessentially English document. So it was; but its original version—though not its later confirmations—contains four clauses relating to Wales and Scotland.[40] It could not be otherwise if peace were to be secured. John's ambitions had included the whole of the British Isles—and much else besides—within his stratagems; opposition to him likewise operated on the same stage. When Llywelyn ab Iorwerth, prince of north Wales, captured Shrewsbury on 17 May 1215, or when later in August–September 1216 young Alexander II of Scotland marched all the way to Dover to swear homage to Prince Louis of France, they were showing that, when the going got rough, they also could play their power games on a truly British stage. Nothing perhaps shows this better than the fact that Alexander and Llywelyn were invited in October 1216 to Northampton to participate in the election of a new English king.[41] The election did not, of course, take place; but the invitation was quite a turn-up for the books. Nor was Ireland left out of the equation. The English barons in Ireland had remained solid in their support for John, or at least neutral, since October 1212. That was a matter of no small political significance. Their reward came quickly from the minority government of Henry III: within a fortnight of John's death the order was given that

[38] F. Liebermann, *Über die Leges Anglorum, saeculo xiii ineunte Londoniis collectae* (Halle, 1884), 5–7, 12–14, 19–22, 33 (note especially the reference to Alfred (p. 20): 'totam monarchiam totius regni Britannie possedit, quod modo vocatur regnum Anglorum); idem, 'A Contemporary Manuscript of the "Leges Anglorum Londoniis collectae"', *English Historical Review* 28 (1913), 732–45.

[39] *Memoriale Fratris Walteri de Coventria*, ed. W. Stubbs, 2 vols. (R.S., 1872–3), II, 203. Cf. the comment of the Tewkesbury annalist (*Annales Monastici*, ed. H. L. Luard, 5 vols. (R.S., 1864–9), I, 59): 'the king made the whole of Ireland and most of Wales subject to him.'

[40] Magna Carta, c.56–c.59. I am not persuaded by the argument (Duncan, *Scotland*, 521) that the Scottish clause 'applied to King Alexander as an English baron'. Cf. J. C. Holt, *Magna Carta* (2nd edn., 1992), 286–8, 341. For Wales, see J. B. Smith, 'Magna Carta and the Charters of the Welsh Princes', *English Historical Review* 99 (1984), 344–62.

[41] Duncan, *Scotland*, 522–3; Lloyd, *Wales*, II, 643.

Magna Carta should be issued for Ireland, and so it was transmitted to Dublin in February 1217.[42] None of this, of course, is to deny that the eye of the political storm of these years was firmly in England; but the integration and overlaps of political structures and ambitions meant that there was now a British Isles dimension to politics, including English politics.

Neither John nor his predecessors, of course, had a policy for, or even a vision of, the British Isles as such. The centre of gravity of their ambitions and anxieties, and those of most of their political elites, were primarily European and English. Within such a world the outer zones of the British Isles were generally of secondary interest, if that; Henry II and John gave them any sustained personal attention only when they were not distracted elsewhere. Even then their interventions were often responsive rather than proactive, prompted by the need to demonstrate their mastery (be it to Welsh princes, as in 1165, or to Anglo-Norman barons in Ireland, as in 1170 or 1210), or by an opportunity which fell into their laps (as with the capture of the king of Scots in 1174) or by the need to clear the decks in Britain in order to pursue greater ambitions on the continent (as seems to have been the case with John's frenetic activities in 1209 to 1212). Nor in truth were the problems which confronted them in different parts of the British Isles at all comparable in character: in Wales and Ireland they dealt with countries which had been (or were in the process of being) considerably colonized and subdued by Anglo-Norman lords and settlers and where native political power was fragmented and anaemic; in Scotland, on the other hand, they confronted a unitary and rapidly modernizing monarchy, which was able to absorb the powerful Anglo-Norman settler groups into its social and political structure and to redesign the institutions of its power substantially on an English model.

In all these respects it is arguably misleading, even mischievous, to treat the British Isles, and specifically England's relations with the outer zones of the British Isles, as a separate or unitary analytic category within the world of the Normans and Angevins, and their barons and churchmen. A few ideologues and day-dreamers apart, Britain or the British Isles was not a conceptual unit within their thought-worlds, let alone their worlds of action. Yet there were elements within the evolving historical situation which were making the British Isles, and England's status within it, an increasingly distinctive issue in the politics of power as the thirteenth century progressed.

First, English domination in the British Isles beyond England, and specifically in Wales and Ireland, was more, much more, than a process of

[42] F. X. Martin and J. F. Lydon in *NHI*, II, 148–57. For the letter of support from the Irish barons, *CDI*, I, nos. 444, 448; and for the version of Magna Carta despatched to Ireland in 1217, H. G. Richardson, 'Magna Carta Hibernie', *Irish Historical Studies* 3 (1942), 31–3.

military and political power. It was accompanied by a process of colonization and settlement which, by 1216, had transformed the social, economic, and ethnic landscape of significant parts of both countries and created communities which were self-consciously and aggressively English but were not of England itself. The consequences, including the political consequences, were profound. Wales and Ireland, or at least the Anglicized and English-controlled parts of them, were now more than detachable parts of the mosaic of British and continental lands which we call 'the Angevin empire'; through the experience of colonization and settlement they had a special relationship with England. It was a token of that relationship that many of the institutions of the governance of England were transferred indirectly (as in Wales) or directly (as in Ireland) or imitatively (as in Scotland) to them. It was a symbol of this special relationship that King John was said to have taken the laws of England with him to Ireland (i.e. English-controlled Ireland) in 1210. Englishness—be it settlers, laws, or institutions—was an exportable commodity within the British Isles.[43] That was not true elsewhere within the Angevin empire. The zone of Anglicization was the British Isles; that served to demarcate it from the rest of the lands of the Angevin rulers.

Another feature which served to integrate parts of Wales and Ireland and even, in a small measure, Scotland into a distinctive relationship with England was the degree to which they shared a common aristocracy and thereby an intertwining of their territorial ambitions and social and political concerns. The barons and knights who were involved in the conquest and settlement of Wales and Ireland and in the aristocratic colonization of Scotland were drawn from the ranks of England's political elites. Many of them retained their estates and/or their affiliations in England. They thereby formed part of an aristocratic elite whose power and ambitions straddled two, three, or even, occasionally, all four countries of the British Isles, and did so at a time when their territorial links with northern France were largely collapsing.[44] This meant that the ambitions and reverberations of English political life quickly had their echoes in the English communities and territorial politics of English-controlled Wales and Ireland. Likewise the affairs of the march of Wales and English Ireland and even, in a measure, of the cross-border Anglo-Scottish estates were part of the weft of English politics. A polity of the British Isles

[43] For these themes see below, Ch. 6.

[44] For this theme see in particular R. Frame, *Ireland and Britain 1170–1450* (1998), esp. chs. 2–4 and 9; and Keith Stringer, *Earl David* (as in n. 37), ch. 9; 'Identities in Thirteenth-century England: Frontier Society in the far North', in *Social and Political Identities in Western History*, ed. C. Bjørn et al. (Copenhagen, 1994), 28–66; 'Nobility and Identity in Medieval Britain and Ireland: The de Vescy family, *c.*1120–1314', in *Britain and Ireland 900–1300. Insular Responses to Medieval European Change*, ed. Brendan Smith (Cambridge, 1999), 199–239.

—however its component parts might be assembled and related to each other—seemed to be in the making.

This development is all the more significant when we place it in the context of the dramatic changes in the map of Angevin political power in the early thirteenth century. The loss of the Angevin monarchy's northern French lands from 1202–4 onwards, and the eventual formal acceptance of that loss in the Treaty of Paris in 1259, meant that the monarchy and the aristocracy were now more England-based in their residence and ambitions, and, arguably, therefore more likely to focus their attention, and the power at their command, on the relationship between England and the outer zones of the British Isles. England was now assuredly the centre of the political firmament of the kings of England in a way which had not been true since the Norman Conquest. The Crown's possessions beyond England were seen as annexes of an England-centred world. Nor can there be any doubt that during the course of the thirteenth century the English political community became more self-consciously, stridently, and even aggressively English in its posture. Such an England-dominated view of the universe was likely to have repercussions on perceptions of England's relations with, and attitude towards, the rest of the British Isles.

There were other long-term structural changes afoot which might profoundly affect perceptions of the nature and mechanics of overlordship, including any actual or dormant claims to the overlordship of the British Isles. These changes have often lain hidden beneath the particularities of events and the conservatism of formulae of dependence; in fact their potential was explosive. The sort of high kingship which Henry I or Henry II had periodically asserted over the other rulers of the British Isles (as indeed over their clients on the continent) had been a fairly relaxed *superioritas*. It had generally been content with a formal and visual acknowledgement of its authority, public submission, and periodic tribute (much as Henry II had secured from the rulers of Ireland, Scotland, and Wales in 1175); it could be and was underwritten both by punitive raids (of which the campaigns of King John in 1209–12 were awesome examples) and by giving a relatively free hand, under ultimate royal control, to Anglo-Norman barons and their followers to undertake such conquest, settlement, and colonization as were feasible.

During the thirteenth century there is a detectable shift in what such overlordship, royal overlordship, might entail. Various elements seem to enter into the equation. One was the growing use of written instruments to define the relationships of power and dependence between the king of England and the native rulers of the outer zones of the British Isles, and to do so on the terms and in the language of the English king and his chancery clerks and lawyers. Written documents define and sharpen relationships; they permit little of that elasticity and informality of interpretation which had been one of the features of earlier high kingships. The sharp increase in the regular use of writing from the later twelfth century also enhanced the capacity of government to rule at a distance and to do so in detail; the records of John's government in Ireland were an early and eloquent comment on what might be achieved. Even more significant in changing the character and perception of overlordship was the much more precise and hard-edged legal content which was being given to the notion of overlordship by lawyers and governmental negotiators. The obligations of client rulers to the king of England were being increasingly expressed in tenurial terms and approximated to those of English tenants-in-chief. A much more precise content was also being given to the jurisdictional obligations of subordinate rulers (such as the prince of Gwynedd or the king of Connacht) to the king of England, securing for the latter appellate powers and the right of intervention in the affairs of his dependants.[45]

There is no need to claim that such measures and trends constituted a coherent and consciously pursued programme for the intensification of the claims of the king of England to an ultimate overlordship of the British Isles. But equally there is no need to deny that these long-term changes in attitudes and assumptions were, or at the very least had the potential for, transforming the nature and claims of that overlordship. Whether these changes would, or would not, lead to a redefinition of the content and practice of overlordship would depend on a host of factors—on the preoccupations and priorities, domestic and foreign, of the kings of England, on political circumstances and openings in native Wales and Ireland, and also, in very different forms, in Scotland, and on the personalities of the rulers, both overlord and client princes. There are very clear indications in Wales in the 1240s and early 1250s how the power of English overlordship could be menacingly and effectively intensified. Even in Scotland during periods of minority and/or political instability it was not always easy to gauge where neighbourly concern ended and a potentially heavy-handed interference began—both in the practice and in the occasional rhetoric of relationships. But by and large the long reign of Henry III (1216–72) was, for a variety of reasons, a period in which an effective *modus vivendi* seemed to be operating in the relationship between the English kingdom and the rest of the British Isles under non-English rule, not least because the English did not press such theoretical claims as they may have entertained, very occasionally, in private, partly because native rulers of Ireland and Wales had adjusted their ambitions to the practical reach of their

[45] Davies, *Domination and Conquest*, chs. 5–6 develops these arguments more fully.

power.[46] Whether this situation continued to prevail and, possibly, to evolve peacefully depended ultimately on two factors: opportunities, actual or contrived (and for wielders of power the difference between the two can be small) and the attitude and preoccupations of the king of England. In Edward I opportunities and royal determination came together in an unforeseen but explosive combination for the exercise of English overlordship in the British Isles.

Edward has divided historiographical opinion in the British Isles from his own day to ours as no other English ruler was to do until the time of Oliver Cromwell. He was soon hailed as Edward the Great, the Conqueror, and such compliments are still not unknown in historical writing; but he was also denigrated in his own day as 'le roy covetous', although mere covetousness appears in the eyes of some Scottish and Welsh historians as one of the lesser of his moral flaws.[47] How, then, did he see his position within the British Isles? We can leave Ireland on one side. His position there was unambiguous: like his ancestors he was lord of Ireland. As to his power and status within Britain we need not assume that his attitude was unchanging, cynical, or conspiratorial. Like most men of power he was the servant of circumstances and, where he could be, the master of opportunities. He had no programme to redefine his position within the British Isles; but equally, as a monarch who was a stickler for his rights and the dignity of his crown in all spheres, it was unlikely that he would brook any perceived challenge to what he saw as his *superioritas*, nor would he pass by any opportunity to exploit his overlordship to the full.

We could perhaps best glimpse how he saw his position in Britain were we to catch up with him between Worcester and Tewkesbury in October 1278. On 13 October he and his queen and a great array of English magnates had been present at the cathedral at Worcester when Llywelyn ap Gruffudd, prince of Wales and recently vanquished and chastened rebel, was married to Eleanor, daughter of Simon de Montfort and recently a prisoner of Edward. Edward I, and his brother Edmund, gave away Eleanor, their first cousin, at

[46] For the significance of the reign in British terms, see Robin Frame, 'Overlordship and Reaction, *c.*1200–*c.*1450', in *Uniting the Kingdom? The Making of British History*, ed. A. Grant and K. J. Stringer (1995), 65–84; Davies, *Domination and Conquest*, 82–7; Davies, *Conquest*, 300–7; idem, 'The English State and the "Celtic" Peoples', *Journal of Historical Sociology* 6 (1993), 1–14.

[47] 'Le roy covetous': *Calendar of Documents relating to Scotland . . . 1108–1509*, ed. J. Bain (Edinburgh, 1881–8), II, 537. The 'noble and wise', 'the good king Edward the Conqueror', 'Edward the Great': *Calendar of Ancient Correspondence concerning Wales*, ed. J. G. Edwards (Cardiff, 1935), 234; *Rotuli Parliamentorum*, 6 vols. (1832), III, 476; *Annals of Connacht 1224–1544*, ed. A. M. Freeman (Dublin, 1944), *s.a.* 1307. For contrasting modern assessments of Edward see, for example, on the one hand F. M. Powicke, *King Henry III and the Lord Edward* (Oxford, 1947), 725, and M. Prestwich, *Edward I* (1988), 567, and on the other *Welsh Assize Roll 1277–84*, ed. J. Conway Davies (Cardiff, 1940), 81 and G. W. S. Barrow, *Robert Bruce* (3rd edn., Edinburgh, 1988), 52.

the church door; paid for the wedding feast; gave a small gift to Llywelyn to mark the occasion; and met some of the expenses of the transport of the young princess's goods. There was, of course, a political point to this public largesse: the prince of Wales was being married in the king of England's presence, by his permission, in a cathedral of his choice within his kingdom, and—with a nice and surely calculated sense of irony—on the feast-day of the Translation of Edward the Confessor, the patron saint of the English royal dynasty.[48]

Among the wedding guests at Worcester were Alexander III, king of Scots, and his queen, Edward I's sister. Three days later at Tewkesbury Alexander offered to do his homage to Edward; but Edward declined to proceed with the ceremony on the rather feeble grounds that his council was not present. The homage was eventually performed at Westminster on 28 October in the king's chamber in time of parliament, in the presence of a large audience of leading English laymen and ecclesiastics.[49] What exactly Alexander pledged himself to on that occasion has been a bone of contention between English and Scottish records and English and Scottish historians ever since.[50] Here we may content ourselves with two comments: deferring the ceremony of homage from the relative privacy of Tewkesbury to the calculated publicity of Westminster was a clever act of political theatre, also making it clear that it was the king of England who determined the venue and the timing of the act;[51] secondly, the official enrolment of the memorandum of the homage proceedings was likewise a pre-emptive act of seeking to ensure that history got it 'right' and that the homage was seen to be, at least in the official English record, 'unconditional'.[52]

The marriage of Llywelyn and the homage of Alexander were, in effect, a package: they expressed, in the most public manner and before carefully selected audiences, the paternal and gracious face of Edward I's belief—shared

[48] For accounts of the ceremony, see esp. *Brut*, *s.a.* 1278 and Thomas Wykes in *Annales Monastici*, IV, 277. The event took place 'annuente rege Anglorum'. The gift given by Edward was one mark (13s 4d.). On the same day he gave alms worth 14s. at the shrines of St Wulfstan and St Oswald at Worcester Cathedral: PRO Chancery Miscellanea (C. 47) 4/1 f.41; cf. *Welsh Assize Roll*, 44. For a full account of the marriage and its background, see J. Beverley Smith, *Llywelyn ap Gruffudd. Prince of Wales* (Cardiff, 1998), 394–402, 448–50.

[49] Most of the key texts relating to this episode are conveniently assembled in Anderson, *Scottish Annals*, 383–4, and Anderson, *Early Sources of Scottish History*, II, 675–6.

[50] *Anglo-Scottish Relations*, 76–83 for the two texts. For contrasting interpretations cf. Duncan, *Scotland*, 590–1; Barrow, *Kingship and Unity*, 156–7; F. M. Powicke, *The Thirteenth Century 1216–1307* (Oxford, 1953), 595.

[51] The fact that the Scottish king secured a concession that 'henceforth the king (of England) and his descendants should not defer to receive the homage of the king (of Scots) and his heirs but should take it wherever he (the king of England) could be found in the realm of England' (Wykes in *Annales Monastici*, 277–8; *Calendar of Patent Rolls 1272–81*, 280) suggests that the parties well appreciated the significance of the deferment of the homage from Tewkesbury to Westminster.

[52] *Calendar of Close Rolls 1272–9*, 493 (letter of 21 Mar. 1278): 'absque conditione aliqua'.

Edward I in Parliament (Wriothesly MS). Photograph: The Royal Collection

surely by the English political nation generally—that he was in effect high king of Britain and lord of Ireland. We have arguably been so concerned with constitutional niceties and ambiguities (important as they undoubtedly were) that we have overlooked the deliberate visual theatre of these events and the messages they were meant to, and did, convey. Contemporaries knew otherwise. As one English chronicler remarked *à propos* Alexander III's homage to Edward I (either overlooking or not noticing its limited character): 'the triumph of so great a surrender should not be hidden from our countrymen for the future.'[53] High kings are well content to allow other kings and princes a place within their empire, so long as they know, remember, and apparently acknowledge their place. What that place should be within the institutions of the Edwardian state was imaginatively, if fictitiously, captured by a sixteenth-century representation of parliament in which Edward I sits on his throne, with the king of Scots and the prince of Wales on either side of him at a lower level.[54] There may be artistic licence in the picture, but it takes us, arguably, nearer to the heart of Edwardian high-kingship than does much historical analysis. Edward I is known to have considered that it would be appropriate for the prince of Wales and the king of Scotland to sit in his parliament at Westminster alongside the magnates of England,[55] and virtually on a par with them. Indeed, his suggestions for the integration of the leaders of the Scottish and Welsh polities into the framework of the kingdom went even further. During the desperate negotiations of the winter of 1282 his spokesmen tried to buy off Llywelyn ap Gruffudd, prince of Wales, with the offer of an earldom in England; the same offer was extended to King John (Balliol) of Scotland in 1296 provided he ceded all rights to the kingdom of Scotland.[56] Had either of these ploys succeeded—and both look more plausible than hindsight might suggest—then high kingship would have moved much closer to becoming a unitary kingship and a single British political nation might have been on the cards.

[53] Wykes, *Annales Monastici*, IV, 277–8.

[54] See Plate opposite.

[55] For the suggestion that the prince of Wales was expected to attend parliament in England after the 1277 settlement, *Eulogium Historiarum*, ed. F. S. Haydon, 3 vols. (R.S., 1858–63), III, 143; *The Chronicle of Walter of Guisborough*, ed. H. Rothwell (Camden Society, 1957), 215; *Annales Monastici*, IV, 278; *Littere Wallie*, ed. J. G. Edwards (Cardiff, 1940), 104; for Scotland, *Anglo-Scottish Relations*, 210–11. Edward remarked of Llywelyn that he was no more than 'one of the greater among the other magnates of our kingdom' (*Treaty Rolls 1234–1325*, ed. P. Chaplais (1955), no. 134, p. 54), and of King John Balliol that 'he came to *our* parliament at *our* command and was present in them *as our subject, like others of our realm*' (my italics).

[56] *Registrum epistolarum fratris Johannis Peckham*, ed. C. T. Martin, 3 vols. (R.S., 1882–5), II, 469–71; E. L. G. Stones and M. N. Blount, 'The Surrender of King John of Scotland to Edward I in 1296: Some New Evidence', *Bulletin of the Institute of Historical Research* 48 (1975), 94–106.

Were we able to stop the clock of history in, say, 1305 it would seem indeed as if such a prospect was about to be realized, but on terms which could hardly have been predicted in 1278. In Wales the native principality had been extinguished more than twenty years since, and it had meanwhile been made abundantly clear to the Marcher lords that their status gave them no immunity from the disciplinary power and supervision of the king of England. Scotland was kingless and had been browbeaten into total and seemingly irreversible submission; an ordinance placed before parliament at Westminster, though generous in its acknowledgement of the relative political maturity of Scotland and its leaders, now decided its future governance.[57] As to Ireland, never had English, and specifically royal, authority been more extensive in its institutional forms there than in the later years of Edward I. There were twelve English-type shires in the country and only the north-west corner of the island was altogether outside shire and liberty structure; English control of most of the diocesan structure of Ireland was likewise, at least formally, unchallenged.[58] We can go further: never had the physical presence of English power, be it in the person of the king himself or that of his appointed representatives, or in mighty castles such as Harlech and Beaumaris in Wales and Roscommon and Ballymote in the west of Ireland, been so ubiquitously and awesomely present in the outer zones of the British Isles as in the last fifteen years or so of Edward I's reign.[59]

It was, of course, the triumph of power; contemporaries were not short of saying so. Sometimes they said it crudely: the magnates had bragged that England could exterminate Scotland without any external help. 'What matter if both the Welsh and the Scots are our foes?' so Edward I is alleged to have boasted, 'Let them join forces if they please. We shall beat them both in a day.'[60] These statements may have been made, as we would say, off the record; but even on the record Edward I's language made no bones of the fact that in this instance might was right.[61] Power and proprietorship were the twin bases

[57] Davies, *Conquest*, ch. 14; Barrow, *Robert Bruce*, 132–6; *Anglo-Scottish Relations*, 240–60.

[58] A. J. Otway-Ruthven, 'Anglo-Irish Shire Government in the Thirteenth Century', *Irish Historical Studies* 5 (1946–7), 1–28, esp. p. 6; J. A. Watt, 'English Law and the Irish Church: the Reign of Edward I', in *Medieval Studies presented to Aubrey Gwynn*, ed. F. X. Martin et al. (Dublin, 1961), 133–67.

[59] See below, pp. 83–7, 172–3. Note the comment of Barrow, *Bruce*, 75 on Edward I in 1296: 'In four months he had traversed the whole eastern part of Scotland, stayed at every burgh and royal castle of note, and demonstrated his might to the people.' Edward had spent a total of 694 days in Wales in 1282–4, far longer than the total visits and campaigns of all his predecessors to the country since the Norman conquest.

[60] Matthew Paris, *Chronica Majora*, ed. H. R. Luard, 7 vols. (R.S., 1884–9), IV, 378; *Chronicle of Walter of Guisborough*, 325–6.

[61] It is noteworthy that the suggestion that the Statute of Wales (1284) was issued in response to the request, and with the consent of, the inhabitants of Wales was deleted between the draft and the final version: W. H. Waters, 'A First Draft of the Statute of Rhuddlan', *Bulletin of the Board of Celtic Studies* 4 (1927–9), 344–8.

of his authority in Britain. The land of Wales had come 'into the lordship of our possession (*in proprietatis nostrae dominium*)' and had been 'annexed and united to the crown of the said kingdom as part of the said body'.[62] As for Scotland, it was 'subjected by right of ownership to our power' and to his 'right and full dominion . . . by reason of property and possession'.[63] In the process the latent high kingship of earlier days—be it the stage-managed submissions of Henry II's day or the apparently genial ceremonies of 1278—was being transformed into a more direct authority. Terminology and titles made the point crisply. Wales and Scotland in succession lost their princely and kingly status; both now came to be described simply and pointedly as 'lands'.[64] The title of the prince of Wales was adopted, or usurped, for the English king's eldest son as heir apparent to the crown of England.[65] Though Edward I was occasionally referred to as 'king of England and Scotland', in reality the kingship of the Scots was in suspense for rebellion, subsumed in effect within the crown of England as that of its sovereign lord.[66] If to that we add the title lord of Ireland, then Edward I was now by 1305 in truth, if not in name, king of the British Isles, 'our realm' as he occasionally referred to it, if only implicitly, in the singular.[67] The transfer of the regalia and holiest relics of the Welsh principality and of the Scottish kingdom to Westminster in 1284 and 1296 respectively, to be located near or at the shrine of Edward the Confessor, the patron saint of the English monarchy, made it visually clear that the other kingships in Britain had been eradicated by, or absorbed in, the English kingship.[68] In

[62] Preamble to the Statute of Wales, 1284. For discussion see esp. Llinos B. Smith, 'The Statute of Wales, 1284', *Welsh History Review* 10 (1980–1), 127–54. Though English spokesmen had no hesitation in referring to what had happened in Wales as a conquest (e.g. *Rotuli Parliamentorum*, I, 93–4), they also defended it as being based on justice rather than might and by reference to the royal right: *Calendar of Charter Rolls*, II, 284; *Littere Wallie* (as above, n. 55), 125 (non hereditario sed jure regio).

[63] *Anglo-Scottish Relations*, 214–17.

[64] See, for example, Berry, *Statutes*, 293: 'Our land of Wales, our land of Ireland, our realm of England'; *Anglo-Scottish Relations*, 102 (1291), 146 (1296), 176 (1300–1), 240–58 (1305): 'the land of Scotland'. Usage is not consistent; but 'land' is the term used throughout the 1305 Ordinance. Cf. the argument put forward during the Great Cause: 'though the land of Scotland be called a "kingdom", the land itself is only a lordship, like Wales, the earldom of Chester, or the bishopric of Durham': *Edward I and the Great Cause* (as above, n. 35), II, 328–9.

[65] J. G. Edwards, *The Principality of Wales 1267–1967. A Study in Constitutional History* (Caernarfon, 1969).

[66] Edward I described as 'king of England and Scotland': Stevenson, *Documents*, II, no. 353. Cf. Ranald Nicholson, *Scotland. The Late Middle Ages* (Edinburgh, 1974): 'His [sc. Edward I's] ideal was an incorporating union under the English crown, a union in which the kingdom of Scotland would disappear.'

[67] *Anglo-Scottish Relations*, 210–11 (1301). Cf. *Rotuli Parliamentorum*, I, 283 (Ordinances of 1311): 'hors du Roiaume d'Engleterre, d'Escoce, d'Irlaunde et de Gales'.

[68] Prestwich, *Edward I*, 203–4, 474; Barrow, *Bruce*, 73. It was significant that it was the 10-year-old Alfonso, the eldest son of Edward I, who was given the honour of presenting the coronet (*aureola*) of Llywelyn ap Gruffudd at the shrine of Edward the Confessor at Westminster in 1284: *Chronicles of the Reigns of Edward I and Edward II*, ed. W. Stubbs, 2 vols. (R.S., 1882–3), I, 92.

both cases it was, as a contemporary English chronicler put it, 'a sign of the resignation and conquest of the kingdom'.[69] It was appropriate, therefore, that at his last parliament in Carlisle in January 1307 Edward promulgated a statute which was to apply in England, Ireland, Wales, and Scotland.[70]

What, of course, remained to be determined was how this composite, pluralistic realm was to be governed, and how and how far—given its profound ethnic, legal, linguistic, social, economic, and political fissures—it could move towards some measure of integration. The experiment of the Edwardian empire was too short-lived to give us the confidence to answer that question; but the hindsight that allows us to know what did not happen should not be permitted to conceal from us what was attempted and even achieved. New categories of enrolments were created in the English chancery to deal with the affairs of Wales and, later, Scotland;[71] the new exchequers at Caernarfon and later Carmarthen, and the much older one at Dublin, were made clearly answerable to the Westminster parent exchequer, and it was the practice of the Westminster exchequer which was to determine the habits of the new one to be established at Berwick;[72] taxes were levied in Wales (and Ireland) in 1292 and 1300 which suggested that the outer parts of Edward's British empire were to be introduced to the same fiscal discipline as the English heartland;[73] the Scots soon learnt that the maltolte on wool exports and later the new custom on alien merchants were to apply exactly in their country as in England;[74] and Westminster and the prince of Wales's palace at Kennington became the clearing-house for individual petitions from the remotest parts of the British Isles.[75] The way in which the resources of Ireland in men, money, and supplies were deployed in the conquest of Wales and later Scotland, or the way in which Welsh troops found ample scope for service in the king's armies in

[69] *Chronicle of Walter of Guisborough* (as above, n. 55), 281.

[70] *Rotuli Parliamentorum*, I, 220–1. For other examples: Berry, *Statutes*, 293, 314, 317; *Calendar of Justiciary Rolls ... re Ireland temp. Edward I*, ed. James Mills, 2 vols. (Dublin, 1905–14), II, 359.

[71] The *Rotuli Wallie* began on 2 November 1277; the *Rotuli Scotie* on 13 June 1291.

[72] Irish exchequer: J. F. Lydon in *NHI*, II, 194–5; Welsh exchequers: W. H. Waters, *The Edwardian Settlement of Wales in its Administrative and Legal Aspects* (Cardiff, 1938), 14–15; R. A. Griffiths, *The Principality of Wales in the Later Middle Ages. I. South Wales 1277–1536* (Cardiff, 1972), 35–44; the Berwick exchequer: Stevenson, *Documents*, II, 163–4.

[73] *The Merioneth Lay Subsidy Roll 1292–3*, ed. K. Williams-Jones (Cardiff, 1976); H. G. Richardson and G. O. Sayles, *Parliaments and Councils of Medieval Ireland*, I (Dublin, 1947), 193–9. Taxes had, of course, been levied in (English) Ireland earlier.

[74] Barrow, *Bruce*, 78 and n. 61; *Calendar of Patent Rolls 1292–1301*, 586; *Cal. Close Rolls 1302–7*, 229–30. The new custom of 1275 had already been applied to Ireland and Wales as well as to England: *CDI*, I, no. 1117. The whole of the British Isles was treated as a single commercial zone in its relations with Flanders in 1297: *CDI*, IV, no. 358.

[75] *Memoranda de Parliamento, 1305*, ed. F. W. Maitland (R.S., 1893); *The Record of Caernarvon*, ed. H. Ellis (1838), 212–25.

Ireland and Scotland, indicated that the British Isles were now a single stage of power which the king of England could treat as a unit for his own financial, military, and commissariat needs. If the power of the king of England was forging these islands into a more closely woven unit, might political integration follow, albeit at a distance? After all, Edward I had shown that he wanted more than conquest and annexation. In Wales in 1283 and in Scotland in the 1290s he demanded the allegiance of his new subjects, high and low, expressed in oaths of fealty, communal and individual.[76] Once allegiance had been secured, a measure of political participation and consultation might be considered—by meeting delegations from the leading men of north Wales in 1296 or by inviting Scottish representatives to the parliament which drew up the Ordinance for the governance of Scotland in 1305.[77]

Where all this might have led we shall never know, though we could make some informed guesses. Neither Edward nor his empire survived much longer. That, however, should not conceal from us that his reign had shown, more so (however briefly) than any earlier reign, that the English monarchy had the power to take the whole of the British Isles more or less under its control, when circumstances played into its hand and opportunities were seized. Contemporaries took that view. The burgesses of Berwick had already described Edward in 1294 as by divine providence ruler of the three realms of England, Scotland, and Ireland (Wales being presumably subsumed under England). One of the many monastic historians who tried their hands at composing a potted history of England in the late thirteenth century, in the context of the English claim to sovereignty over Scotland, expressed it more telegraphically: to him, Edward was simply 'the lord of the whole island'. Most impressive of all, not least because of the provenance of the comment, was the entry in the Annals of Connacht for 1307: 'Edward the Great, king of England, Wales and Scotland, duke of Gascony and lord of Ireland, rested in Christ. The crown of the king of England, Wales, Ireland and Scotland was afterwards given to Edward, son of Edward.'[78]

Diplomatically inaccurate this multiple title might be; but substantively it had the ring of truth. Edward I's power seemed to extend, at least

[76] *Littere Wallie*, 151, 154–7; Barrow, *Bruce*, 76 ('As in 1291 every substantial holder of land in Scotland was required to swear fealty to the king of England in his capacity—albeit unstated in his official style—of lord of Scotland.').

[77] *Calendar of Patent Rolls 1292–1301*, 223 (3 December 1296); *Anglo-Scottish Relations*, 240–3.

[78] *Calendar of Documents relating to Scotland*, II, no. 696; *Memoriale Fratris Walteri de Coventria* (as cited above, n. 39), 1–19 at p. 18 (Hic monarcha effectus et totius insule dominus, Walenses saepius se bellantes devicit, Scotos subvenit, et accepit homagium de magnatibus Scotiae, et omnia castra recepit in manu sua, et omnes insulas); *Annals of Connacht*, *s.a.* 1307; *Miscellaneous Irish Annals A.D. 1114–1437*, ed. S. Ó hInnse (Dublin, 1947), 135 (*s.a.* 1307).

metaphorically speaking, to the four corners of the British Isles. But the obituary notice in the Annals of Connacht has a further truth to it: Edward was described as king of four separate countries, *not* as king of the British Isles, nor even of Britain. In fact, Edward's formal title remained simply and exclusively king of England; his power over the other countries of the British Isles was regarded as subsumed in, or annexed to, that title. What had taken place was an English take-over of the British Isles. What remained to be seen was whether a take-over founded on power could be converted into a credible and sustainable union.

2

ISLAND MYTHOLOGIES

Nefyn is a tiny fishing village on the northern shore of the Llŷn peninsula in north-west Wales. There in late July 1284 Edward I held a celebratory round table. A large gathering of barons and knights from England and overseas assembled at Nefyn; no expense was spared; jousts were led by the earls of Lincoln and Ulster; and doubtless—Welsh weather permitting—a jolly time was had by all. The occasion for the jollities was, of course, the celebration of the final victory over the Welsh some eighteen months or less earlier. Nefyn was, and is, a picturesque place but desperately remote, as the foreign knights who picked up their supplies at Chester *en route* thither could doubtless testify.[1] So why was it chosen as the venue for the victory jamboree? It was in part, perhaps, because it was an ancient commotal centre with its own demesne land and one of the very few places in north-west Wales to show some incipient signs of urban life and maritime activity.[2] The availability of some minimal local supplies would have considerable appeal for the commissariat managers of Edward I's household. Nefyn had also been one of the residences of the native princes of north Wales; Edward seems to have made a point of appropriating those residences, sometimes physically transferring them into the new bastions of his power, as he did when he removed Llywelyn ap Gruffudd's hall at Ystumgwern into Harlech castle.[3]

But those who organize extravagant celebrations let their imaginations run riot; it surely required a rush of the romantic imagination to choose Nefyn, of all places, as the venue for the victory parade. Nefyn, as the contemporary accounts insist, lay in farthest Snowdonia between mountain and sea, the kind

[1] For accounts, see esp. *Annales Monastici* (as above, Ch. 1, n. 39), II, 402; III, 313; William Rishanger, *Chronica et Annales 1259–1307*, ed. H. T. Riley (R.S., 1865), 110; *Annales Cestrienses*, ed. and trans. R. C. Christie (Lancashire and Cheshire Record Society, 1887), 114. Note esp. the phrases 'apparatum maximum et expensas', 'in signum triumphi contra Wallensium protervam'. Edward was at Nefyn 27–31 July 1284: *Itinerary of Edward I*, 3 vols. (List and Index Society, 1974–7), I, 193.

[2] T. Jones Pierce, *Medieval Welsh Society*, ed. J. B. Smith (Cardiff, 1972), ch. VI; idem, 'Two Early Caernarvonshire Accounts', *Bulletin of the Board of Celtic Studies* 5 (1929–31), 142–55.

[3] *Royal Commission on Ancient Monuments in Wales and Monmouthshire. Caernarvonshire*, 3 vols. (1956–64), III, 83–4. Likewise, Prince Llywelyn's hall at Aberconwy was refurbished to provide a privy palace for Edward I's son, Edward: A. J. Taylor in *The History of the King's Works*, ed. H. M. Colvin, 6 vols. (1963–82), I, 353–4.

of place where a valiant knight might go on a perilous quest, into 'wild Wales', the land of Gog and Magog. But there was more to it than wildness and remoteness. It was at Nefyn that Gerald of Wales claimed to have discovered a copy of the prophecies of Merlin. Not far away at Caernarfon, in 1283, the body of Magnus Maximus, 'father of the noble emperor Constantine', had allegedly been discovered and, according to one report, had been reinterred in the church on Edward I's personal command. In June of the same year work had begun on what was the most remarkable statement of Edwardian imperial ideology, the castle of Caernarfon, its polygonal towers and banded masonry deliberately reminiscent of the walls of Constantinople, and its principal tower to be crowned by a triplet of turrets each bearing an imperial eagle. If to that we add that some contemporaries believed that the crown of King Arthur was one of the trophies secured from the Welsh after the conquest of 1282–3, it is not difficult to see how imaginative sensibilities might have become overexcited.[4]

Nor need we assume—as seems to be currently fashionable[5]—that the hard-headed and hard-hearted Edward I was altogether immune from such excitement. After all, he and his queen had been personally present at the abbey of Glastonbury on 18–19 April 1278 when the bodies of Arthur and Guinevere were disinterred, and had personally applied their seals to the certificates of authentication attached to the coffins prior to their reinterment before the great altar.[6] Flatterers were indeed beginning to wonder whether Edward I was not a new Arthur in the mould of Merlinic prophecies. When Edward married Margaret of France in September 1299, one chronicler based his account of the festivities almost verbatim on Geoffrey of Monmouth's famous description of the coronation feast of King Arthur at Caerleon.[7] But there was no need to enter the realm of fiction; the facts spoke eloquently enough for themselves, especially by the mid-1290s. The chronicler at Bury

[4] Nefyn's location: *Annales Monastici*, III, 313 (infra Walliam in ultimis finibus de Snowedune, supra mare); prophecies of Merlin: Gerald of Wales, *Opera*, VI, 124 (*Itinerary through Wales*, book 2, ch. 6); body of Magnus Maximus: *Flores Historiarum*, ed. H. R. Luard, 3 vols. (R.S., 1890), III, 59; Caernarfon castle: Taylor in *King's Works in Wales*, 370–1; Arthur's crown: *Annales Monastici*, II, 401; Rishanger, *Chronica*, 107; *Flores Historiarum*, III, 59.

[5] M. Prestwich, *Edward I*, 120–2. Contrast R. S. Loomis, 'Edward I, Arthurian Enthusiast', *Speculum* 28 (1953), 114–27. During his secret negotiations with the Scots in 1321, Thomas, earl of Lancaster, adopted the pseudonym 'King Arthur': J. R. Maddicott, *Thomas of Lancaster 1307–22* (1970), 302.

[6] There is a detailed description of the event in Adam of Domerham, *Historia de rebus gestibus Glastoniensibus*, ed. T. Hearne (Oxford, 1727), 587–9. See also J. C. Parsons, 'The Second Exhumation of King Arthur's Remains at Glastonbury, 19 April 1278', *Arthurian Literature*, ed. J. P. Carley and Felicity Riddy, 12 (1993), 173–7. I thank Dr Juliet Vale for drawing my attention to this article.

[7] Cf. *H.R.B.*, c.57 and Rishanger, *Chronica*, 395–7.

St Edmunds certainly saw the promised land at Edward I's feet by 1296: 'England, Scotland and Wales are under his sway. He has thereby acquired the former monarchy of the whole of Britain, for so long fragmented and truncated.'[8]

A new empire had been born, or, rather, an old empire—the monarchy of the whole of Britain—had been reborn. Empire-builders do not live by power alone; they yearn for a mythology and an ideology to explain and justify their success. The kings of England, like other empire-builders before and since, could look in several directions. They might, in the style of the structural amnesia of early medieval king-lists, adjust the past in order to claim by hereditary right what they had in fact secured by conquest. Few did it quite so outrageously as the Glastonbury chronicler who claimed that David I of Scotland (1124–53) had died without an heir—which, of course, he had not—and so the title to the kingship and land of the Scots had descended through his sister, Matilda, wife of Henry I, to the king of England as heir to, as well as lord of, Scotland![9] They might alternatively and additionally turn to feudal language and conventions: it was, of course, the rebellion of vassal rulers which was the pretext for the confiscation of the principality of Wales in 1282 and of the kingdom of Scotland in 1296. Contemporaries and historians alike have been much exercised, especially with regard to Scotland, about the propriety of such arguments. In truth, surely, it requires an exceptional degree of historical innocence to see feudal rituals, obligations, and terminology—especially between rulers—other than in terms of the structuring of the realities of power. As the story of the Great Cause—the process to decide the succession to the Scottish throne in 1291–2—shows, the definition of such relationships can be rapidly and casuistically adjusted to follow where power and ambition (including in this case the ambitions of the contenders for the Scottish throne)[10] had already led.

[8] *The Chronicle of Bury St Edmunds, 1212–1301*, ed. A. Gransden (1964), 133. Cf. the comments of Pierre Langtoft, quoted below, p. 43.

[9] *The Great Chartulary of Glastonbury*, ed. A. Watkin, 3 vols. (Somerset Record Society, 1947–56), I, iii (non solum dominum sed heredem). Cf. the claim of the author of the London recension of the Laws of Edward the Confessor that King Ine married a woman called Walla (hence the land of Cambria was henceforth called Wallia!) and 'was the first to secure the monarchy of the whole kingdom after the arrival of the English in Britain': F. Liebermann, *Die Gesetze der Angelsachsen*, 3 vols. (Halle, 1903–10), I, 658. Others could, of course, play these games. Thus Robert Bruce claimed to be the true descendant of the royal house of Wessex: see the remarkable Scottish apologia published in P. Linehan, 'A Fourteenth-century History of Anglo-Scottish Relations in a Spanish Manuscript', *Bulletin of the Institute of Historical Research* 48 (1975), 106–22.

[10] *Anglo-Scottish Relations*, 112–14; *C.D.S.*, II, nos. 482, 483–8, 489. Note that John Balliol acknowledges in his fealty and homage that Edward I is 'sovereign seignour du reaume de Escoce' (*Foedera* I, ii, 181).

Perhaps more convincing as justificatory arguments—because less contaminated by the casuistries of the lawyers—were appeals to God, reason, justice, civility, and good order. Wales, so commented Edward I, was subject to us not only by power (*potentia*) but also by justice (*justitia*).[11] Justice should, perhaps, be left to the gods; but economic prosperity and governmental good order are more humanly measurable and thereby exportable commodities. In both fields the English realm most certainly had—and equally certainly knew that it had—a great deal to offer the rest of Britain. The Anglo-Normans, and the English after them, rarely commented on their mission and achievement in this respect in so many words; but when they did so their observations could be bluntly frank. The benefits of conquest were their own justification. Of Wales, they said in the mid-twelfth century that 'they perseveringly civilized it after they had vigorously subdued it'; the result vindicated the means employed: 'one might have thought it in no wise inferior to the most fertile part of Britain', in short a second England.[12] In political terms, likewise, it was in the name of good order and sound laws that the imposition of English rule and English norms across the rest of the British Isles was justified: 'to reduce the land and its inhabitants to obedience', 'to reform the state of the country', or to introduce 'a better pattern of life' are just a few of the phrases which bespeak such a mentality.[13] And in their mission as the apostles of good order, civility, and economic enterprise the English could generally rely on the sanction and support of the Church: thus it was under the blessing of the bull *Laudabiliter* (1155–6) that the English set out to bring Ireland under their control, while in Wales over a century later the fulminations and exhortations of Archbishop Pecham both preceded and followed Edward I's armies as they reduced Wales to the king's will.

There were, therefore, several avenues of argument open to English kings and apologists to explain and justify their claims to domination of the rest of Britain and Ireland and to the pursuit of those claims. But in a past-oriented and a past-validating society, claims to empire and supremacy, as to all other forms of power, had ultimately to be located in the past. So it was on this occasion. The argument from history could operate at different levels and on various chronological registers. The rich records of the English chancery could be systematically ransacked to provide documentary chapter and verse to bolster the claim to the overlordship of Britain. It was in this spirit, for example, that a clerk was set to work in the 1270s to make a selection from the *Curia*

[11] *Calendar of Charter Rolls*, II, 284.

[12] *Gesta Stephani*, ed. K. R. Potter and R. H. C. Davis (Oxford, 1976), 15.

[13] *Gesta Stephani*, 15 (Wales); *Foedera*, I, ii, 737 (Scotland); Gerald of Wales, *Expugnatio*, 100–1, 145–7 (Ireland).

regis rolls of cases relating to English jurisdiction over Wales, or again in the 1290s to assemble the dossier containing correspondence relating to Wales since 1240 which we know as *Liber A* or *Littere Wallie*.[14] Scotland presented a much more difficult target for the propagandists of English overlordship than did Wales: it had not been within the reach of English jurisdiction since the days of systematic record-keeping, and therefore a much longer time perspective and the deployment of very different kinds of historical evidence were necessary to underpin the case for overlordship. So it was that in 1291 Edward I ordered the ransacking of the chronicles and muniments of English monasteries to provide him with the evidence to be *dominus superior* of Scotland.[15] The returns and the potted histories of Anglo-Scottish relations which resulted from the exercise are surely one of the most remarkable medieval examples of the deployment and distortion of the past in the service of the present. But ultimately the search for a usable and justificatory past must necessarily proceed beyond mere history into the dark worlds of origins and mythology. So it was to be in Stuart England with the Ancient Constitution and the Immemorial Law; so it was in the Middle Ages with what the chronicler of Bury St Edmunds had called the monarchy of the whole of Britain. If the English wished to ground their claim to the domination of Britain in a historical or mythological past, then they could not do so without engaging with the term 'Britain' or without treading on the toes of alternative historical mythologies. That was the challenge that became increasingly clear as the thirteenth century drew to its close.

The idea of Britain exercised a powerful hold over the medieval mind. It had a depth, a resonance, a precision, and an incontestability which did not belong to its imprecise, contestable, and Johnny-come-lately competitors—England, Scotland, Wales. Britain had long constituted a separate, definable world on its own, an *alter orbis* as it was still known in Anselm's day.[16] It had the further advantage of being a precise, even neutral, geographical term which was apparently immune from the vagaries and inconstancies of political fortune in a way which was not true of, say, Francia and Germania or *Wallia* or *Scotia*. Early medieval writers from Gildas through Bede and 'Nennius' to Geoffrey of Monmouth were very much at home with the concept of Britain: it was the natural geographical framework for their histories. A rapid pen portrait of this

[14] PRO Curia Regis Rolls (K.B. 26), no. 159; *Welsh Assize Roll*, ed. J. Conway Davies, 13–30; *Littere Wallie*, ed. J. G. Edwards, xxvii–xxxiii.

[15] *Edward I and the Throne of Scotland*, ed. Stones and Simpson (as above, ch. 1, n. 68), ch. VI; R. A. Griffiths, 'Edward I, Scotland and the Chronicles of English Religious Houses', *Journal of the Society of Archivists* 65 (1979), 191–9 (now reprinted in idem, *Conquerors and Conquered in Medieval Wales* (Stroud, 1994), ch. 11).

[16] R. W. Southern, *Saint Anselm and his Biographer* (Cambridge, 1963), 128–30.

best and fairest of isles—its length and breadth in miles, its twenty-eight cities, its rivers, its associated islands—became a recognized *topos* with which to introduce their works.[17] One could be very precise about such an island: Bede assessed the whole circuit of its coast at some 4,875 miles; the Welsh Triads, the Triads of the Isle of Britain as they were appropriately known, were even more specific: Britain extended from the promontory of Blathaon (probably in Caithness) to that of Penwith (near Land's End) and from Crigyll in Anglesey to Sarre End in Kent.[18] Then again Britain had the great advantage of being a classical Latin word, Britannia, and a province of the Roman empire. It thereby provided a bridge to the classical Roman world and the respectability and antiquity that Roman origins offered. So it was that it was not in the forests of Germany but with Julius Caesar's invasion of Britain that Bede opened his Ecclesiastical History of the English People, and it was with the *status universae Britanniae* that he closed his account.[19] Bede's choice of terms and of chronological framework was profoundly significant. He had in effect hitched the history of the *gens Anglorum* to an earlier, pre-English, and Roman history of Britain. Bede was, of course, important not only for his own sake but for the huge shadow he cast over historical thinking in England for so many centuries into the future, even to our own day. Perhaps the academic apotheosis of his view of the past was the decision to inaugurate the Oxford History of *England* with a half-volume, recently upgraded to a full one, on Roman *Britain*.

But Britain was more than a convenient and historically redolent term; it was also, throughout the early Middle Ages, a political aspiration. It presented a prospect of unity and simplicity in what was a fragmented and fissile world of ethnic divisions and short-lived hegemonies. In short, it was a potent element of political mythology. An occasional king of Northumbria or Mercia in the seventh and eighth centuries might be accorded the title of king of Britain or, even more extravagantly, 'emperor of the whole of Britain'. But it was in the tenth century that the kings of Wessex-England began to explore the full, and fulsome, possibilities of such claims. After he had recovered York

[17] Gildas, *The Ruin of Britain and other documents*, ed. and trans. M. Winterbottom (1978), 16–17; Bede, *Ecclesiastical History*, ed. B. Colgrave and R. A. B. Mynors (Oxford, 1969), I, c. 1; Nennius, *British History*, ed. and trans. J. Morris (1980), 18–19; *H.R.B.*, ch. 5. For Gildas as 'the father of the concept of *Ynys Prydein* (the Island of Britain)', see esp. Patrick Sims-Williams, 'Gildas and the Anglo-Saxons', *Cambridge Medieval Celtic Studies* 6 (1983), 1–30.

[18] *Trioedd Ynys Prydein. The Welsh Triads*, ed. Rachel Bromwich (2nd edn., Cardiff, 1978), 228–35. According to the *Brut*, *s.a.* 1114 (p. 37), the army which Henry I assembled in that year came from 'all the island of Britain, from the promontory of Penwith in Cornwall to the promontory of Blathaon in Scotland'.

[19] Bede, I, c. 2; V, c. 23 (p. 560). Cf. J. N. Stephens, 'Bede's Ecclesiastical History', *History* 62 (1977), 1–14.

in 927, Athelstan inscribed his coins with the words *rex totius Britanniae* and in his charters he could be even more expansive: 'I, Athelstan, king of the English elevated by the right hand of the Almighty, which is Christ, to the throne of the whole kingdom of Britain'. Several of Athelstan's successors followed suit. Thus Edgar's coronation rite exhorted him to be honoured 'above all kings of Britain', while one of his charters saluted him as 'king and emperor of . . . the kings and peoples dwelling within the boundaries of Britain'.[20] Inflated such titles may have been, but perhaps not preposterous if we consider the position and pretensions of, say, Edgar in the 970s. In any case, men's ambitions and vanities are part of the historian's agenda; rulership of Britain was clearly part and parcel of such ambitions and vanities. The fashion for such pan-Britannic claims may have declined after the late tenth century; but it by no means disappeared. Even on the eve of the Norman conquest, the title *rex totius Britanniae* was accorded to Edward the Confessor in one group of his charters, and his near-contemporary biographer assumed that he was the ruler of Britain, nothing less.[21] Such ideas seem to have cut much less ice with the Normans; they were more concerned with power than with grandiose labels. But the idea of Britain would not go away; it was simply transferred from the realm of political rhetoric to that of historiography. Thus when Henry of Huntingdon came to write his History of the English in about 1130, he constructed his past to lead inexorably to an imperial and British monarchy. 'The kingdom of Wessex,' he commented under the year 519, 'in course of time subjected all to itself and obtained the monarchy of all Britain'—precisely the achievement which the Bury St Edmunds chronicler was to attribute to Edward I in 1296, just as the author of the Leges Anglorum was to make free use of the phrase in John's reign.[22]

A single Britain was more than a political aspiration; it was also an ecclesiastical dream. Indeed in the late eleventh and early twelfth century, it was churchmen above all who kept the idea alive and for their own purposes. It was after all an idea with an apostolic lineage to it. From the earliest correspondence of Pope Gregory the Great and St Augustine of Canterbury, the unit which was, at least theoretically, the object of salvation and ecclesiastical organization was Britain. Indeed what else could one call it? So it was that

[20] *English Historical Documents, c.500–1042*, ed. D. Whitelock (2nd edn, 1979), 548–9, 560, 563; Eric John, *Orbis Britanniae and Other Studies* (Leicester, 1966), esp. ch. 1; Henry Loyn, *Society and Peoples. Studies in the History of England and Wales, c.600–1200* (1992), ch. 21; B. Yorke, 'The Vocabulary of Anglo-Saxon Overlordship', *Anglo-Saxon Studies in Archaeology and History* 2 (1981), 171–200.

[21] F. Barlow, *Edward the Confessor* (1970), 135–7.

[22] Henry of Huntingdon, *Historia Anglorum* (as above, ch. I, n. 26), 96–7; for chronicle of Bury St Edmunds and the author of the Leges Anglorum, see above, pp. 16–17, 32–3.

Augustine was given the designation 'archbishop of the Britains', and one of his most distinguished successors, Theodore, that of 'archbishop of the island of Britain and the see of Canterbury'.[23] And so the examples could be multiplied. What is more, those examples and the Ecclesiastical History of Bede—with its clear yearning for a single and orthodox Church of Britain—were assiduously studied at Canterbury in the eleventh and twelfth centuries. Such texts and such titles were now deployed in order to bolster Canterbury's claim to primacy over York and to metropolitan power over the whole of Britain and indeed Ireland also. For about eighty years after 1070 the Norman archbishops of Canterbury showed remarkable, if spasmodic, tenacity in the pursuit of such claims. Lanfranc, Anselm, and their successors recurrently flaunted titles such as 'primate of the whole of Britain'; their spokesmen, such as Eadmer and John of Salisbury, frequently referred to Canterbury as 'the mother of Britain' or 'the first see of Britain'. Just in case there was any ambiguity as to the meaning of that phrase, it was specifically spelt out by Archbishop Anselm: 'primate of the whole of England, Scotland, Ireland and the adjacent isles'.[24] Men of the mind are always more likely to be seduced by such grand abstractions than men of muscle. But even ecclesiastics were shrewd enough to realize that their ambitions might find even more favour if they could be supported by arguments of political expediency. And so they were. 'It would be expedient for the solidarity of the kingdom,' so Archbishop Lanfranc is alleged to have argued, 'that all Britain should be subject to one primate.' In short, Britain should have one king and one archbishop.[25]

Such ambitions were shattered in the twelfth century. Canterbury's hopes for primacy over the British Isles were denied it by the papacy, first by the establishment of four archbishoprics for Ireland and later by taking the Scottish Church directly under its own wing. It was left merely with Wales, and even there its hold was recurrently challenged. The 'mother of Britain' had

[23] Bede, II, c. 3–4; IV, c. 17.

[24] From many examples one might cite the following: *Councils and Synods*, ed. D. Whitelock, M. Brett, and C. N. L. Brooke (Oxford, 1981), II, 619; *The Letters of Lanfranc*, ed. H. Clover and M. T. Gibson (Oxford, 1979), 50–1; Margaret Gibson, *Lanfranc* (Oxford, 1978), 121; Eadmer, *Historia Novorum in Anglia*, ed. M. Rule (R.S., 1884), 26, 42, 189; Hugh the Chantor, *The History of the Church of York 1066–1127*, ed. C. Johnson (1961), 7, 126–7; John of Salisbury, *Letters*, ed. W. J. Millor et al., 2 vols. (1955–79), II, 466, 499; *Episcopal Acts re Welsh Dioceses*, ed. J. Conway Davies, I, 240 (D.38). It is interesting to note how Bede's phrase 'all of the church of the English' (IV, c. 2) was transmuted by Eadmer into 'all the bishops of Britain' (*Historia Novorum*, 282). For a full discussion of Canterbury's claims, see M. T. Flanagan, *Irish Society* (as cited above, Ch. 1, n. 17), ch. 1. Simultaneously the archbishops of York were claiming that all the bishoprics of Scotland were their suffragans, in accordance with Gregory the Great's grand plan for the ecclesiastical organization of Britain: *Regesta Regum Scottorum, I, The Acts of Malcolm IV*, ed. G. W. S. Barrow (Edinburgh, 1960), 16–17.

[25] Hugh the Chantor (as in n. 24), 126–7.

contracted into the Church in England, the *ecclesia anglicana*. As for political visions of Britain, the Normans never seem to have been deeply enamoured of them; after all, their origins, their affections, and their ambitions lay more in northern France than in the grim outer zones of *ultima Thule*. But just at the moment that the concept of Britain was retreating from the world of ecclesiastical and political realities, it was given a huge life-saving and indeed life-enhancing injection in literary circles. I refer, of course, to the appearance of Geoffrey of Monmouth's *History of the Kings of Britain* in the late 1130s.[26] *We* regard Geoffrey's *History* as a great literary hoax. Though some of his near contemporaries regarded Geoffrey as a disreputable scoundrel, the vast majority of them—starting with the sober and balanced Henry of Huntingdon—were swept off their feet by his stories. And so were their successors for generations, indeed centuries, to come. We could regard this, with the naturally dyspeptic jealousy of academic historians, as mere literary success; even at that level we should stand in awe: there survive 215 manuscript copies of Geoffrey's *Historia*, leaving the Venerable Bede, his nearest competitor, trailing far behind at 164.[27]

But there was more to the *Historia* than literary seductiveness and success; it also posed a profound political challenge. This is not merely or mainly a matter of whether contemporaries believed Geoffrey's account to be true or not; it is, after all, in the world of the imagination that some of the most powerful political universes are created and some of the greatest political challenges are met. Therein lies Geoffrey's true significance. We can identify at least four challenges that his work presented, all of them revolving around the challenge implicit in the concept of Britain. First there was King Arthur. With the appearance and triumphant success of Geoffrey's work, Arthur became the paradigm of what truly great kingship could be; measured by his standards, his modern successors turned out to be wimps. He was everywhere: one day, so it was said, Peter des Roches came across him, 'once lord of the monarchy of the whole of Britain', while out hunting; Edward I and his wife gazed at his remains at Glastonbury in 1278.[28] He was an ambivalent, even threatening, spectral presence: after all, his great victories had been won at the expense of the Saxons, 'whose very name,' so Geoffrey has him assert, 'is an insult to

[26] Citations are from *HRB* in Neil Wright's edition, as cited in the List of Abbreviations. The book and chapter headings of Lewis Thorpe's translation (Harmondsworth, 1966) are cited for convenience in brackets.

[27] Julia Crick, *The Historia Regum of Geoffrey of Monmouth. III. A Summary Catalogue of the Manuscripts* (Cambridge, 1989), 9; idem, *IV. Dissemination and Reception in the Later Middle Ages* (Cambridge, 1991).

[28] *Chronicon de Lanercost, 1201–1446*, ed. J. Stevenson (Edinburgh, Maitland Club, 1839), 23; above, p. 32.

heaven and detested by all men'.[29] Arthur was in truth more of a threat dead than alive; the prospect of his return to reclaim his inheritance and to be crowned as king in London was tied into the prophecies of Merlin, the second chilling challenge in Geoffrey's *Historia*. The prophecies were deeply disconcerting stuff: it was little wonder that the threat at the end of the first version of Geoffrey's book that the British people would regain the island (Britain) at some point in the future through the merits of their faith should be replaced in the subsequent First Variant Version by the reassurance that the Britons had lost the crown of the kingdom for ever.[30] But the reassurance did not work. The sneaking fear persisted that the Welsh boast—that 'by means of Arthur they will win back . . . this land all together. . . . They will give back its name to the land. They will call it Britain again'—might come true and Merlin's prophecy be realized.[31] Arthur, Merlin, and the word Britain were an eminently dangerous combination: they were a deadly threat to English supremacy since they predicated the return of Britain and the Britons to their former glory. That alone helps to explain the ghoulish account in a London chronicle of what happened to the decapitated head of Llywelyn, the last native prince of Wales, in December 1282: it was taken 'to the city of London where Brutus used to be crowned, placed upon a stave and crowned with a crown of ivy and then placed on the Tower of London, in fulfilment of the prophecy of the said Merlin'.[32] Those who indulge in such sick charades are deeply insecure people: Geoffrey and Merlin had made them so.

The third challenge implied in Geoffrey's text lay in its conception of the political order. The *Historia* assumes throughout a single Britain ruled by a succession of single kings: 'the island of one crown', 'the diadem of Britain', 'the kingship of the whole island' (which King Arthur had held) are among its recurrent themes. Geoffrey was too clever an artist to define closely what he meant in political terms by Britain; in particular, he was suitably ambiguous

[29] *HRB* c. 145 (IX c. 4).

[30] *HRB* c. 204–5 (XII c. 17); The *Historia Regum Britanniae of Geoffrey of Monmouth. First Variant Version* (Cambridge, 1988), c. 186/7, c. 204.

[31] From 'The Description of England' (as cited in Ch. 1, n. 26). John Gillingham has suggested that 'The Description' should be dated *c.*1140: 'The Context and Purposes of Geoffrey of Monmouth's *History of the Kings of Britain*', *Anglo-Norman Studies* 13 (1991), 99–118 at p. 112. Cf. the prophecy of Merlin according to *HRB* c. 114 no. 20 (VIII c. 3 at p. 175)—notably the threat to delete the name of England (*nuncupatio extraneorum*) and to restore the name of Britain (*nomine Bruti*).

[32] *Flores Historiarum* (as cited above, n. 4), III, 51; *Chronicles of Edward I and Edward II* (as cited above, ch. 1, n. 68). The comment of the latter (*The Annals of London*) on the significance of the defeat of the Welsh merits quotation in this context: 'And so the glory of the Welsh who were once called Britons has been totally transferred [to the English]. . . . And whatever the prince of Wales ought to have achieved according to the prophecies [of Merlin] has now been effected by King Edward.'

about Scotland.[33] But such evasive ambiguities were part of his stock-in-trade; they did not detract from the fact that his central political image was the single monarchy of Britain, to be contrasted surely with the petty quarrelling kingdoms of Bede's *Historia*, just as his assumption of the ethnic unity of the Britons contrasted with the ethnic jumble of Bede's world. No one could claim to be king of Britain until that fractured unity had been restored. And it was an aboriginal unity, which brings us to the fourth gauntlet which Geoffrey threw down. Bede may have thought that he was bold to have started his *History of the English People* with the invasion of Julius Caesar, thereby linking the world of the Anglo-Saxons with that of Roman antiquity. Geoffrey, of course, was much more ambitious: he reached the Romans in Britain only in chapter 54 of his book; before that lay over a thousand years of British history and a whole galaxy of kings stretching back to Brutus, great-grandson of Aeneas and first king of Britain.

We can, of course, dismiss such a farrago with a smile, because we have replaced such mythologies of creation and evolution by our own. Contemporaries could not afford such luxuries. In past-oriented and past-validating societies, control and exploitation of the past are critical to credibility in the present. To lose out on the history of Britain from Brutus to Julius Caesar, or even to Hengist and Horsa, was not only to forfeit a really good story, it was also to introduce discontinuity and usurpation into what should be a seamless web of legitimacy. The awkward issue that had to be negotiated was what has been called 'the passage of dominion', the smooth grafting of the glorious history of Britain's past to the saga of English victory, leading to a future consummation in the restoration of an Arthurian monarchy of the whole of Britain. The British past had to be captured and possessed by the English if their claim to the domination of Britain, and with it the revival of Arthur's empire, was to be historically and mythologically legitimized. Mythologizing propaganda, maybe; but we who live in an age of media hype and spin doctors should be the last to poke fun at or underrate such activity.

Three examples may serve to illustrate how the task was undertaken. The first was the letter which Edward I sent to Pope Boniface VIII in May 1301, to explain his right as 'immediate and proper lord of the realm of Scotland'. It began its potted history in the days of Eli and of Samuel the prophet with 'a certain valiant and illustrious man of the Trojan race called Brutus', and moved through kings such as Belinus and Locrinus until it reached Arthur, 'king of the Britons and the most renowned of princes'. Arthur's role was

[33] Single Britain: *HRB*, cc. 143, 159, 187, 192, 200 (IX, c. 1, c. 16; XI, c. 11; XII, c. 3, c. 11); Scotland: *HRB*, c. 199 (XII, c. 10).

pivotal: he trounced the Scots, installed his own nominee as king of Scotland, and required him to carry the sword at Arthur's coronation, as a sign of the subjection of Scotland to the kings of Britain. From Arthur the story moved easily, and brazenly, to Alfred and his successors, kings of England—no longer of Britain—who 'enjoyed both monarchy and dominion in the island' (that is, Britain). Thereafter the historical argument to sustain the case for English overlordship of Scotland from Edward the Elder to Edward I could be, and was, easily cobbled together from a hand-picked sheaf of English sources.[34]

The second example represented visually what had been written in prose in the letter of 1301. It was composed at much the same time, probably at St Mary's Abbey, York, whither the central offices and governmental records had been transferred during Edward I's campaigns against Scotland. It is in effect a pictorial genealogical history of the kings of Britain/England. It starts with twenty large circular medallions, outlining the classical ancestry of the rulers of Britain, beginning with Jason's quest for the golden fleece and ending with Brutus, the descendant of Aeneas, setting out to found a new Troy, Albion. There then follow 220 small circular medallions, one each for the rulers of Britain from Brutus to Edward I. So was constructed the seamless web of the history of the kings of Britain, with the kings of England neatly and effortlessly grafted onto the line of their Trojan and British predecessors. But the roll communicated a more immediate historical lesson. It concluded (though this portion of the roll subsequently became detached) with a further 72 small medallions. On these medallions are represented the kings of England and Scotland and the intermarriages between the two houses across the centuries. The last of those marriages—that of Edward I's son and heir to Queen Margaret, the 'Maid of Norway', heiress to the Scottish throne—should have led to the ultimate political consummation of these marriage alliances, the dynastic union of the two crowns, albeit that the separateness of the two countries was to be respected. The death of the Maid, of course, defeated such a prospect and led to Edward I's claim that he was a chief or superior lord of Scotland. It was to further such a claim, and to illustrate it pictorially, that the roll was prepared, quite likely (as would seem from its outstanding quality) as a presentation copy for the king himself.[35] The English

[34] *Anglo-Scottish Relations*, pp. 192–219. Cf. *Edward I and the Throne of Scotland 1290–1296*, ed. E. L. G. Stones and G. G. Simpson, II, 298–9. The Brutus argument (derived ultimately from *HRB*) was not deployed in the Anglo-Scottish polemical war until 1300–1. It is interesting to note that Edward I's son was given a copy of *HRB* in 1301: Hilda Johnstone, *Edward of Carnarvon 1284–1307* (Manchester, 1947), 18.

[35] Bodleian Library, Oxford, Bodley Rolls 3; British Library, Cotton Galba Charter XIV.4. The relationship between the two rolls was established by W. H. Monroe, 'Two Medieval Genealogical Roll-Chronicles in the Bodleian Library', *Bodleian Library Record* 10 (1981),

needed the solace of history—a history of Britain *ab origine*—as the ideological arm of their subjugation of the island.

The third example is a manuscript volume which found a home in All Souls College, Oxford, in the library where the figure of King Arthur beamed down, appropriately enough, from the stained-glass windows.[36] It communicated the same message as the other two. It is a composite volume compiled probably in the early fourteenth century. It contained, *inter alia*, an unfinished copy of Geoffrey's *Historia*, a potted history of English kings from Saxon times, a copy of Edward I's 1301 letter to the Pope regarding his claim to Scotland, conventional notes about the dimensions and divisions of England (which, incidentally, since they indicated that England extended from Cornwall to Caithness and from St David's to Dover, made it clear what they thought of Scotland and Wales) and, finally, a copy of the section of Peter Langtoft's Chronicle which dealt with Edward I's reign, especially, and vituperatively, his dealings with Scotland. It is the conjunction of distant past and recent present, and indeed the continuity from the one to the other, which are the intriguing features of this composite volume. And at the centre of it lies a vision of a single Britain, past and now, hopefully and imminently, present. It was that vision—with its clear echoes of King Arthur—which prompted Peter Langtoft, canon of Bridlington, to a paean of poetic ecstasy in the later years of Edward I as he saw the fulfilment of Merlin's prophecy: 'Now are all the islanders joined together, And Albany reunited to the regalities / Of which King Edward is proclaimed lord. Cornwall and Wales are in his power / And Ireland the Great at his will. There is neither king nor prince of all the countries / Except King Edward who has joined/judged them. Arthur never had the lands so fully.' The Arthurian empire had been reconstituted and indeed surpassed; the monarchy of the Island of Britain was once more unitary.[37]

But the story did not end there, as Peter Langtoft bitterly conceded. The bid to reconstitute the empire of Britain failed. The reason for the failure lay in part in the events of the first part of the fourteenth century; to these we will return later. But the reason lay more decidedly and comprehensively in the

115–21. The MSS are described in L. F. Sandler, *Gothic Manuscripts 1285–1385*, 2 vols. (1986), I, 26–7.

[36] All Souls College, Oxford, MS 39, described in Andrew G. Watson, *A Descriptive Catalogue of the Medieval Manuscripts of All Souls College Oxford* (Oxford, 1997), 76–9. For the stained glass in the library, see above, pp. 1–2.

[37] Pierre de Langtoft, *Chronicle*, ed. and trans. T. Wright, 2 vols. (R.S., 1866–8), II, 264–7. Langtoft felt that Edward I should model himself on Arthur: 'In ancient histories we find written / What kings and what kingdoms King Arthur conquered / And how he shared largely his acquisitions / There was not a king under him who contradicted him, / Earl, duke or baron who ever failed him / In war or in battle.'

past, specifically in the existence of alternative mythologies which the English failed to dislodge. We can overlook the objection of the terminological pedants that the Britain of Langtoft's dream and Edward I's ambition did not, of course, correspond to the Roman province of Britannia at any point in its history. Much more serious, indeed insuperable, was the fact that power of itself does not automatically entitle the powerful to appropriate a mythology, try as they might. The original owners and sitting tenants of British mythology were still in residence and would lay claim to their inheritance for centuries to come. They were, of course, the Britons, otherwise and latterly known as the Welsh. They stood squarely and stubbornly between the English and the latter's attempt to appropriate the mythology of the island of Britain.

We may start with terms and language, for to control language and terminology was, as we shall see, to appropriate mythology. Until at least the middle of the twelfth century the people whom we know as Welsh regularly, if not invariably, called themselves Britons and the language they spoke the British speech.[38] Britain, *Britannia*, was the name of *their* island; the name of the other place, whose existence had to be temporarily if inconveniently recognized, was—if it was given a name at all—*Anglia* or even *Saxonia*.[39] Clinging on to such terms—Britain, British, Britons—when reality had so patently moved on some centuries since was not just an act of cultural archaism; it was also a profound historical, political, and prophetic statement. Historically it proclaimed that the Britons were the aboriginal and still authentically the only true proprietors of the Island of Britain. Welsh historical lore—a lore sedulously cultivated by its professional, and often hereditary, class of remembrancers for the better part of a millennium—assumed the Island of Britain as its basic and irreducible unit; its poetry, prose tales, and hagiography take that assumption for granted; so, even more evidently, does the mnemonic distillation of its historical lore, known appropriately as *Trioedd Ynys Prydain*, the Triads of the Isle of Britain.[40]

But in a past-dominated society, historical lore was also a political statement. So it was on this occasion; and the prime message from that statement—and the one that Geoffrey of Monmouth was later to filch—was that of the

[38] I hope to explore this theme fully, with supporting documentation, later.

[39] For the Britannia/Anglia or Saxonia contrast, see, for example, Asser, *Life of King Alfred*, ed. W. H. Stevenson (Oxford, 1904), 63, 65; *Vitae Sanctorum Britanniae et Genealogiae*, ed. A. W. Wade-Evans (Cardiff, 1944), 92; *The Book of Llan Dâv. Liber Landavenis*, ed. J. Gwenogvryn Evans (facsimile, Aberystwyth, 1979), 192.

[40] From a very extensive literature, reference may be made here to *Trioedd Ynys Prydein* (as cited above, n. 18), esp. xcviii–cxxiv; B. F. Roberts, 'Geoffrey of Monmouth and the Welsh Historical Tradition', *Nottingham Medieval Studies* 20 (1976), 29–40; P. P. Sims-Williams, 'Some Functions of Origin Stories in Early Medieval Wales', *History and Heroic Tale*, ed. T. Nyberg et al. (Odense, 1985), 97–131.

sovereignty and unity of Britain as a single—indeed, ultimately, the only truly legitimate—unit of power. Thus it was the theme song 'The Sovereignty of Britain' which, according to the Welsh law-texts, the bard of the household of a Welsh king was to intone when the booty was being distributed after a royal raiding party; it was as 'the great king of the Britons who ruled the whole of Britain' that past rulers such as Arthur and Maelgwn were remembered, and that was long before Geoffrey got to work; it was as one 'born of the famous race of Britons, the race which once withstood the Roman army vigorously and forced Julius Caesar to flee as a fugitive' that Ieuan ap Sulien introduced himself in Latin verse in the late eleventh century.[41] Ecclesiastically such statements were likewise echoed in the memories of St David as 'archbishop of the whole British race' and by claims—vigorously pursued by the Norman bishops of St Davids—that his see was 'the first and greatest of the provinces of the whole of Britain' and 'the greatest glory of the realm of Britain'.[42] The literature of Wales throughout the medieval period, and indeed beyond, was similarly saturated in references to a pan-British past: so it was, for example, that the author of one of the great Welsh medieval prose tales introduced Bendigeidfran as 'crowned king of this Island [of Britain] and exalted with the crown of London'; equally the measure of the calamity of the killing of Llywelyn ap Gruffudd, prince of Wales, in 1282 could be indicated only by comparing it with the killing of Arthur and Bendigeidfran, twin rulers of Britain.[43]

And so the examples could be multiplied across the centuries. They show how memories, continuous if contrived memories, of a glorious past weighed heavily and inspiringly on the Welsh mind; they were the ideological framework for its political ambitions. They also carried with them sentiments of despair and prophecy, likewise centred around Britain and its history. Despair sprang from the memory of the oppressions (Welsh *gormesoedd*) which the Island of Britain had suffered. The third of those oppressions, according to the Triads, was 'the Saxons, with Horsa and Hengist as their leaders'. And 'none of those oppressions,' it added mournfully, 'went back.' Indeed oppression might presage annihilation, genocide. That was the apocalypse which the Welsh chronicler anticipated in 1114 when Henry I set out on an expedition

[41] *Llyfr Iorweth. A Critical Text of the Venedotian Code of Medieval Welsh Law*, ed. A. R. Wiliam (Cardiff, 1960), 10; *Vitae Sanctorum* (as cited in n. 39), 68–70, 136; M. Lapidge, 'Welsh Latin Poetry', *Studia Celtica* 8–9 (1973–4), 68–106 at p. 83.

[42] Rhigyfarch, *Life of St David*, ed. J. W. James (Cardiff, 1967), 24–5; *Episcopal Acts re Welsh Dioceses*, ed. J. Conway Davies, I, D 131; D 139.

[43] *Pedeir Keinc y Mabinogi*, ed. I. Williams (2nd edn., Cardiff, 1951), 29; T. Roberts, 'Englynion Marwnad i Lywelyn ap Gruffudd', *Bulletin of the Board of Celtic Studies* 26 (1974–6), 10–12.

against the Welsh. He had, so the chroniclers recorded ominously, assembled his forces 'from the whole island of Britain', and his intention was nothing less than 'to exterminate all the Britons so that the Britannic name should never more be remembered'.[44] Contemporary events were clearly interpreted within an age-old pan-Britain mythology. The suicidal despair which such threats generated could be countered only by an extravagant exercise of prophecy and optimism. At the heart of this prophecy (Welsh, *armes*) lay once again the island of Britain. So it is that one of the earliest surviving statements of the political prophecy is the remarkable tenth-century poem, *Armes Prydein*.[45] Its theme was to be a hardy perennial of Welsh political aspiration for centuries to come. Gerald of Wales gives a glimpse of it in his account of the sins of the Welsh. 'They boast, and most confidently predict, that they will soon reoccupy the island of Britain. It is remarkable how everyone in Wales entertains this illusion.'[46] They continued to entertain the illusion even after the Edwardian conquest; indeed, the catastrophe of conquest made it all the more necessary for them to cling on to it. 'The Welsh habit of revolt,' said an English chronicler in 1316 with the weariness of a district commissioner reporting on recalcitrant natives, 'is a long-standing madness. . . . This is the reason. The Welsh, formerly called the Britons, were once noble crowned over the whole realm of England; but they were expelled by the Saxons and lost both name and kingdom. . . . But from the sayings of the prophet Merlin they still hope to recover England. Hence it is that they frequently rebel.'[47]

So long as the Welsh clung on to such mythologies and prophecies and so long as they, unlike the English chronicler, knew the difference between England and Britain, then there was little prospect that the English could conjure up or appropriate an effective British mythology (at least to the satisfaction of anyone except the English themselves) to explain the dominance which they were coming to enjoy in the island. If that was the case *vis-à-vis* Wales, it was of course proportionately even more so with regard to Scotland and Ireland. How far the complex, and sometimes contradictory, origin legends and mythologies which are to be found in John of Fordun's *Chronicle of the Scots Nation* of the 1380s draw on much older sources is a moot point

[44] *Trioedd Ynys Prydein* (as cited above, n. 18), 84–7; *Brut*, *s.a.* 1114 (p. 37).

[45] *Armes Prydein*, ed. I. Williams, trans. Rachel Bromwich (Dublin, 1972); D. N. Dumville, 'Brittany and "Armes Prydein Vawr"', *Études Celtiques* 30 (1983), 145–59.

[46] Gerald of Wales, *Opera*, VI, 216 (Description of Wales, book 2, cap. 7). Cf. the statement of the aim of Gruffudd ap Rhys in 1116: 'to restore and to renew the Britannic kingdom', *Brut* (RBH), *s.a.* 1116 (pp. 86–7). Cf. similar references, *Brut*, *s.a.* 1098.

[47] *Vita Edward Secundi*, ed. and trans. N. Denholm-Young, 69. For a contemporary echo of these views, see the letter from Gruffudd Llwyd to Edward Bruce in J. B. Smith, 'Gruffydd Llwyd and the Celtic Alliance, 1315–18', *Bulletin of the Board of Celtic Studies* 26 (1974–6), 463–78 at pp. 477–8.

among Scottish historians themselves.[48] Some of the traditions were certainly very old; others were no doubt massaged, updated, and even created to meet the changing conditions of the twelfth and thirteenth centuries, not least the gradual forging of the country which we call Scotland and the need to mount a defence against the theoretical and practical pretensions of English overlordship. What is clear for present purposes is that even if we confine our sights to the period between the account of the inauguration of Alexander III in 1249 (when a highland remembrancer recited Alexander's genealogy back to Guidheal Glas son of Neolus, king of Athens, and Scota his wife, daughter of Pharaoh of Egypt) and the Declaration of Arbroath of 1320 (with its famous account of the 113 kings, 'the line unbroken by a single foreigner', who had ruled the Scots from the moment of their arrival in Scotland 'twelve hundred years after the people of Israel crossed the Red Sea'), the Scots had elaborated their own self-contained and exclusive mythology.[49] Such a mythology, of course, made no concession to the Saxons nor, ultimately much more important, to the Britons. Indeed it claimed that Scotland was no part of Britain and that the Scots had indeed driven out the Britons; 'From that time,' so it was triumphantly concluded, 'the Scots, as a new race and possessing a new name, had nothing to do with the Britons.'[50] That was to scupper Geoffrey of Monmouth as well as Edward I. Forging a route around such a complex wall of counter-mythology would require great ingenuity and/or overwhelming power. The same, of course, would be even more true of Ireland. Though Geoffrey of Monmouth claimed that Arthur's conquest of Ireland in effect made the island part of any revived Britannic empire, and though Gerald of Wales likewise asserted that it was as plain as a pikestaff that Ireland was part of Britain, in truth Ireland fitted uncomfortably and at best marginally into any pan-Britain mythology.[51] As for the Irish themselves, they had of course long since constructed their own historical mythology; in so far as there was a place at all in its later redactions for the English or the Normans it was quite

[48] See esp. E. J. Cowan, 'Myth and Identity in Early Medieval Scotland', *Scottish Historical Review* 63 (1984), 111–35; D. Broun, 'The Origin of Scottish Identity', in *Nations, Nationalism and Patriotism in the European Past*, ed. C. Bjørn et al. (Copenhagen, 1994), 35–56; idem, 'The Origin of Scottish Identity in its European Context', in *Scotland in Dark Age Europe*, ed. B. E. Crawford (St Andrews, 1995), 21–31; idem, 'The Birth of Scottish History', *Scottish Historical Review* 66 (1997), 4–22; R. J. Goldstein, *The Matter of Scotland. Historical Narrative in Medieval Scotland* (Lincoln, Nebr., 1995).

[49] J. Bannerman, 'The King's Poet and the Inauguration of Alexander III', *Scottish Historical Review* 68 (1989), 120–49; A. A. M. Duncan, *The Nation of Scots and the Declaration of Arbroath 1320* (1970).

[50] *Anglo-Scottish Relations*, 227. For the Scota legend, see also R. J. Goldstein (as cited above, n. 48), 75; P. Linehan (as cited above, n. 9).

[51] *HRB* c. 153 (IX c. 10); Giraldus Cambrensis, *Expugnatio Hibernica*, book 2, ch. 6 (pp. 148–9).

simply—very much on the analogy of the Welsh *gormesoedd*—as the last of the foreign tyrants around whose invasions the chronology of the Irish past had been constructed.[52]

What this amounts to claiming is that English power as it spread its tentacles and claims into the outer zones of the British Isles would have great difficulty in forging a pan-British ideology to explain its position, if only because there were well-developed and deep-rooted native mythologies already in place. How then did the English respond? In Scotland they did so in part by rewriting the history of what we would call Anglo-Scottish relations since the tenth century on their own terms, claiming sovereign lordship of the country on the basis of this reinterpretation and, in part, as in the letter of 1301 or again under Henry IV in 1400, by trying to turn Geoffrey of Monmouth's tall stories to their advantage.[53] Ireland was even more awkward: we can see as much in the way that Gerald of Wales tosses and turns in his explanation of the English invasion. A miscellany of arguments was assembled: some drew on Galfridian history (especially the submission of Ireland to King Arthur); others on the remarkable claim that since the Irish originally came from the Basque country, which was now part of English Gascony, they therefore had, as it were, a genetic obligation of obedience to the English; then there was the more recent free submission of Irish kings to Henry II; and to cap it all there was the papal claim to authority over all islands, a claim which presumably had been vested in the king of England in Ireland's case through *Laudabiliter*. Such a panoply of arguments was more a tribute to literary ingenuity than to ideological conviction.[54]

But it was the Welsh challenge which would have to be met if the English were to erect a convincing British mythology. It was the Welsh after all who claimed to be the true descendants of the Britons and who were the begetters of the mythology and prophecy of Britain. There were basically two solutions to that challenge. One was to hijack much, if not most, of the Matter of Britain and to convert it into a colourful backcloth for the history of England before the coming of the English. That was indeed undertaken on a large scale from the later twelfth century. In the process King Arthur was converted, as he was

[52] Kathleen Hughes, *The Early Celtic Idea of History and the Modern Historian* (Cambridge, 1976); D. Ó Corráin, 'Irish Origin Legends and Genealogy: Recurrent Aetiologies', in *History and Heroic Tale* (as cited above, n. 40), 57–96; John Carey, *The Irish National Origin-Legend. Synthetic Pseudohistory* (Cambridge, 1994). For the Lebor Gabála (Book of Invasion), the pseudohistory of ancient Ireland which was elaborated in the eleventh and twelfth centuries on the basis of eighth-century tradition, see also briefly D. Ó Corráin, 'Nationality and Kingship in Pre-Norman Ireland', *Historical Studies* 2 (1978), 1–35, esp. pp. 5–7.

[53] *Edward I and the Throne of Scotland 1290–1296* (as cited in Ch. 1, n. 68), ch. 6; *Anglo-Scottish Relations*, 192–219, 346–65.

[54] Giraldus Cambrensis, *Expugnatio*, 148–9, 252–3.

by Roger Howden, from king of the Britons into king of England, and was so memorialized in stained glass at All Souls College. Even the Edwardian conquest of Wales was, by a similar mythological sleight of hand, interpreted as confirmation of Merlinic prophecy of the re-establishment of the monarchy of all Britain.[55] Such contrivances confirmed that there was indeed an ideological awkwardness to be circumvented; the disingenuousness of the answers suggested that there was no easy or convincing solution. The alternative, as in all such situations, was to cut the Gordian knot by denying that there was a problem. From at least the tenth century that has been ultimately the English solution to the British problem. The solution was first crisply propounded by Ealdorman Aethelweard in the late tenth century in his translation of the Anglo-Saxon chronicle: 'Britain,' he remarked with triumphalist brevity, 'is now called England (*Anglia*), thereby assuming the name of the victors (*nomen victorum*).'[56] We can trace this sentiment hardening into an orthodoxy through the chronicles and collections of the twelfth century.[57] By the time of Roger of Wendover in the early thirteenth century it was a decision ascribed to a conclave of Anglo-Saxon kings who had decreed unanimously that the island should henceforth be called England 'rather than Britain after Brutus'.[58] For the author of an early thirteenth-century redaction of the Laws of Edward the Confessor, this triumph of the name England represented more than the imposition of the victor's terminology; it announced the creation of a new people and a new polity. 'And so a single folk (*gens*) and a single people had been created throughout the whole kingdom of Britain. As a result everyone substituted the name "kingdom of the English" for what had hitherto been called "the kingdom of Britain".'[59] It was the final solution to the British problem. It solved it by eliminating it.

[55] For Howden's transformation of King Arthur from 'rex Britonum' to 'rex Anglie', see J. Gillingham, 'The Context and Purposes of the History of the Kings of Britain' (as cited above, n. 31), 103, n. 23; for All Souls's stained glass, above, pp. 1–2; for the deployment of the Edwardian conquest as confirmation of Merlin's prophecies, above, n. 32.

[56] *Chronicle of Aethelweard*, ed. A. Campbell (1962), 9.

[57] Among many examples one might cite the following: Henry of Huntingdon (*Historia Anglorum*, ed. D. Greenway, 12–13): 'This most celebrated of islands, formerly called Albion, later Britain, and now England'; William of Newburgh (*Historia rerum Anglicarum*, ed. R. Howlett, 2 vols. (R.S. 1884–5), I, 131–4): 'the English people expelled the Britons from the island, so that it is now called England, not Britain'; Gervase of Canterbury (*Historical Works*, ed. W. Stubbs, 2 vols. (R.S. 1879–80), II, 21): 'And so the name of Britain was deleted and England was so named after the English.' Even continental authors picked up the phrase: Chrétien de Troyes, writing in the 1170s, introduces Cligés by noting how he went from Greece 'to England, which was called Britain in those days'.

[58] Roger of Wendover, *Flores Historiarum*, ed. H. O. Coxe, 4 vols. (English Historical Society, 1841–4), I, 92–3.

[59] F. Liebermann, *Gesetze* (as cited above, n. 9), I, 659.

A people which can engineer such a solution is supremely self-confident; it is, as it were, in the driving-seat of history and terminology. So indeed the English were from at least the tenth century, if not considerably earlier. We might begin as usual with Bede, not only because of the intrinsic interest of his views but also because his account, spliced with the Anglo-Saxon chronicle, became the canonical interpretation of early English history. Britain, *Britannia*, was indeed the framework of Bede's *History*; it could not be otherwise, for the very concept and word England had yet to be invented. Yet it was on the *gens Anglorum*, *nostra gens*, 'our people', as he proudly called it, that he primarily concentrated, as he readily conceded; and for all the doffing of his cap to the term Britain, the cleavage between the Britons and the English was fundamental to his work and the coming of the English to Britain, *adventus Anglorum in Britanniam*, was the key turning-point in the history of the island.[60] The future form of English history was taking, or was being given, shape.[61] Bede's view of history, and thereby of the English as an object of God's grace, was ultimately salvational. But as England was forged through the power of the Wessex dynasty into a single, unitary kingdom in the century or so after Alfred, the English or *Angelcynn* were also shaped into a political community. That is why scholars have been at pains of late not only to highlight the formidable institutional power of the Old English 'state' but also its strong and deliberately promoted sense of political and mythological unity. It was becoming a powerfully imagined community, a nation-state.[62] In that process it was *Engla-lond* and *Angelcynn*, not some nostalgic and contentious *Britannia*, let alone *Britonnes*, which were ultimately the victorious concepts and terms. England and the English had in effect usurped Britain, or as much of it as was worth usurping.

Language, as so often, said it all. When the Welsh harped on—as they did throughout the Middle Ages and beyond—about their intention to give back to Britain its name, they were in effect acknowledging that the battle for

[60] Bede, I, c. 22; II, c. 1; V, c. 23 ('Brettones . . . gentem Anglorum')–c. 24 ('de historia ecclesiastica Brittaniarum, et maxime gentis Anglorum').

[61] From a large literature, see esp. H. E. J. Cowdrey, 'Bede and the "English People"', *Journal of Religious History* 11 (1981), 501–23; P. Wormald, 'Bede, the bretwaldas and the *Gens Anglorum*', in *Ideal and Reality in Frankish and Anglo-Saxon Society*, ed. P. Wormald et al. (Oxford, 1983), 99–129; J. Campbell, *Essays in Anglo-Saxon History* (1986), chs. 1–2.

[62] James Campbell, 'Was it Infancy in England? Some Questions of Comparison', *England and Her Neighbours 1066–1453. Essays in Honour of Pierre Chaplais*, ed. M. Jones and M. Vale (1989), 1–17; idem, 'The Late Anglo-Saxon State: A Maximum View', *Proceedings of the British Academy* 87 (1995), 37–65; idem, 'The United Kingdom of England. The Anglo-Saxon Achievement' in *Uniting the Kingdom? The Making of British History*, ed. A. Grant and K. J. Stringer (1995), 31–47; P. Wormald, '*Engla Land*: The Making of an Allegiance', *Journal of Historical Sociology* 7 (1994), 1–24; Sarah Foot, 'The Making of *Angelcynn*: English Identity before the Norman Conquest', *Transactions of the Royal Historical Society*, 6th ser., 6 (1996), 25–49.

Britain had been lost and that the reversal could be undone only by the return of some Arthur-like figure. The battle was in effect lost in the tenth century. The title of the king who was in power and pretension superior to all other kings in Britain proclaimed the victory. Athelstan may have had a die cast with the legend 'king of the whole of Britain', but the title that emerged triumphant was that of king of the English, *rex Anglorum*. After the reform of the coinage by Edgar in 973 it was to become, and remain, the unchanged style of the English kings.[63] Hereafter the king was simply *rex* (no more pretensions to *basileus* or *imperator* or other such grand terms), and it was the English people, *populus anglicanus*, which was called upon to salute its king at the coronation. When the Normans succeeded, they were likewise, regardless of the effective reach of their power, well content with the same title in Britain—king of the English.[64]

The victory of Englishness, and with it in effect the displacement of the concept and terminology of Britain, is evident in other directions. It was in the late tenth century that the very word *Engla-lond* and its Latin equivalent *Anglia* apparently first made their appearance and quickly became established.[65] When, in the decades between about 1120 and 1150, a remarkable group of historians set about to fill in the huge gap in historiography since the age of Bede, their agenda was firmly and exclusively English: they wrote the history of the English and of the deeds of the English kings; they wrote out of love of their country and of 'we English'; their heroes were men such as Egbert, Alfred, Edgar, and even Hereward.[66] Henry of Huntingdon may be allowed to speak for them all: it was with great pride that he announced in his narrative, *The History of the English*, under the year 836, that he had arrived at the stage when one could talk of a monarchy of England, *monarchia Anglie*.[67] So much for those who had made such a fetish of 'the monarchy of Britain'. If you have your England, and are so comfortable with it, what need of Britain? Even ecclesiastical propagandists, who were the most vociferous and tenacious upholders of the concept of a unitary Britain and Ireland in

[63] James Campbell (ed.), *The Anglo-Saxons* (1982), 167; E. John, *Orbis Britanniae* (as cited above, n. 20), 51–3; N. Banton in *Studies in Church History* 18 (1982), 71–85.

[64] F. Barlow, *Edward the Confessor*, 135–6; D. C. Douglas, *William the Conqueror* (1964), 248.

[65] R. R. Davies, 'The Peoples of Britain and Ireland 1100–1400. 2. Names, Boundaries and Regnal Solidarities', *Transactions of the Royal Historical Society*, 6th ser., 5 (1995), 1–20, esp. pp. 7–11.

[66] R. W. Southern, 'Aspects of the European Tradition of Historical Writing. 4. The Sense of the Past', *Transactions of the Royal Historical Society*, 5th ser., 23 (1973), 243–63, esp. 246–56; James Campbell, *Essays in Anglo-Saxon History*, ch. 13; Rees Davies, *The Matter of Britain and the Matter of England* (Oxford, 1996).

[67] Henry of Huntingdon, *Historia Anglorum*, 264. Henry consciously introduces a chronology which differentiates the monarchy of Britain (whose history he concludes with Egbert) from the Wessex-based monarchy of England: ibid., lix–lxi, 97.

terms of ecclesiastical organization, were eventually forced to readjust their ambitions. It was partly that the language of ecclesiastical pretension could not indefinitely remain out of alignment with the terminology of state power: even Eadmer, vigorous defender of Canterbury's pan-British claims that he was, referred to his lord of Canterbury as 'archbishop of the English' and to 'the whole church as it is constituted in England'.[68] And an English church, with a Welsh appendage, is what it became in the twelfth century, as Canterbury was denied the last vestiges of its theoretical claim to supremacy over Scotland and Ireland.[69] The Church of the Britains had contracted into the *ecclesia anglicana*, and it was the liberties of that Church that King John guaranteed in the opening clause of Magna Carta.

The triumph of this English definition of self-identity was to have profound consequences; in some fashion the history of Britain may be said to have lain under its shadow ever since. It marked, in effect, the abandonment of a British ideology and with it the concept of a monarchy of the whole of Britain. When such ideas re-emerged in the sixteenth and seventeenth centuries and thereafter, it was on very different terms.[70] There was a price to pay. The ideological and mythological basis of the claim of the English to control over, and overlordship of, the rest of Britain—notably Wales and Ireland, since Scotland survived as a separate kingdom—was left unexplained and unresolved. That left the question of the disjunction between the terms 'Britain' and 'England' hanging in the air. It could be solved, at least by the English, by declaring unilaterally that Britain was now England. That is what Ealdorman Aethelweard, Henry of Huntingdon, and scores of others did; it was also in effect the solution announced by the King Arthur window at All Souls College. For those who found the claim that the part is equivalent to the whole was more than logic could bear, the alternative solution was to redefine the whole. So it was that the English spokesman at the Council of Constance asserted that the Scots 'are undoubtedly part of the English nation, since they have no way of denying that Scotland is part of Britain, though not such a large part'.[71] It was in the same spirit that a sixteenth-century pamphleteer declared that 'this realm now called Englande [is] the only supreme seat of the empire of Great

[68] Martin Brett, *The English Church under Henry I* (Oxford, 1975), 12.

[69] Above, pp. 37–9.

[70] Jenny Wormald, 'The Creation of Britain: Multiple Kingdoms or Core and Colonies?', *Transactions of the Royal Historical Society*, 6th ser., 2 (1992), 175–94; essays by Marcus Merriman, Jenny Wormald, Conrad Russell, Nicholas Canny, and John Morrill in *Uniting the Kingdom?* ed. Grant and Stringer (as cited above, n. 62); *Conquest and Union. Fashioning a British State 1485–1725*, ed. S. G. Ellis and S. Barber (1995).

[71] C. M. D. Crowder, *Unity, Heresy and Reform 1378–1460. The Conciliar Response to the Great Schism* (1977), 117.

Britagne.'[72] But by and large the English were content with their own self-definition; if their power and control extended elsewhere in the British Isles and indeed beyond, they were content to exercise them without theorizing about them or justifying them at undue length, let alone elaborating a mythology to sustain them. That has been in a measure both the strength and the weakness of the English domination of the British Isles. It was—and is—a domination which was so powerfully grounded in its own, exclusive, and early-formed historical mythology that it found it well-nigh impossible, or indeed necessary, to come to terms with the identities and mythologies of the rest of the peoples and countries of the British Isles.

[72] Quoted in Roger A. Mason, 'Scotching the Brut: Politics, History and National Myth in Sixteenth-Century Britain', in *Scotland and England 1286–1815*, ed. Roger A. Mason (Edinburgh, 1987), 68.

3
ORBITS OF POWER

The British Isles are comprised of two substantial land masses—Britain and Ireland—and a galaxy of surrounding islands of varying size and importance. How this geographical complex ought to be organized into units of power and governance and into communities of loyalty and affection was—and remains—an open question. Countries are not laid up in heaven; they are shaped and reshaped here on earth by the stratagems of men and the victories of the fortuitous. But once they take root and are bolstered by the habits and mechanisms of unity and by a common mythology, they soon acquire an image, if not of immemoriality, at least of almost inevitable and organic development. As Benedict Anderson has put it, chance is thereby converted into destiny.[1] So it is with the four countries of which the British Isles are taken to be composed and around whose existence and identities our historiographies naturally focus. It need not, of course, have been so. Power and loyalties in these islands could have been differently and, arguably, more rationally organized. By 1093 some of the options were already closed and some of the labels and names, which have such a powerful grip on our minds, were beginning to acquire a geographical and even a political fixity. But the map of power, boundaries, loyalties, and countries had greater fluidity about it than our normally 'Whiggish' historiographical habits frequently acknowledge.

Let us begin with England. Recent scholarship has shown triumphantly the unity, power, and precociousness of the pre-conquest English 'state' which the Normans inherited and exploited ruthlessly to their own ends.[2] As we are taught to gaze in admiration at the undoubted achievements of this 'state', we should, nevertheless, bear in mind certain reservations about its past and future. It is, for example, as well to recall that it was a relatively recent artefact, created largely in the tenth century by a process which was more one of conquest than of reconquest and involving a major reorganization of power, personnel, and structures of authority in what we know as midland and southern

[1] Benedict Anderson, *Imagined Communities* (rev. edn., 1991), 12.

[2] For recent expositions of the case see esp. Patrick Wormald, 'Engla Lond: The Making of an Allegiance' (as cited above, Ch. 2, n. 62); and James Campbell, 'The United Kingdom of England. The Anglo-Saxon, (as cited above, Ch. 2, n. 62), 31–47.

England. Indeed, the very word England, *Engla-land*, *Anglia*, apparently only makes its first recorded appearance in surviving texts in the late tenth century.[3] Even more to the point of the current argument, it was not predetermined what the eventual shape of this new country called England might turn out to be. For ambitious dreamers, a greater England might well include Lothian, for as late as 1091 the Anglo-Saxon Chronicle referred to 'Lothian in England'; parts of north-east and south-east Wales might also fall into its ambit; and when Pembrokeshire appears as a county accounting at the royal exchequer in 1130, it would seem that the phrase 'Little England beyond Wales' might acquire the ring of administrative truth.[4] But perhaps a lesser rather than a greater England was a more feasible prospect in 1093. Particularly was this so in the north. England, after all, was a country created in the south; how far north it would extend was still open to question. York was the northernmost borough and mint of pre-conquest England, and the river Humber was sometimes regarded as the boundary of the country.[5] That might be to err on the side of modesty; but beyond the rivers Ribble in the west and Tees in the east one still entered in the 1090s into an area which William Kapelle has called 'the free zone', a land of regional supremacies, frontier outposts (of which Newcastle and Carlisle were the most striking and recent examples), raids and counter-raids, and deep uncertainties.[6] Neither Northumbria nor Cumbria was inevitably part of England. There was nothing in the social, cultural, linguistic, or tenurial configuration of either district which indicated into which orbit of power and loyalty—or indeed more than one such orbit—they might be subsumed.[7]

Part of the uncertainty was whether this northern area of what is now England would fall, in part or in whole, within the orbit of the kings of Scots.

[3] On the earliest recorded usage of the word, J. A. Burrow, 'The Sinking Island and the Dying Author: R. W. Chambers Fifty Years On', *Essays in Criticism* 40 (1990), 20, n. 11.

[4] Lothian: *Anglo-Saxon Chronicle*, *s.a.* 1091; north-east Wales: *Victoria County History (VCH). County of Chester*, I (1987), 254, 262, 301–18; south-east Wales: *VCH Hereford*, I (1908), 263–9; P. Courtney, 'The Norman Invasion of Gwent: a Reassessment', *Journal of Medieval History* 12 (1986), 297–313; Pembrokeshire: *Pipe Roll 31 Henry I*, ed. J. Hunter (1833), 136–7 (accounts were also submitted for Carmarthen this year, ibid., 89–90). The term 'Pembrokeshire' became an accepted part of official and literary terminology: e.g. *The Song of Dermot and the Earl*, ed. G. H. Orpen (Oxford, 1892), l. 409; David Crouch, *William Marshal* (1990), 78, n. 29 (for the title 'comes de Penbrocsir'); *Pipe Rolls I Richard I*, 163; *1 John*, 182; *2 John*, 226.

[5] In his historical mythology, Geoffrey of Monmouth made the Humber into the boundary between Deira and Albania on the one hand and Loegria on the other: *HRB*, c. 72 (Bk IV, c. 19).

[6] W. E. Kapelle, *The Norman Conquest of the North and its Transformation* (1979), 7.

[7] Cf. the opinion of Geoffrey Barrow: 'In the first half of the twelfth century we may not confidently speak of Scotland, Alba, Scotia, Ecosse as extending south of the Firth of Forth. Nor may we confidently speak of England, Anglia, Angleterre as extending much, if at all, beyond Stainmore common in the north-west corner of the north Riding of Yorkshire': *The Anarchy of King Stephen's Reign*, ed. Edmund King (Oxford, 1992), 237.

The enterprise and appetite of those kings in the tenth and eleventh centuries were, in their fashion, quite the equal of those of the Wessex dynasty in England. They had shifted the centre of gravity of their power to the east and the south, gobbled up Lothian and Strathclyde, and clearly saw no reason why their ambitions should not extend further southwards.[8] But how meaningful it is to talk of a country called Scotland, and what sort of a future it might have (if any), is quite another matter. First of all, there is the awkwardness of terminology. The Anglo-Saxon Chronicle might refer to a place called Scotland; but it is not until the late twelfth or even the thirteenth century that the term *Scotia*, Scotland, begins to acquire as it were the connotations and range which we associate with it. Until then its usage was restricted to the area north of the Forth—indeed, in the strictest sense, to the kingdom's core between the Forth, the central Grampians, and the Spey. Lothian was no part of it, nor, for that matter, was Strathclyde or Galloway.[9] He would have indeed been a bold person—perhaps a brave heart—who would have claimed that the assemblage of provinces loosely acknowledging the authority of Malcolm Canmore at his death in 1093 would necessarily and securely constitute a single country. The odds against it were considerable. Geographically, not only was there the fault line of the highland–lowland division,[10] but there was also the undoubted fact that the most obvious boundary in northern Britain was the great moss between Clyde and Forth, the Scottish Sea as it was appropriately named.[11] Ethnically the country that would come to be known as Scotland was an assemblage of at least four or five major peoples, each with its own language, customs, laws, traditions, and affiliations; the tensions between them could, and did, break through to the surface when the political going got tough, as in 1094 or 1138 or 1174.[12] Politically, indeed, while

8 Duncan, *Scotland*, ch. 4.

9 *Anglo-Saxon Chronicle*, *s.a.* 932. This is apparently the earliest known usage of the English word 'Scotland' to refer to a part of Britain. For the meanings of the word *Scotia* see *R.R.S.*, 38–9; G. W. S. Barrow, *The Anglo-Norman Era in Scottish History* (Oxford, 1980), 153–4; and D. Broun, 'Defining Scotland and the Scots before the Wars of Independence', in *Image and Identity. The Making and Re-making of Scotland through the Ages*, ed. D. Broun et al. (Edinburgh, 1998), 4–17, esp. pp. 6–9.

10 The twelfth-century tract, *De Situ Albanie* (which draws on earlier geographical lore) assigns a major significance to the eastern boundary of Dál Riata, known significantly as the Ridge of Britain (*Dorsum Britanniae*): B. T. Hudson, *The Kings of Celtic Scotland* (1994), 5.

11 The memory of the Scottish Sea as the southern boundary of the original *Scotia* remained alive for centuries. Thus Walter Bower (*Scotichronicon*, ed. D. E. R. Watt et al. (Aberdeen, 1987–98), vol. VI, 354–7) records the tradition that the bridge over the Forth at Stirling 'lies between *Britannia* and *Scotia*; forming the border of them'. Likewise when John, lord of the Isles, and James, earl of Douglas, concluded an indenture with Edward IV of England in 1462 they claimed as their reward all the realm of Scotland 'beyond the Scottish sea', *Acts of the Lords of the Isles 1336–1493*, ed. J. and R. W. Munro (Scottish Record Society, 4th series, 22 (1986)), 114.

12 Anderson, *Scottish Annals*, 117–18 (1094); 198 (1138); 256 (1174). For Scotland as a country of 'four or five disparate peoples', Duncan, *Scotland*, 111.

it might have been appropriate, at least programmatically, to refer to the kingship of the Scots, it was certainly premature to speak of a kingdom of Scotland. Rulers with titles of kings or *reguli* were to be found in areas such as Galloway and Argyll, and were a recent memory in Strathclyde; it remained to be seen whether large tracts of the north and the west could be attached, more or less loosely, to an east- and south-centred kingship or would move in an independent or quasi-independent western sea orbit.[13] Dynastically, the title to the single kingship of the Scots (such as it was) by no means went unchallenged: the battle of Stracathro of 1130 is often regarded as a decisive episode in determining the issue; but it was not until the young MacWilliam heiress (the descendant of a discarded segment of the Scottish royal line) was done to death in the most brutal fashion in the market-place at Forfar in 1230 that the security of the ruling dynasty and the unity (loose-limbed as it was) of the country that we can now call Scotland could be said to be assured;[14] and it was not to be until 1266 that the western isles and mainland were finally added to the kingdom.

If the ultimate shape and cohesion of the countries we call England and Scotland were by no means predetermined in 1093, the situation in Wales and Ireland was even more problematic. Here we are confronted with a paradox. It could be asserted with some confidence that Wales and Ireland (with the exception of some pockets of alien settlement) were culturally and ethnically more credible and united as units than were either England or Scotland. They both had, to a very considerable extent, a single language, a single law, a single literary tradition, a profoundly influential common mythology, and a learned class of jurists, poets, and remembrancers who acted as the keepers of the high culture of their respective societies to a remarkable degree. But in terms of power and politics, Wales and Ireland were deeply fragmented and conflict-ridden societies. They even rationalized and mythologized their divisions: the Welsh, inspired by their practice of arranging all life and learning

[13] See generally R. A. McDonald, *The Kingdom of the Isles. Scotland's Western Sea Board c.1100–c.1336* (East Linton, 1997).

[14] For inter-segmentary competition in the Scottish royal dynasty before 1130, B. T. Hudson, *The Kings of Celtic Scotland*, 146. For recurrent revolts in Moray or Ross, often associated with the claims of the MacWilliam family (descendants of Malcolm III's first wife), in 1130, 1179, 1181, 1187, 1211–12, and 1215: Anderson, *Early Sources*, II, 174, 312–13, 389, 404; Anderson, *Scottish Annals*, 278, 294–5; *R.R.S.*, II, 11–15, 19–20. For the crisis of 1230–1, Anderson, *Early Sources*, II, 471–83; Duncan, *Scotland*, 529–30; K. J. Stringer in *Medieval Scotland. Crown, Lordship and Community. Essays presented to G. W. S. Barrow* (Edinburgh, 1993), 96–7. For some very pertinent observations on the political fragility of medieval Scotland, see D. P. Kirby in *English Historical Review* 91 (1976), 837–41, and, most recently, R. Andrew McDonald, '"Treachery in the Remotest Territories of Scotland": Northern Resistance to the Canmore Dynasty, 1130–1230', *Canadian Journal of History*, 33 (1999), 162–92.

in triads, referred schematically, and inadequately, to the three main divisions (Gwynedd, Powys, Deheubarth) and courts (Aberffraw, Mathrafal, Dinefwr) of their country; the Irish inherited, and tried periodically to update, the traditional notion of their country as divided into 'five fifths'.[15] Neither formula could do any sort of justice to the complexity and ever-shifting kaleidoscope of power structures in their respective countries. Geography, of course, compounded the problem, be it the mountain ranges of Wales or the great midland bog and watery landscape of Ireland.[16] Recognizable Wales and Ireland might be to contemporaries as geographical units, but in other respects they were, as Katharine Simms has observed of Gaelic Ireland, 'states of mind', and profoundly disturbed states of mind at that.[17] Nor was it certain that parts of them—small parts, maybe, in area but critical strategically and economically—might not be absorbed into other better-organized and more effectively acquisitive units, be it a greater England or a western-sea empire or empires.

Wales and Ireland provide another cautionary note as one approaches the question of the organization of power in the British Isles in the Middle Ages. Neither, self-evidently, would qualify as a nation-state, even an inchoate one; in neither was unity more than an aspiration or at best a spasmodic and largely unstructured hegemony; in both, regional and kin-group loyalties could be exceptionally powerful. Language is instructive in this respect: words such as 'province' (let alone 'provincial'), 'region', and 'delegated power' bespeak and assume unitary countries and/or states; the corresponding Welsh and Irish medieval terminology—*gwladoedd*, *tuatha*—assumes no such hierarchy of power but rather a plural federation of units (smallish units if you will) and peoples which might coalesce or, equally, disaggregate but which remained in some degree the natural units of loyalty and affection, often far more so than transient 'kingships' and hegemonies.[18] In other words, one man's province may be another man's country; it depends how he views the world and deploys language. So it was in the British Isles in the late eleventh century; the map of power and loyalty had not necessarily or finally settled into a four-countries mode.

England, or at least the England covered by the Domesday commissioners, had gone farthest down that road. Vestiges there certainly were of earlier

[15] Wales: *The Latin Texts of the Welsh Laws*, ed. H. D. Emanuel (Cardiff, 1967), 316, 332, 349; Gerald of Wales, *Opera*, VI, 166–7 (Description of Wales., book 1, ch. 2); Ireland: *NHI*, II, 13–14; F. J. Byrne, *Irish Kings and High Kings* (1973), 42–7.

[16] See the pioneering study of A. P. Smyth, *Celtic Leinster: Towards a Historical Geography of Early Irish Civilisation* (Dublin, 1982).

[17] K. Simms, 'Guesting and Feasting in Gaelic Ireland', *Journal of the Royal Society of Antiquaries of Ireland* 108 (1978), 67–100 at p. 67.

[18] For *gwladoedd* etc. see Davies, *Conquest*, 12–14. The term is common in the vernacular poetry and annals.

organizational and political differences and divisions; perhaps the most famous is the reference in the so-called Laws of Henry I to the threefold division of the country in terms of law between West Saxon, Mercian, and Danish law. But vestiges these were and they were brushed away with remarkable briskness and brusqueness.[19] The periodic clearing out of the props of earlier power structures and elites across the tenth and eleventh centuries and the remarkably ubiquitous and pervasive presence of royal authority in every part of the land gave England, at least south of Humber and Mersey, the least provincial character of any part of the British Isles. The same was markedly less true of the country we know as Scotland, in spite of the concentration of much of its historiography on the growth of the power of a unitary kingship and on the evidence (itself much of it the archive of success) of 'state-building'. The tradition of 'submission to one king' is indeed a remarkable feature of early Scottish history, and recent work on the history both of Dalriada in the west and of thanages (the districts under the control of royal officers called thanes) in the east has taught us not to underestimate the organizational abilities of early Scottish kingships.[20] But what is surely equally striking is the continued strength and resilience of 'provincial' identities and powers.[21] The 'Scotland' of the early charters is very considerably a Scotland of provinces: Fife, Fothrif, Menteith, Gowrie, Lothian, Moray, Cumbria, and so forth.[22] The men of each province formed their own community and composed their own army;[23] the provincial earl—or king as he might occasionally be called in a Gaelic source—was often the descendant of a Celtic *mormaer* and was the natural leader of his province.[24] A kingdom, albeit a loosely knit one, might be composed of such provinces; but equally the integrity of a country might be challenged, or at the very least substantially qualified, by such provincial identities. The history of Galloway, for example, suggests as much. A province whose ruler still

[19] Paul Hyams notes that 'the day of the provincial coutumier within the *regnum* of England may already have passed by the second decade of Henry I's reign': 'The Common Law and the French Connection', *Anglo-Norman Studies* 4 (1981), 77–92 at p. 81.

[20] 'Submission to one king': Duncan, *Scotland*, 111, 116; Dalriada: J. Bannerman, *Studies in the History of Dalriada* (Edinburgh, 1974); thanages: A. Grant, 'Thanes and Thanages from the Eleventh to the Fourteenth Centuries', *Medieval Scotland* (as cited above, n. 19), 39–82.

[21] Note A. A. M. Duncan's comment, admittedly regarding an earlier period, on Scotland as 'a scatter of provinces held together uncertainly by the most masterful of the provincial kings', 'The Kingdom of Scots', in *The Making of Britain. The Dark Ages*, ed. L. M. Smith (1984), 131–44 at p. 131.

[22] See, for example, *Early Scottish Charters prior to A.D. 1153*, ed. A. C. Lawrie (Glasgow, 1905), 12, 14, 23, 54, 66, 83, 86, etc.; *Regesta Regum Scottorum*, I, 36.

[23] For a reference to the *vexillum Moraviae*, *Registrum Episcopatus Moraviensis* (Bannatyne Club, 1837), no. 264; the army of Fife: *Early Scottish Charters*, 67.

[24] Mormaer: *Early Scottish Charters*, 78, 84. Robert Bruce is called mormaer of Carrick in the *Annals of Connacht*, ed. A. M. Freeman (Dublin, 1944), *s.a.* 1306. See generally Duncan, *Scotland*, 164–8.

occasionally titled himself king or prince, commanded his own army and fleet, insisted that his own bishopric of Whithorn be subject to the jurisdiction of York rather than be part of the *ecclesia scotticana*, and accepted the direct and active overlordship of the king of the English when it suited him was, to put it mildly, a very semi-detached member of the country that was coming to be known as Scotland.[25] Even in the early decades of the thirteenth century, though Galloway was by now more manifestly part of the kingdom, its lord could exercise quasi-regal authority, refer to 'our army', and move easily between the Scottish and English courts in pursuit of his grandiose ambitions to lord it over a western-sea principality embracing English Cumbria, the Isle of Man, and much of Ulster.[26]

As for Wales and Ireland, it is the strength of what we would call provincial identities and loyalties which comes across most strongly from the early sources. We hear, for example, in Wales of the men of Llŷn, Arfon, Ystrad Tywi, Ceredigion, and so forth, and of the fearsome pride of the men of Powys in their own privileges, just as in Ireland the men of Leinster, Munster, Breifne, and so forth figure prominently in the Annals of Tigernach.[27] In so far as contemporaries conceived of larger units or loyalties, those concepts might well be drawn from the realm of history or mythology such as *Ynys Prydein* (the Island of Britain) or *fir Erenn* (the men of Ireland). This is how these men constructed their world. We have no right to impose even

[25] Galloway has been the subject of some excellent recent studies, esp. *Galloway. Land and Lordship*, ed. R. D. Oram and G. P. Stell (Edinburgh, 1991); R. D. Oram, 'A Family Business? Colonisation and Settlement in Twelfth- and Thirteenth-century Galloway', *Scottish Historical Review* 72 (1993), 111–45; idem, 'In Obedience and Reverence: Whithorn and York *c*.1128–*c*.1250', *Innes Review* 42 (1991), 83–100; K. J. Stringer, 'Periphery and Core in Thirteenth-Century Scotland: Alan Son of Roland, Lord of Galloway and Constable of Scotland', in *Medieval Scotland* (as cited above, n. 14), 82–114; 'Reform Monasticism and Celtic Scotland: Galloway, *c*.1140–*c*.1240', in *Alba: Celtic Scotland in the Medieval Era*, ed. E. J. Cowan and R. A. McDonald (East Linton, 1999). Dr Stringer has also kindly given me advance sight of his edition of the Acta of the Lords of Galloway in *Freedom and Authority: Scotland c.1050–c.1650. Historical and Historiographical Essays presented to Grant G. Simpson*, ed. T. Brotherstone and D. Ditchburn. Note that Fergus of Galloway entitled himself *rex Galwitensium* when he founded the abbey of Dundrennan, *c*.1142.

[26] The ambivalent relationship between the rulers of Galloway on the one hand and the kings of England and Scotland on the other from at least the time of Henry II suggests that Galloway could, and indeed occasionally did, pose as much of a problem to the kings of Scotland as the duchy of Brittany did to the kings of France in the fourteenth century. In 1296 Edward I released the 88-year-old Thomas of Galloway, after sixty years of imprisonment, in order to use him to foment disaffection against the Scots in Galloway: G. W. S. Barrow, *Robert Bruce*, 112.

[27] Contemporary historical sources such as the *Brut* or *Historia Gruffud vab Kenan* (ed. D. Simon Evans (Cardiff, 1977)), refer regularly to the men of the individual regions or *gwladoedd* of Wales—such as Ystrad Tywi, Ceredigion, Meirionnydd, Llŷn, Brycheiniog, Tegeingl, Dyffryn Clwyd, etc. For the poem in praise of 'the privileges of the men of Powys' (*Breiniau gwŷr Powys*), *Gwaith Cynddelw Brydydd Mawr*, I, ed. Nerys A. Jones and Ann P. Owen (Cardiff, 1991), 128–42. For the men of individual Irish districts, see *Annals of Tigernach* (as in Ch. 1, n. 31) *s.a.* 1134, 1137, 1156, 1161, 1163, etc.

the categories of the thirteenth century, let alone those of our day and convenience, on their world. To construct the history of the British Isles as the history of four countries is to foreclose on the options that were still possible in the late eleventh century, not least in terms of the organization of power and loyalties.

There is another reason why we should tread warily down the four-countries route: it looked as if it cut across the grain of the ethnic divisions of the British Isles.[28] We return here to our earlier paradox. The kings who ruled the two most effective and coherent units of power in the British Isles exercised authority over multiple peoples but arrogated unitary labels to describe the power they exercised and the peoples who were subject to their rule. The one called himself simply 'king of the English' (*rex Anglorum*), the other 'king of the Scots' (*rex Scottorum*). Both titles were originally propagandist fiction; both ultimately and successfully established the image of a single people under a unitary ruler. The English did so most successfully and at a remarkably early date, partly because the mythology of a recently acquired regnal unity was underpinned by the institutions of common governance. A country had been created out of an assemblage of peoples, polities, and loyalties in a remarkably short period. This newly invented country, England, proved resilient enough as a unit of power to withstand the traumas of Danish and Norman invasions and supremacies. Equally, and arguably even more significantly, the concept of a single people, the English, proved sufficiently elastic to accommodate within itself, sooner or later, all those who acknowledged the political supremacy of the man who called himself 'king of the English', regardless of their own ethnic lineage and affiliations. The ultimate triumph of the concepts of 'England' and 'the English' was to create the illusion that they were inevitable, even immemorial realities, whereas, as with all countries and peoples, they were contingent historical creations. It could have been otherwise.

The same was true of the country which would eventually be called Scotland. Its king bore the deceptively simple and apparently all-encompassing title 'king of the Scots'; but the blandness of the title concealed a more complex reality. Contemporaries occasionally recognized as much. 'The Scottish army,' according to the English chronicle commenting on the battle of the Standard in 1138, 'was composed of Normans, Germans, English, Northumbrians, Cumbrians, men of Teviotdale and Lothian, Picts (who are commonly called Galwegians) and Scots.'[29] Not all the population groups so

[28] R. R. Davies, 'The Peoples of Britain and Ireland 1100–1400. 1. Identities', *Transactions of the Royal Historical Society*, 6th ser., 4 (1994), 1–20.

[29] Anderson, *Scottish Annals*, 181. Ailred (Anderson, ibid., 200) adds the Islesmen and the men of Argyll and Moray. For the tensions between 'the English, the Scots, the Picts and the rest of the barbarians' after the battle, ibid., 208.

listed may have shared the same degree of coherence and identity; but the comment was a timely reminder of the ethnic and regional fissures that lay barely below the surface of what we often characterize, by way of shorthand, as a single Scottish society. Indeed, the king himself in the address clauses of his writs in the twelfth century might greet as many as five separate ethnic groups within his kingdom, and that was to err on the side of modesty.[30] Exercising a measure of federative overkingship over such an assemblage of peoples required tact, force, and good luck. When a contemporary observed that King David I (1124–53) 'ruled the Scots with affection, the Galwegians with terror', what he was acknowledging was the ethnic fault-lines in the kingdom and the ethnic discrimination which could so easily characterize royal policy.[31] The outcome of any attempt to forge a single ethno-political identity out of such a varied assemblage of peoples was by no means a foregone conclusion. The prospect of a single Scottish nation was an aspiration to be worked at; it was not a historical given.

Nor was Scotland itself in 1093. It was still a country very much in the making. It does not require a huge leap of the historical imagination to conceive of a different ordering of geographical and political power in northern Britain from the one that actually came to prevail. One orbit of power could well have coalesced around the original Scotia (north of the Forth) and Lothian; it would have been a southern- and eastern-oriented community, increasingly in close liaison with an Anglo-French world which it so persistently mimicked and with which it had natural cultural and social relations. Much of the rest of what was to be Scotland could well have entered into northern and western orbits of power, be it a greater Gaeldom and/or a Hiberno-Scandinavian empire. Nor need such orbits have been confined within the limits of latter-day Scotland or indeed any of the other countries of the British Isles. On several occasions in the twelfth and early thirteenth centuries, for example, a unit of power embracing, to a greater or lesser degree, Ulster, the Isle of Man, Anglesey, Cumbria, Galloway, and the Western Isles seemed a distinct possibility. In terms of power structures, ease of communications, ecclesiastical and economic connections, ethnic and cultural links, such a unit would have made a great deal of sense. The swashbuckling career, martial alliances, and religious patronage of John de Courcy and his associates

[30] For multiple address clauses in twelfth-century Scotland see, for example, *Early Scottish Charters*, 76, 91 (French, English, Scots, Galwegians), 95, 162; *R.R.S.*, I, 74, 272 (French, English, Scots, Welsh, and Gallovidians); II, 77.

[31] Anderson, *Scottish Annals*, 193. Cf. the account by Richard of Hexham of the fierce disputes within David I's army in 1138: 'The English and the Scots and the Galwegians and the rest of barbarians . . . took the opportunity to kill, wound or rob the other' (*Chronicles of Stephen*, etc., III, 165–6).

at the end of the twelfth century showed that such a prospect could be cultivated by Anglo-Norman adventurers as well as by Scandinavian kings.[32]

Had any of these eventualities happened, where and when would have been our Scotland? We know, of course, that none of these possibilities in fact materialized, or rather that none of them became an established feature of the political geography of northern Britain. We therefore exercise the historian's prerogative of hindsight to tell the story of the British Isles in a way that rules out the possibility. In fact there was—and is—no finality or irreversibility about the countries we have come to know as England, Scotland, Wales, and Ireland. They had, it is true, already by 1093 acquired in varying measure some of the distinctive features of their identities; but there was still much that was contingent and uncertain about their shape and character.

We might more readily recognize as much if we consider briefly the geographical template on which the power structures of the British Isles were constructed in our period. The least problematic part of that template consisted of a southern region extending southwards from the Mersey and the Humber to the Channel. This was the richest, most fertile, and most accessible part of the island. It had already been forged before the eleventh century into a remarkably close-textured political, governmental, social, and economic area, its local and regional differences to a considerable degree overlaid by a common wash of organizational mechanisms, economic links, social forms, and credal habits. This was the England of the Domesday commission, though the folios of its survey showed that it was an England which could extend its ambit northwards, to Yorkshire and beyond in particular, and possibly to the east into the lowland tongues of what is now eastern Wales. It was a southern-constructed and southern-dominated orbit of power. Its southern orientation, in terms of culture as well as power, was reinforced and exaggerated by the Norman conquest and settlement of England and by the cross-Channel affiliations of its kingship and its ruling secular and ecclesiastical elite.

Once a power unit had been shaped whose focal points were Westminster and Winchester, the problem of 'the north' would loom large on the agenda of British power politics. Particularly at issue was the area to the north of the River Tees and to the south of the Firth of Forth on the one hand, and to the

[32] For John de Courcy and his world, see the outstanding study by Seán Duffy, 'The First Ulster Plantation: John de Courcy and the Men of Cumbria', in *Colony and Frontier in Medieval Ireland. Essays presented to J. F. Lydon*, ed. T. Barry, R. Frame, and K. Simms (1995), 1–27. For the mid-thirteenth century, E. J. Cowan posits 'the prospect . . . of a self sustaining kingdom, well defended and well provided, extending all the way from Man to the Butt of Lewis and encompassing a considerable chunk of the western seaboard', 'Norwegian Sunset—Scottish Dawn: Hakon IV and Alexander III' in *Scotland in the Reign of Alexander III 1249–1286*, ed. N. H. Reid (Edinburgh, 1990), 103–31 at p. 125.

north of Stainmore and to the south of Solway Firth or even further north on the other. There could have been several solutions. One, which our four-countries approach rather tends to rule out, would have been the evolution of one or two independent units of power between a Wessex-based England in the south and a Fife- and Angus-centred Scotia in the north. After all, a mainly Brythonic kingship of Cumbria, extending at best from the River Duddon in the south to the Clyde in the north, had survived in some sense until the early eleventh century,[33] while in the east an enlarged Northumbrian kingdom, extending once more to embrace Lothian, would make quite a lot of geographical and ethnic sense. With the slaughter of Malcolm III and his son near Alnwick in November 1093 a second option could be entertained: not only might the aggressive Anglo-Norman kingship fully reclaim Northumbria and annex southern Cumbria—as it had indeed already indicated by the establishment of advanced outposts at Newcastle on Tyne in 1080 and Carlisle in 1092 respectively—but it might also toy with the idea of laying claim to the mainly Anglian district of Lothian. After all, both William the Conqueror and his sons had shown that Lothian, and indeed rather beyond, was well within the reach of their military forays.[34]

Yet the distant north lay far from the centre of the activities, ambitions, and concerns of the Norman and Angevin kings of England. For the kings of Scots, however, during much of the twelfth and thirteenth centuries to annex this area was a primary ambition. They regarded southern Cumbria as rightfully theirs, filched from them by the kings of England, while Northumbria, possibly indeed as far as Durham, would complement the southern drive which had been the main thrust of their territorial expansion since the tenth century. Their dream came true after 1135 and more particularly 1141. Until 1157 the king of Scots controlled this area as an integral part of his kingdom, holding court at Carlisle, minting his coins there, exploiting the silver mines of Alston to spectacular effect, building great stone keeps at Carlisle and elsewhere, setting his sights on control of the bishopric of Durham, and issuing his commands in the district as king of Scots. Even the aristocratic elites and monasteries of the region came to terms with what seemed to be a permanent transfer of political allegiances.[35] The Tyne, or even the Tees, and the Duddon,

[33] A. MacQuarrie, 'The Kings of Strathclyde, *c.*400–1018', *Medieval Scotland* (as cited above, n. 14), 1–20; G. W. S. Barrow, 'The pattern of lordship and feudal settlement in Cumbria', *Journal of Medieval History* 1 (1975), 117–38.

[34] For a recent review, with full references, see Judith Green, *The Aristocracy of Norman England* (Cambridge, 1997), ch. 3.

[35] For references see above, Ch. 1, n. 23. Also Judith Green, 'Anglo-Scottish Relations, 1066–1174' in *England and Her Neighbours 1066–1453. Essays in Honour of Pierre Chaplais*, ed. M. Jones and M. Vale (1989), 53–73; idem, 'Henry I and David I', *Scottish Historical Review* 75 (1996), 1–19.

or even the Ribble, rather than Tweed and Solway Firth, could well have been the borders of the new Scotland. Henry II, of course, put paid to such ideas; but the kings of Scots certainly did not abandon their ambitions. When the political going got tough in England—as when Richard I was short of cash in 1194[36] or when political disenchantment with John reached its climax in 1215–16[37]—the prospect of a Scottish annexation of the north was resurrected. The problem was to be formally solved by the Treaty of York in 1237; but it was more substantively dealt with in reality by the generally cordial relations between the two kingships and the two kingdoms for most of the two centuries between 1097 and 1296, and by the development of extensive cultural, political, tenurial, ecclesiastical, and social links between Scotland and England, including those in the Anglo-Scottish borders.[38]

If what we know as the northern counties of England constitute one of the areas of contention in the power politics of the medieval British Isles, the west was altogether a much more complex and intractable problem. Historiographically it is also, as a common problem, a much neglected one, partly because discussion of it has been fragmented by the constructs which we call the histories of Ireland, Wales, and Scotland, partly because its plurality and diversity are singularly unamenable to the categories and approach which have done such good service for the unitary histories of England and even Scotland. How then may we define and very broadly characterize this western zone of the British Isles? It may be said to include, in its most ample form, most of northern and western Scotland, the Isles, Galloway, the Isle of Man, Wales, and Ireland. Such an extensive and variegated zone could not be expected to show the political and economic unity and even uniformity which may be said in broad terms to characterize lowland England and even lowland districts of southern and eastern Scotland. Yet it may be possible to identify certain general features of this western zone which stand in contrast with those of the heartland areas controlled by English and Scottish kings in the early twelfth century.

Geographically the orientation of the zone was westwards, in marked contrast to the southern and eastern orientation of the English and Scottish power

36 Anderson, *Scottish Annals*, 311–21; Duncan, *Scotland*, 239–41. Cf. above, Ch. 1, n. 27.

37 Anderson, *Scottish Annals*, 331–3; Anderson, *Early Sources of Scottish History*, II, 404–13. Seisin of the three northern counties was given to the king of Scots by Eustace de Vescy, the king of Scots' brother-in-law, and the rod used as the physical expression of his transfer of Northumberland was deposited in the king's treasury: Duncan, *Scotland*, 521–4. Carlisle fell to the Scottish king in 1216–17, and the canons of the cathedral were accused of becoming 'partisans and adherents of the king of Scotland' and of having 'received him as patron and lord and paid him homage', *Patent Rolls 1216–25*, 111.

38 The work of Keith Stringer in particular has been seminal in exploring this theme. See esp. his *Earl David of Huntingdon. A Study in Anglo-Scottish History* (Edinburgh, 1985), ch. 9, and for a cartographic representation *Atlas of Scottish History to 1707*, ed. P. G. B. McNeill and H. L MacQueen (Edinburgh, 1996), 418–22.

structures. The highway of power in this zone—the means to a more than local or regional supremacy—lay essentially in the western seaway. The greatest power-brokers of this zone were major sea-lords such as Somerled of Argyll and the Isles (d.1164) who commanded a fleet of up to 160 galleys and who even set his sights on challenging the king of Scots. Appropriately enough, it was the galley which was chosen as the motif on some of the seals and funerary sculpture of these lords of the western seas.[39] Power in the west and the north lay considerably in pillaging and the collection of tribute, augmented by the seizure of the goods and men (and women) of one's competitors. Alliances were readily formed across the seaways of the zone: Olaf of Man (d.1153), for example, married the daughter of the ruler of Galloway and in turn married his own daughter to the lord or *regulus* of the Isles.[40] As such alliances suggest, it was politically and culturally a more intimate and interconnected world than our national historiographies suggest. We can see as much, for example, in the fulsome tribute that the native Welsh chronicle pays to the great king of Leinster, Diarmait mac Maél na mBo, on his death in 1072, or in the remarkable career of Gruffudd ap Cynan (d.1137), son of a Welsh princeling but born to a Viking mother in Dublin.[41] The western sea zone was as ethnically diverse as any part of the British Isles and yet it shared broad features which differentiated it sharply from the zones to the south and east. The units of power within it were relatively small, fluid, and vulnerable; hegemonies could be impressive but short-lived; social organization and

[39] R. A. McDonald and S. A. McLean, 'Somerled of Argyll: a new look at old problems', *Scottish Historical Review* 71 (1992), 3–22; R. A. McDonald, 'Images of Hebridean lordship in the twelfth and early thirteenth centuries: the seal of Raonall MacSorley', *Scottish Historical Review* 74 (1995), 129–43. See also K. A. Steer and J. Bannerman, *Late Medieval Monumental Sculpture in the West Highlands* (Edinburgh, 1977), 180–4 for representations of galleys in stone-carving. A vivid echo of the maritime boastfulness of this world is the comment on a Manx ruler that he 'humbled the Scots so thoroughly that no shipbuilder or boatbuilder dared employ more than three iron bolts', *Chronicon regum Mannie* (as cited in Ch. 1, n. 10), *s.a.* 1068.

[40] R. A. McDonald, 'Matrimonial Polities and Core–Periphery Interactions in Twelfth- and Early Thirteenth-century Scotland', *Journal of Medieval History* 21 (1995), 227–47; idem, *The Kingdom of the Isles* (as cited above, n.13), 44–6. Likewise at the end of the twelfth century Rhodri ab Owain Gwynedd of north-west Wales married the daughter of the king of Man in an attempt to secure the support of the Manx fleet to further his ambitions in Gwynedd: *Brut, s.a.* 1193; Lloyd, *History of Wales*, II, 588. Similarly John de Courcy, *princeps Ulidiae* as he was called, furthered his ambitions by marrying Affreca, daughter of Godred of Man: T. E. McNeill, *Anglo-Norman Ulster* (Edinburgh, 1980), 6.

[41] *Brut, s.a.* 1072 ('the most praiseworthy and bravest king of the Irish'); *The Annals of Tigernach*, *s.a.* 1071 describe Diarmait as 'king of Britons and the Hebrides and Dublin'. For this whole theme see K. L. Maund, *Ireland, Wales and England in the Eleventh Century* (Woodbridge, 1991) and Seán Duffy's important review, 'Ostmen, Irish and Welsh in the Eleventh Century', *Peritia* 9 (1995), 378–96. For a full modern Welsh edition of the life of Gruffudd ap Cynan, see *Historia Gruffud vab Kenan* (cited above, n. 27); for an English translation, ed. A. Jones (Manchester, 1910); for discussion, *Gruffudd ap Cynan. A Collaborative Biography*, ed. K. L. Maund (Woodbridge, 1996).

power were largely kin-based; cultural and legal norms were instilled and upheld by hereditary classes of jurists, poets, and remembrancers. It was a world which must have struck the leaders of society in the southern British Isles as conservative, archaic, and even barbaric.[42]

One of the major and still-to-be-answered issues in the history of the British Isles in the twelfth and thirteenth centuries was what long-term power structures would eventually emerge in this fragmented and turbulent zone, and how, and how far, a meaningful relationship—of power, economic links, and culture—could be forged between this western sea orbit and the two major regnal structures which were fast developing, or had already developed, in what one may term lowland southern and eastern Britain. Could it be that credible and sustainable indigenous hegemonies might be developed in this western zone, different in structure and intensity, maybe, from the kingships of Scotland and England but capable of exploiting and developing the specific resources and opportunities of the west? The kind of high kingship achieved by Turlough O Connor of Connacht (1106–56) and his son Rory (1156–86) over much of Ireland, and the mechanisms they deployed to exercise it, or the remarkable power assembled by Somerled, *regulus* of Argyll and lord of the Isles, prior to his death in 1164, or the principality of Wales being created by the Gwynedd dynasty in the thirteenth century, or, for a later period, the Lordship of the Isles under the rule of the MacDonalds suggest that historians should not perhaps be so dismissive of the possibility as they normally are.[43] Alternatively and—at least with the advantage of hindsight—more credibly, might the western zone, or goodly parts of it, be annexed to, if not absorbed into, the aggressive and well-organized power structures which were the kingships of England and Scotland or, better, of the English and the Scots? If so, what would be the nature and effectiveness of the annexation, what would be the demarcation line of their respective zones of influence and annexation, and what would be the eventual shape of the orbits of power in the British Isles?

We can perhaps best answer these questions, however cursorily, by taking snapshots of the map of power in the British Isles at selected moments and focusing the lens in particular on the northern and western zones. The first

[42] See below, Ch. 5.

[43] O Connor: *NHI*, II, esp. 33–7; D. Ó Corráin, *Ireland before the Normans* (Dublin, 1972), 150–74; Helen Perros, 'Crossing the Shannon Frontier: Connacht and the Anglo-Normans, 1170–1224', in *Colony and Frontier in Medieval Ireland* (as cited above, n. 32), 117–39. Somerled: R. A. McDonald (as cited in n. 39 above). Gwynedd: Davies, *Conquest*, chs. 9 and 12; D. Stephenson, *The Governance of Gwynedd* (Cardiff, 1984); J. Beverley Smith, *Llywelyn ap Gruffudd*, chs. 3 and 6. Lordship of the Isles: A. Grant, 'Scotland's "Celtic Fringe" in the Late Middle Ages: The MacDonald Lords of the Isles and the Kingdom of Scotland', in *The British Isles 1100–1500. Comparisons, Contrasts and Connections*, ed. R. R. Davies (Edinburgh, 1988), 118–41.

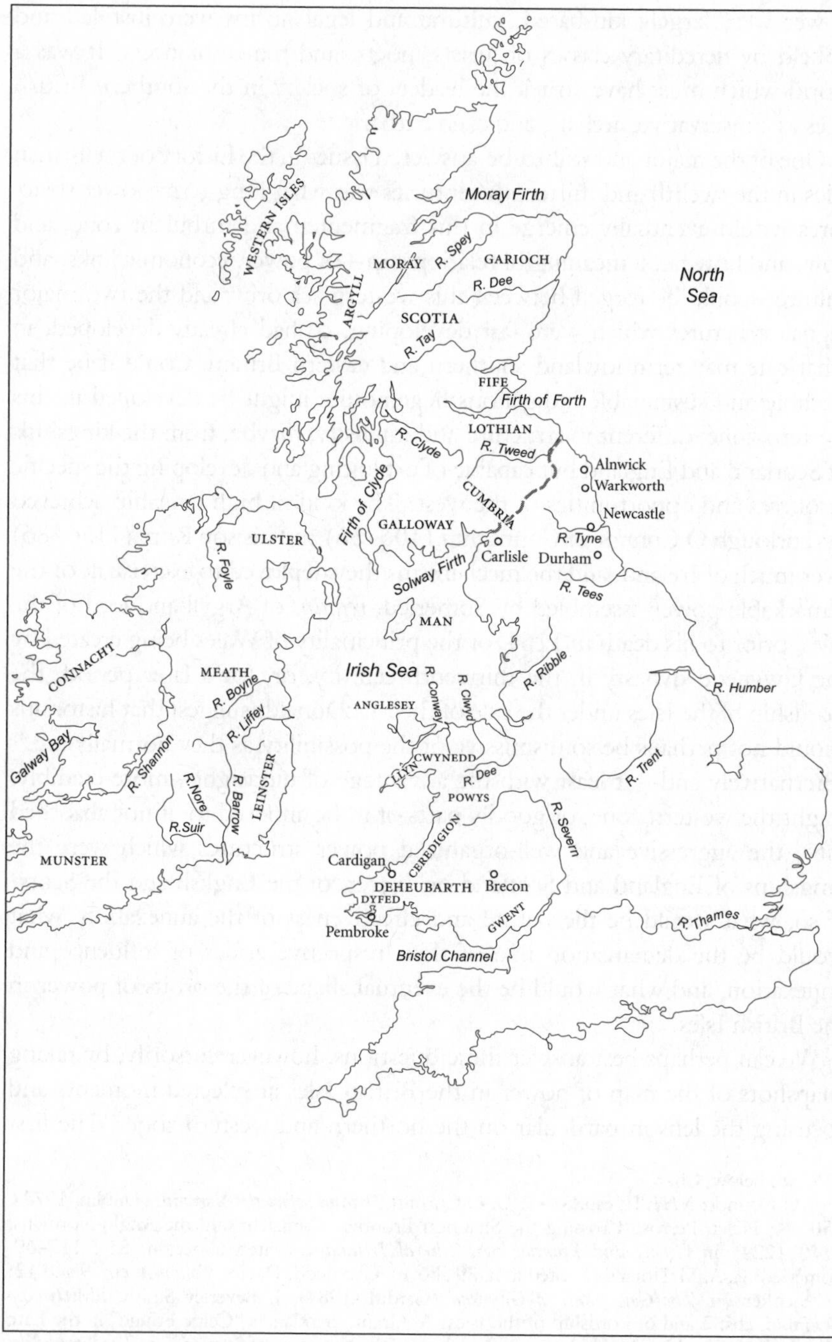

Map 1. The regional divisions of the northern and western British Isles *c.*1100

snapshot (Map 1) might be taken at the turn of the eleventh century; its point might be more effectively made if it were allowed to be composed of three sequences. The first sequence is dated in 1093 and is a record of violent deaths—those of Rhys ap Tewdwr, ruler of Deheubarth and at that time the most powerful native dynast in Wales, near Brecon, and of Malcolm III, king of the Picts and the Scots, and his eldest son at Alnwick. Both were killed by Norman forces, led respectively by Bernard of Neufmarché and Robert Mowbray. The second incident took place in Anglesey five years later. Magnus Barelegs, king of Norway, arrived with a fleet in the island, 'thinking', as the Welsh chronicler reports, 'to conquer all the island of Britain'. But others clearly had the same intention: Hugh of Avranches, earl of Chester, and Hugh of Montgomery, earl of Shrewsbury, were already ravaging the island with the help of a fleet from Ireland. In the ensuing fight on the foreshore Earl Hugh of Shrewsbury was killed by the redoubtable King Magnus, and the Norman momentum in north Wales received a severe setback. The third and final snapshot in this historical montage is dated five years later. It records the death in Ulster of King Magnus, killed on a foray there by the men of the province.[44]

These three episodes across a period of ten years reveal how the map of power in the British Isles, especially in the west and the north, was being reshaped at the close of the eleventh century. It is only by bringing the whole of the British Isles into the picture that the scale and the significance of the individual episodes can be appreciated and the change in the balance of power identified. Three major power groups were competing for control and supremacy: an aggressive Anglo-Norman kingship and its insatiably acquisitive aristocracy; a predatory Scottish kingship; and marauding Scandinavian war-bands. The sheer military gusto and appetites of these groups seemed to know no bounds. Great swathes of the British Isles lay within the orbit of their ambitions, though not fully within their reach or expectation. How much this was a single stage of power can be glimpsed by the way they wove their alliances and arranged their marriages. Magnus Barelegs may have been king of Norway, but it was one of the daughters of Murtogh (Muirchertach) O'Brien, king of Munster, whom he took as his bride. Another of Murtough's daughters was married to Arnulf of Montgomery, the Norman lord of Pembroke and Holderness, who was casting a greedy eye towards Ireland. The king of Scots was also an actor on this stage: he had been compelled to

[44] 1093: above Ch. 1, n. 1; 1098: Brut, *s.a.* 1098; Anderson, *Early Sources*, II, 101–15; Rosemary Power, 'Magnus Barelegs' expedition to the West', *Scottish Historical Review* 65 (1986), 107–32. 1103: Annals of Ulster (cited above, Ch. 1, n. 2), *s.a.*; S. Duffy, 'Irishmen and Islesmen in the kingdoms of Dublin and Man 1052–1171', *Ériu* 423 (1992), 93–133.

quitclaim all the islands to the west of Scotland to Magnus and he bought the friendship of Murtogh with the gift of a camel.[45]

By the end of 1103 the outcome of this struggle for mastery in the outer zones of the British Isles was, at least for the next generation, fairly clear. The disastrous Scottish defeat of 1093 in effect eliminated the Scottish threat to the northern zone for over forty years. English power now went unchallenged up to the Tweed and the Solway Firth. Indeed, the king of Scots was now virtually a satellite client of the English king, socially and militarily beholden to him, and soon opening up his kingdom to his barons, knights, churchmen, burgesses, and their habits and practices. As to the Scandinavians, the death of Magnus Barelegs in Ulster in 1103 was the prelude to the downgrading of their activities and dominance in the western sea orbit; it was not until 1263 that the king of Norway returned in person to these waters. As for Wales and even Ireland, contemporary observers had little doubt that they were now, at the very least potentially, within the orbit of the English king's power, albeit on its outer rim. That is why the Welsh annalist saluted Henry I in terms of awe as 'the man who had subdued under his authority all the island of Britain and its mighty ones' or why William of Malmesbury reported of the kings of distant Munster that 'they would write nothing but what would please him and do nothing but what he commanded.'[46] There could be no doubt where the centre of gravity of power in the British Isles now lay nor how far its reverberations extended. The English domination of the whole of the British Isles seemed to be well under way. A single orbit of power was coming into view. What was open to question was what forms it would assume and how long would it take to complete.

If we were to take our next snapshot of the geography of political power in 1166 (Map 2) we would find that the answers to those questions were not altogether as straightforward as a prophecy based on the events of 1093–1103 might have suggested. The English king, it is true, was still very much the dominant power in the British Isles. In that respect, as in so many others,

[45] *Annals of Inisfallen* (as cited in Ch. 1, n. 1), *s.a.* 1103 (p. 261), 1105; *Brut*, *s.a.* 1102 (p. 23); *The Ecclesiastical History of Orderic Vitalis*, ed. M. Chibnall, 6 vols. (Oxford, 1969–80), VI, 30–1; Duncan, *Scotland*, 127. The complex pattern of alliances and the interconnectedness of events in the western orbit of the British Isles in these years is particularly evident in 1102–3: the Montgomeries were crushed by Henry I in spite of fostering links with the native Welsh and calling on the help of a fleet from Murtough; Murtough O'Brien himself was heavily defeated by the O'Loughlins at the battle of Mag Coba in 1103; and before the year was out his ally and son-in-law, Magnus 'Barelegs', the king of Norway and pretender to an extensive supremacy over the western seaways of the British Isles, was killed in Ulster. Cf. D. Ó Cróinín, *Early Medieval Ireland* (1995), 280–1.

[46] As cited above, Ch. 1, nn. 12–13.

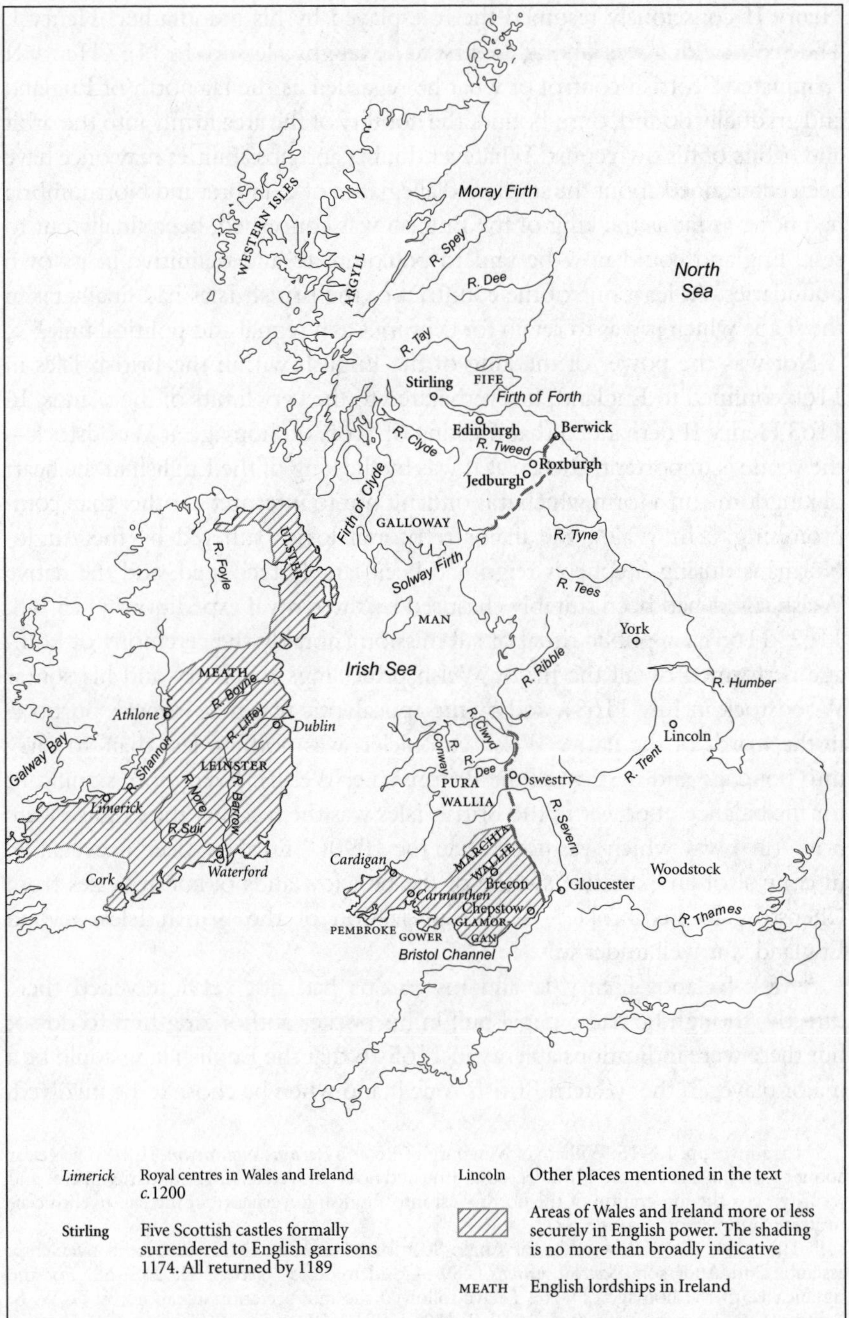
Moray Firth
North Sea
WESTERN ISLES
ARGYLL
R. Spey
R. Dee
R. Tay
Stirling
FIFE
Firth of Forth
Edinburgh
Berwick
R. Tweed
Roxburgh
Jedburgh
R. Clyde
Firth of Clyde
GALLOWAY
R. Tyne
Solway Firth
R. Tees
ULSTER
R. Foyle
MAN
York
Irish Sea
R. Ribble
R. Humber
MEATH
R. Boyne
Athlone
Dublin
R. Liffey
R. Clwyd
R. Conwy
Lincoln
Galway Bay
R. Shannon
LEINSTER
R. Nore
R. Barrow
R. Dee
PURA WALLIA
Oswestry
R. Trent
Limerick
R. Suir
R. Severn
MARCHIA WALLIE
Waterford
Cardigan
Woodstock
Cork
Brecon
Gloucester
Carmarthen
Chepstow
R. Thames
PEMBROKE
GOWER
GLAMORGAN
Bristol Channel
Limerick Royal centres in Wales and Ireland c.1200
Stirling Five Scottish castles formally surrendered to English garrisons 1174. All returned by 1189
Lincoln Other places mentioned in the text
Areas of Wales and Ireland more or less securely in English power. The shading is no more than broadly indicative
MEATH English lordships in Ireland

Map 2. English power in the British Isles *c.*1200

Henry II consciously resumed the role played by his grandfather, Henry I. The Scottish king was among the first to be taught a lesson. In 1157 Henry II terminated Scottish control of what he regarded as the far north of England and gradually bound, or re-bound, the nobility of the area firmly into the orbit and habits of his own court. Whatever doubts and possibilities may once have been entertained about the status and allegiance of Cumbria and Northumbria had now, as far as the king of the English was concerned, been finally put to rest. England could now be said to be complete and definitive in its own boundaries. At least one of the countries of the British Isles had finally taken the shape which it was to retain for centuries as a regnal and political unit.[47]

Nor was the power of the king of the English within the British Isles in 1166 confined to England; it reverberated to the very limits of the islands. In 1163 Henry II demanded that the king of Scots do homage at Woodstock—the venue is important, chosen as it was by the king of the English in the heart of kingdom—in a form which it is difficult not to interpret as other than compromising.[48] In Wales, the major territorial losses suffered by the Anglo-Normans during Stephen's reign had been largely recouped, and the native Welsh rulers had been suitably chastised by three royal expeditions (1157–8, 1163, 1165), by public ritual of submission (notably the ceremony of homage performed by all the major Welsh princelings to Henry and his son at Woodstock in July 1163), and by the apocalyptic fear that Henry's purpose, in the words of the native Welsh chronicler, was nothing less than 'to carry into bondage and destroy all the Britons' (i.e. Welsh). Even more significant for the balance of power in the British Isles was the fact that the English were now—in a way which was not true in the 1090s—firmly, indeed irreversibly, in control of an extensive swathe of the best lowlands of south Wales from Chepstow to Pembroke.[49] The Anglicization of the British Isles beyond England was well under way.

As for Ireland, Henry II and his barons had not yet intervened there directly, though he had a papal bull in his pocket authorizing him to do so; but there were indications aplenty in 1165–6 that the English king could be a major player in the western British zone if and when he chose to be involved.

[47] Cf. above, pp. 13–15. William of Newburgh (*Historia Rerum Anglicarum*, II, 106) was clear about the significance of the 1157 decision: 'England now enjoyed its full boundaries in ease and security.' For the integration of the north-west into English governance in the late twelfth century, see Summerson, *Carlisle*, 82.

[48] The major chronicle sources for Anglo-Scottish relations in these years are conveniently assembled in Anderson, *Scottish Annals*, 239–47; idem, *Early Sources*, II, 233–68. For the significance of the homage of 1163 I have followed the interpretation advanced by G. W. S. Barrow, *Kingship and Unity. Scotland 1000–1306* (1981), 48, and K. J. Stringer, *Earl David of Huntingdon*, 11.

[49] Davies, *Conquest*, 51–3, 96–100, and map 3; *Brut*, *s.a.* 1165.

Among the visitors to his court in Aquitaine in 1166 were Dermot MacMurrough, the dispossessed king of Leinster, and the bishop of the Isles acting on behalf of the king of Man.[50] By their presence they were recognizing where the centre of gravity of the British Isles, even of its western zone, lay. Henry II did not respond to their invitations at that stage, but the fact that in the previous year he had employed troops from Scotland and a fleet from Dublin for his Welsh expedition showed that he and his advisers, for all their continental preoccupations, were well aware of the opportunities and challenges presented by the outer zones of the British Isles.[51]

But the Welsh expedition of 1165 also helps us to qualify the picture of unremitting English dominance of the British Isles. That expedition was a failure; no further royal expedition entered Wales for another forty-five years. It was a reminder, if one were needed, that effective and sustained control in the western zone did not come easily. It may well be, of course, that the area did not figure high on the agenda of the Angevin rulers of England and was not sufficiently appetizing for their aristocracy. So much is suggested by the fact that Henry II did not act on the bull *Laudabiliter* (which gave him the right to intervene in Ireland) or on Dermot MacMurrough's invitation, and that it was a group of desperadoes, down on their luck and yearning for new worlds to conquer, who eventually took up the challenge.[52]

But it was in Scotland that it was becoming ever more apparent that the British Isles were not likely easily to form a unitary orbit of power and that the English attempt to dominate the north and western zones would not go unchallenged. The English king, it is true, treated his Scottish neighbour as a junior partner and, as we have seen, seized on any opportunity to demonstrate and underscore his superiority.[53] But the Scottish monarchy presented an altogether different order of challenge from that presented by Irish kings and Welsh princes. Its unitary roots lay deeply and effectively in the past. Furthermore, during the course of the twelfth century it had undergone a transformation into a monarchy of a contemporary northern European character, whose authority was increasingly underwritten by the adoption of English practices of governance and tenure and by impressive colonization by an Anglo-Norman and Flemish aristocracy and its followers. Its status as a

[50] *NHI*, II, 64; *Chronicles of the Reigns of Stephen, Henry II, and Richard I*, ed. R. Howlett, 4 vols. (R.S., 1884–9), IV, 228–9 (Robert of Torigni).

[51] As Gerald of Wales (*Expugnatio Hibernica*, 78–9) shrewdly observed, the blockade of Dublin by a grand alliance of Irish leaders, King Godred of Man, and the Norse of the northern isles, was prompted by 'their fear of threat of English domination, inspired by the successes of the English'.

[52] See generally M. T. Flanagan, *Irish Society, Anglo-Norman Settlers, Angevin Kingship* for an outstanding discussion.

[53] See above, pp. 5–7.

middle-range European power was indicated by the marriage alliances which its dynasty concluded in this period with the ruling houses of Brittany and Flanders.[54]

In terms of the template of power in the British Isles, the 1160s were a particularly significant decade in the shaping of the country that was becoming Scotland. For it was during these years that the Scottish monarchy first truly showed that it had the appetite and the means to intervene directly in the power structures of the north-western British Isles. In 1160 Malcolm IV led three expeditions into Galloway and persuaded its ruler to step down; in 1164, in one of the decisive battles of the twelfth century in northern Britain, Somerled, lord of Argyll and the Isles, was slain as he attempted an invasion of the Scottish kingdom up the River Clyde. What has been appropriately called 'the winning of the west' was under way.[55] It would be a campaign that would last for over a century and it was not without its reverses as well as its success. But it was becoming clear that what had hitherto been a largely eastern- and southern-centred Scottish monarchy was staking a claim to a direct share of power in the far west and south-west of Scotland. The consequences for the map of power in the British Isles were momentous. Scotland, unlike Wales and Ireland, was becoming more than a geographical expression; it was beginning to acquire the kind of regnal solidarity in which there was a match between the pretensions of its ruler and the reach of his military and political power. In short, Scotland was beginning to approximate to what was already the established English model. It is highly significant to note, therefore, that it is in the 1160s that the expression 'kingdom of Scotland' (*regnum Scotie*) is first recorded as being used 'in an unambiguously territorial context'.[56] What this meant for the political geography of the British Isles as a whole was that there were now at least two major nodal centres of power. How they related to each other and how they coped with the overlap of their interests, especially in the north-west, would henceforth be a major theme in the history of Britain.

If we move the clock of history forward by a century to the mid-1260s (Map 3), we will find that the map of power in the British Isles had changed significantly. In many respects it was a simpler, more clear-cut map than that

[54] See in general Duncan, *Scotland*, esp. chs. 7–8; and Barrow, *Kingship and Unity*, chs. 2–3. For more detailed studies, *R.R.S.*, II, introduction and 'The Reign of William the Lion', idem, *Scotland and its Neighbours in the Middle Ages* (1992), 67–91.

[55] Anderson, *Early Sources*, II, 244–7, 254–8; idem, *Annals*, 241–3; G. W. S. Barrow, *Kingship and Unity*, ch. 6. The Chronicle of Man claimed that Somerled's ambition was 'to subdue all Scotland to himself'.

[56] G. W. S. Barrow, *Anglo-Norman Era in Scottish History*, 153.

Map 3. The northern and western British Isles *c.*1266

of 1166, and certainly than that of 1093; but there were also within it features which suggested a potential for future tension.

It was in the west that the most dramatic change had taken place. The western sea orbit had now in effect been shared between the English and Scottish spheres of influence; Scandinavian power, still so dominant in 1093 and not inconsiderable in 1166, had been eliminated; and the native polities of Wales, western Scotland, and Ireland had been encompassed, more or less successfully, within the power orbits of the kings of England and Scotland. It was in Ireland, of course, that the change was most dramatic and far-reaching.[57] Starting in the late 1160s, the country had been absorbed into the dominions of the Angevin kings of England. Ireland was now formally annexed to the crown of England, the king adding the title 'lord of Ireland' to his style and even retaining that title when he handed the lordship itself as an appanage to his son (as Henry III had done in 1254).[58] Most of the country was now, directly or indirectly, under English rule; parts of it were densely settled by third- and fourth-generation English colonists; and the essential features of English law, institutions, land tenure, economic practices, ecclesiastical habits, and culture had been transplanted to the island. Two observations from very different sources may serve to sum up the scale of the achievement. In 1248 an Irish annalist conceded that 'the sway of the Galls [i.e. the English] was over all Ireland'; his conclusion is understandable when we recall that Jordan of Exeter was building a castle, founding a Dominican friary, and establishing a manor in the far north-west in modern county Mayo at that very time.[59] Speaking of this very period, Robin Frame concludes that 'Ireland was an integral part of the wider Angevin polity.' The 'expansionary impetus' of that polity had now firmly encompassed the southern region of the western zone of the British Isles in its ambit.[60]

At very much the same time the northern region of the same zone was being brought equally decisively into the orbit of the other major power centre in the British Isles, the kingdom of Scotland. By 1266 the west and the Highlands had been largely brought to heel in a series of campaigns; the last major revolt in Galloway had been crushed in 1234–5 and the region—once so semi-detached from the kingdom of Scotland and so easily within the destabilizing reach of English power in Cumbria and Ulster—was being fully

[57] In all that relates to the history of Ireland I am deeply indebted in particular to the writings and insights of Robin Frame. His essays have recently been collected in *Ireland and Britain 1170–1450* (1998).

[58] *NHI*, II, 179–80.

[59] *Miscellaneous Irish Annals (A.D. 1114–1437)*, ed. S. Ó hInnse (Dublin, 1947), 129; G. H. Orpen, *Ireland under the Normans 1169–1333*, 4 vols. (Oxford, 1911–20), III, 197–8.

[60] Robin Frame, *Ireland and Britain*, 46, 54.

absorbed administratively and governmentally into the Scottish kingdom; finally, the defeat of Haakon IV at the battle of Largs in 1263 and the cession of the Isle of Man and the Western Isles to the king of Scots at the Treaty of Perth in 1266 announced the virtual end of even theoretical Scandinavian pretensions in the western sea province of the British Isles and the near-completion of the kingdom of Scotland (except for the northern isles).[61] No more eloquent comment on the significance of these events in terms of Scotland's regnal solidarity could be made than the provision of the 1266 treaty that henceforth the inhabitants of the Isles were 'to be subject to the laws and customs of the kingdom of Scotland, and shall be governed and judged in accordance with them henceforth'.[62]

The momentousness of the reshaping of the map of political supremacy in the western zone of the British Isles in the century to 1266 cannot be overestimated. From the Scottish angle it is easy to see why one historian has concluded that 'the two Alexanders [i.e. Alexander II (1214–49) and Alexander III (1249–86)] presided over one of the most successful programmes of territorial consolidation and expansion to be seen in the British Isles since the Norman Conquest itself.'[63] Even more far-reaching, of course, was the English domination and colonization of Ireland. The fates of Ireland and England, and of the Irish and the English, were henceforth inextricably interlinked. England's Irish problem had been launched; so had Ireland's English problem.

So it was that the whole of the northern and western sea province—an area which had been but very loosely attached to southern and eastern Britain in 1093 and even in 1166—had now been absorbed, to a greater or lesser measure, into a single power orbit, that of the British Isles. A single orbit maybe, but one which remained divided into two, albeit unequal, power blocs, the English and the Scottish. By 1266 these two power blocs had reached an effective working relationship with each other. England's control of its northern regions—once so fiercely contested with the king of Scots—had been finally regularized by the Treaty of York of 1237;[64] and by and large, in

[61] The classic accounts are to be found in Duncan, *Scotland*, chs. 20–1 and Barrow, *Kingship and Unity*, ch. 6. For further details see esp. A. A. M. Duncan and A. L. Brown, 'Argyll and the Isles in the Early Middle Ages', *Proceedings of the Society of Antiquaries of Scotland* 90 (1956–7), 192–218; R. A. McDonald, *The Kingdom of the Isles*, chs. 3–4.

[62] The terms of the Treaty are excerpted in Anderson, *Early Sources*, II, 655, n. 4. For comment, see R. I. Lustig, 'The Treaty of Perth: A Re-examination', *Scottish Historical Review* 58 (1979), 35–57.

[63] Keith J. Stringer in *Uniting the Kingdom?*, ed. Grant and Stringer, 93.

[64] For the text of the Treaty see *Anglo-Scottish Relations*, ed. E. L. G. Stones, no. 7. The importance of definitive boundaries is reflected in the story that Henry III offered Alexander II eighty marks' worth of land 'in another part of England, so that the territories of his kingdom might not be mutilated in the northern region': Matthew Paris, *Chronica Majora*, III, 373.

spite of periodic huffing and puffing and some rather high-handed paternalism, the English king did not press his conviction that he was the senior partner in the Anglo-Scottish relationship. But questions remained. How secure and stable were these power blocs, especially in the far west, given the periodic indications of resurgent native power in both Ireland and Wales, and the recentness of Scottish authority in the Western Isles and in south-west Scotland?[65] Would the demarcation of spheres of power between England and Scotland in the western zone of the British Isles—especially in Ulster, the Isle of Man, Galloway, and even the Isles—stand the test of time?[66] Perhaps most crucially, could the existence of two major power blocs be squared in the long run with the claim, dormant maybe but certainly not altogether forgotten, of the English kings to the ultimate super-overlordship (as it has been called) of the whole of the British Isles?

The prospect that the British Isles might be moving in the direction of a broad-based political and cultural community derived plausibility from another direction. We have been so conditioned by the assumptions of a historiography of conflict and the cultivation of national identities in our study of the evolution of the medieval British Isles that we may well underestimate the forces that were making for integration. The distribution of great aristocratic estates and marriages, the transfer of ecclesiastical and governmental institutions and personnel, the rapid development of economic and commercial networks, and the toing and froing of all sorts of men were but some of the reasons why the British Isles were becoming a more integrated society in 1266 than they had been a century earlier.[67] Thus, to take an ecclesiastical example, twenty-three English monasteries held property in Scotland in the 1260s and native-born Englishmen occupied the bishoprics of Aberdeen, Dunblane, Glasgow, and the Isles.[68] Two English earls who died in the 1260s may represent the kind of territorial, tenurial, and economic links which could bind together the different parts of the British Isles in aristocratic terms. Richard de Clare, earl of Gloucester (d.1262) was not only owner of vast estates in southern England but also lord of Glamorgan and much else in Wales, and of the vast lordship of Kilkenny in Ireland; he moved easily between all his estates. So did his contemporary Roger de Quincy (d.1264), simultaneously

[65] The English and Scottish kings could on occasion act in concert to protect their mutual interests in the west, as in the common action against the descendants of Somerled in the 1250s, whose naval power threatened both to destabilize the Western Isles and to attack English settlements in north-west Ireland: *CDI*, II, no. 652.

[66] The complicated interplay of political ambitions in this whole north-western sea-world will be greatly illuminated by the forthcoming studies of Dr Seàn Duffy.

[67] This is a topic which Robin Frame (see *Ireland and Britain*, esp. chs. 2–4, 9) and Keith Stringer (see n. 38 above) have made particularly their own. Cf. above, Ch. 1, n. 44.

[68] Keith J. Stringer in *Uniting the Kingdom?*, ed. Grant and Stringer, 87–8.

earl of Winchester and constable of Scotland, and holder of large estates in both countries.[69] And so did many of their major tenants. Likewise, when we recall that it could be contemplated that Henry III might go on a hunting party to Connacht in north-west Ireland, or that Philip Lovel graduated from being a steward in Galloway to being treasurer of England, or that Gruffudd ap Rhys, the Welsh lord of Senghenydd in Glamorgan, found himself imprisoned in the earl of Gloucester's castle in Kilkenny, we are catching glimpses of some of the forces that were making for the growing integration of the British Isles.[70] This integration, it is true, was pre-eminently in the service of the ambitions of the ruling dynasties and aristocracies of England and Scotland. But there was *ex hypothesi* no reason why such integration could not be extended, at least indirectly, to the ruling native elites of Wales and Ireland. After all, to give one example, when Felim O'Connor of Connacht was summoned to serve Henry III in Wales in 1245, the local annalist noted that he 'was held in honour by the king and was well pleased when he returned westwards'.[71] Had such a policy of inclusion and accommodation been pursued imaginatively, might the British Isles have gradually evolved into a single, albeit loose-limbed, political unit?

In fact the prospects for such an outcome were already extremely remote, indeed arguably nil, by 1266. The British Isles may have been more integrated and the map of power in it more simplified in 1266 than in 1166; but it was also—in terms of identities, perceptions, and sentiments—most assuredly a world of four countries and four peoples.[72] Nomenclature had become simpler and more assertively precise. The names of the four units into which we divide the British Isles naturally and, perhaps, unthinkingly were, of course, already old terms, though they had not always carried the connotations we ascribe to them. But it can be argued that it was in the thirteenth century they acquired the measure of definitiveness and a centrality in terms of political propaganda and aspiration that they have retained since. England was far and away the

[69] Richard de Clare: M. Altschul, *A Baronial Family in Medieval England: The Clares 1217–1314* (Baltimore, Md., 1965), chs. 2, 8, 9. Note that he held court in the Welsh March in 1245 and visited Ireland in 1253; his daughter was born at Llantrisant in Glamorgan. Roger de Quincy: G. G. Simpson, 'The *Familia* of Roger de Quincy, Earl of Winchester and Constable of Scotland', *Essays on the Nobility of Medieval Scotland*, ed. K. J. Stringer (Edinburgh, 1985), 102–30. Beyond the work of Frame and Stringer referred to above, n. 67, the English and aristocratic presence in Ireland and Wales is also explored in J. R. S. Phillips, 'The Anglo-Norman Nobility', in *The English in Medieval Ireland*, ed. James Lydon (Dublin, 1984), 87–105, and R. R. Davies, *Lordship and Society in the March of Wales 1284–1400* (Oxford, 1978), esp. chs. 1, 2, 4.

[70] *CDI*, I, no. 1512 (1223); Matthew Paris, *Chronica Majora*, V, 270–1; Altschul, *A Baronial Family*.

[71] *Annals of Connacht*, 88. This theme is explored in Davies, *Domination and Conquest*, ch. 3.

[72] Cf., R. R. Davies, 'The Peoples of Britain and Ireland 1100–1400. 1. Identities', *Transactions of the Royal Historical Society*, 6th ser., 4 (1994), 1–20, esp. pp. 18–19.

most institutionally mature of these units, with a lineage as an effective single country which extended back to the early tenth century and with a sense of the ethnic unity of its people which was even older. Now, in the thirteenth century, it flaunted its Englishness more stridently and even intolerantly than before. The royal title was changed from king of the English to king of England. Phrases such as 'the English church' (*ecclesia anglicana*), 'the law' or 'laws of England', 'the common utility of the whole of England', 'the magnates of England', 'the nation of the realm of England', or 'the commune of England' became part of the normal discourse of the period.[73] England could be personified, its honour defended, and its fate at the hands of aliens deplored in the literature of the period. Favoured aliens could be given the status of 'a pure Englishman', and an alleged foreign plot 'to delete the name of the English' could be exploited to raise hysteria.[74] Much of this language and rhetoric was, of course, prompted by, and directed at, royal incompetence and alien favourites. But the cultivation and promotion of such a strident and self-confident Englishness would also inevitably shape the English attitude to the rest of the British Isles.[75]

At much the same time that England was cultivating and flaunting its self-identity, Scotland was doing the same. Indeed, the advance in the sense of Scottish self-identity was arguably even more dramatic, because it was achieved from a less promising base-line and over a much shorter time-span. The country was now regnally and territorially defined. 'Under the two Alexanders (1214–86),' according to Geoffrey Barrow, 'the name *Scotia*, *Ecosse*, "Scotland" ceased to refer only to the country north of Clyde and Forth and came finally and definitively to be synonymous with the kingdom of the Scots . . . the political entity to which all Scots belonged, and whose laws they obeyed.'[76] Borrowing freely from the experience of its southern neighbour, this 'entity' was fast acquiring the identifying emblems of unitary political maturity—not least a sense of its own 'rightful boundaries and marches', an insistence that there was a 'common law of Scotland' and 'usage throughout our kingdom of Scotland', and a sense of a single 'community of the

[73] P. Chaplais, *English Royal Documents: King John—Henry VI, 1199–1461* (Oxford, 1971), 13. For examples of the phraseology, W. Stubbs, *Select Charters . . . of English Constitutional History* (9th edn., Oxford, 1913), 320, 324–5, 327, 374, 379.

[74] *Rotuli Parliamentorum*, I, 135; *The Song of Lewes*, ed. C. L. Kingsford (Oxford, 1890), ll. 281–2.

[75] For this theme, see M. T. Clanchy, *England and its Rulers 1066–1272* (1983), ch. 10, and M. Prestwich, *English Politics in the Thirteenth Century* (1990), ch. 5. A different perspective on the period is given in Donald Matthew, *The English and the Community of Europe in the Thirteenth Century* (Stenton Lecture, 1996).

[76] Barrow, *Kingship and Unity*, 153.

realm'.[77] The maturity and cohesion of that political community, and thereby of the country, were tested by minority kingship and petulant English pressure; and they survived.[78] Scotland had come fully of age as a country. It was now difficult to conceive that it could hereafter be—as it had been at various stages during the last two centuries—merely a client kingdom of England. The map of power and authority in the British Isles had thereby been permanently altered.

If England and Scotland had taken a definitive shape and identity as countries, what of Wales and Ireland? Neither enjoyed the measure of political unity and regnal solidarity which had been formative in defining England and Scotland as countries. Both had fallen within the power zones of the English kings and aristocracy and were substantially under their control, direct or indirect. They were in effect treated as annexes of an England-based power bloc. This was made formally explicit as far as Ireland was concerned in 1254 when Henry III decreed that 'the land of Ireland shall never be separated from the *Crown of England* and no one but Edward [Henry III's son] and his heirs, *kings of England*, shall ever claim or have any right in that land' (my italics). That statement—which also applied in effect to the royal lands in Wales—put paid to any notions (which had certainly been occasionally floated earlier) that Ireland might be a separate and detachable kingdom; it also announced that Ireland was inseparably annexed to an England-centred kingdom and crown.[79]

Ireland and Wales were therefore in large measure regarded as dependencies of England. But they were not, nor could they be, *of* England, since England had defined itself exclusively on its own terms. The large and powerful English communities in Ireland and Wales were fiercely and defiantly English, but even they were beyond England. Wales and Ireland were therefore recognized as separate, albeit dependent, territories, 'lands' (*terrae*) as they were normally called in contemporary English documents.[80] But were they, or could they

[77] Boundaries: *Foedera etc.*, I, ii, 735; laws and usage: W. D. H. Sellar, 'The Common Law of Scotland and the Common Law of England', in *The British Isles 1100–1500*, ed. R. R. Davies, 82–100, esp. pp. 86–7; Hector L. MacQueen, 'Scots Law under Alexander III', in *Scotland in the Reign of Alexander III 1249–1286*, ed. Norman H. Reid (Edinburgh, 1990), 74–103, esp. pp. 82–4; community of the realm: Barrow, *Kingship and Unity*, 122–6.

[78] For the minority of Alexander III see esp. Grant G. Simpson, 'Kingship in Miniature: A Seal of the Minority of Alexander III, 1249–57', in *Medieval Scotland. Crown, Lordship and Community*. ed. Grant and Stringer, 131–40. For the remarkable seal of the Guardians in 1286, with its invocation to St Andrew to be 'leader of the compatriot Scots', G. W. S. Barrow, *Robert Bruce*, 17.

[79] *CDI*, II, no. 371. For comment: *NHI*, II, 179. For Wales, see J. G. Edwards, *The Principality of Wales 1267–1967* (cited above, Ch. 1, n. 65).

[80] Cf. Ch. 1, n. 64.

aspire to be, countries? As geographical expressions, maybe; as independent political units—comparable with England or Scotland—self-evidently not. But countries are not defined merely by power and political sovereignty, but by the traditions, sentiments, and aspirations of those who live in them. In that respect the middle years of the thirteenth century witnessed important programmatic declarations in both Ireland and Wales that they were indeed countries, indeed potentially independent or quasi-independent political units.

At a famous meeting at Cáeluisce in 1260 Brian Ó Neill of Tyrone claimed, and was accorded, the title of 'the kingship of the Gaels of Ireland'; even the English chancery recorded the fact that Brian 'presumptuously bears himself as king of the kings of Ireland'. Brian's dream came to a bloody end at the battle of Down on 16 May 1260; but even the dream was a significant indication that the concept of Ireland as a separate, indeed independent, country, rather than being a lordship dependent on the English crown, was still alive.[81] Simultaneously, and with a far greater degree of success, the princes of Gwynedd set out on a deliberate campaign to create a native principality of Wales, with its own distinctive laws and customs and its own internal structures of power. They arrogated the title 'prince of Wales' to themselves and eventually in 1267 extracted from an exhausted English government the recognition of the existence of such a principality and such a title. Wales, albeit a truncated Wales, was apparently in the process of being converted from a geographical expression and a cultural aspiration into a political idea and even a power structure. In that process, the control and definition of the word 'Wales' were critical.[82] In short, political aspiration in the various parts of the British Isles in the thirteenth century thought of the island as a collection of four countries.

It was also the working assumption of contemporary political language and practice. So it was, for example, that Magna Carta drew a clear distinction between the law of England and that of Wales, or that the status of refugees in the different countries of the British Isles was an important issue in diplomatic negotiations.[83] Whatever the realities of orbits of power, especially the English one, and whatever doubts there might be about the status of Wales and

[81] *Annals of Connacht*, 127; *Close Rolls 1259–61*, 64. On his death the Connacht annalist called him 'king of the Gaels of Ireland' (ibid., 131) and the O'Brien's family bard lamented his death with the words 'Eire after thee is an orphan' (Orpen, *Ireland under the Normans*, III, 276).

[82] J. Beverley Smith, *Llewelyn ap Gruffudd. Prince of Wales*, esp. ch. 6; Davies, *Conquest*, esp. ch. 12. I hope to return to some of the ideas hinted at here on a later occasion.

[83] Law: Magna Carta: clause 56; *Foedera*, I, i, 84 (1201 agreement with Llywelyn ab Iorwerth); refugees: *Anglo-Scottish Relations*, ed. Stones, no. 1 (Treaty of Falaise). In a famous letter in 1224 Llywelyn responded to a letter from Henry III by declaring that 'he has no less liberty than the king of Scotland, who receives outlaws from England with impunity': *Calendar of Ancient Correspondence concerning Wales*, ed. J. G. Edwards (Cardiff, 1935), 24.

Ireland as political units, it was now firmly in terms of four countries that contemporaries viewed the British Isles, most revealingly of all in their incidental comments.[84] The consequence of accepting, and acting upon, such an assumption was far-reaching, all the more so for being unchallenged. It meant that the idea of a single monarchy of Britain, or indeed of the British Isles, was well and truly dead and buried. In such circumstances four countries could be welded into one only by means of power, violent or otherwise.

By the later years of Edward I's reign that indeed seemed to have happened. There was no inevitability about the process, no grand pre-ordained plan, merely a seizing of opportunities and challenges as they arose fortuitously. But it was more than a mere chapter of accidents. It was the resolving of the tensions and ambiguities inherent in the equation of power in the British Isles by the mid-thirteenth century—an archipelago shared unequally between two kingdoms and power zones, and between four countries and peoples.[85] By 1296 the British Isles seemed (very recently and suddenly, it is true) to have been converted into a virtually unitary and exclusive orbit of power. Wales had been finally conquered in 1282–3; Edward I's victory tour through the country in 1284 had encompassed almost literally its four corners. So had his march through the country in 1294–5 (Map 4). There was occasional disturbing news from Ireland; but the justiciar (or governor-general)'s detailed account of his travels in that country in June–August 1290 was an awesome demonstration of the reach and amplitude of English authority in the island (Map 5).[86] As for Scotland, Edward had reported proudly in July 1291 that 'the realms of England and Scotland have, by God's favour, been *united* [my italics] by reason of the superior lordship that the king [of England] had in Scotland.' When the Scots refused to accept the consequences of that self-evident truth, Edward's forces comprehensively defeated them at Dunbar on 27 April 1296, and Edward, in the words of a contemporary, 'conquered and searched the kingdom' as far as Elgin, much more thoroughly and further than any English king had ever been before (Map 6).[87]

The comprehensiveness and purpose of the whole exercise could not be in doubt; it was the final solution of the British problem.[88] The principality of

[84] Thus Earl Ranulf of Chester (d.1232) declared that no ecclesiastical taxes would be collected in his lands, 'although England and Wales, Scotland and Ireland were compelled to pay': Matthew Paris, *Chronica Majora*, III, 189.

[85] Cf. Davies, *Domination and Conquest*, chs. 3, 5, 6.

[86] *CDI*, III, no. 559, pp. 274–6.

[87] *Cal. Close Rolls 1288–96*, 200; Stevenson, *Documents on the History of Scotland*, II, 31, 163–4; Barrow, *Bruce*, 72–6.

[88] See above, Ch. 1, where the evidence is rehearsed at greater length.

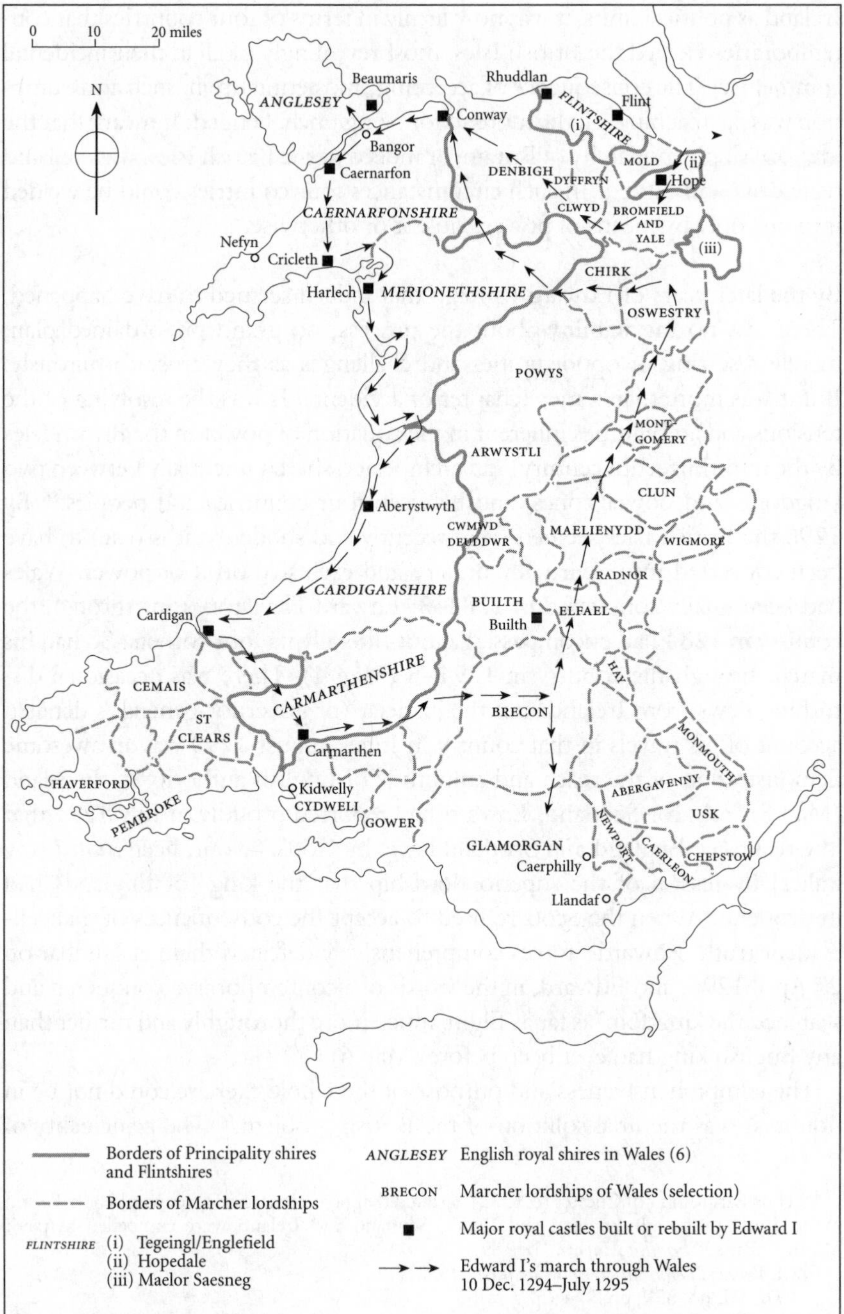

Map 4. Wales in the late thirteenth century

Map 5. Ireland in the late thirteenth century

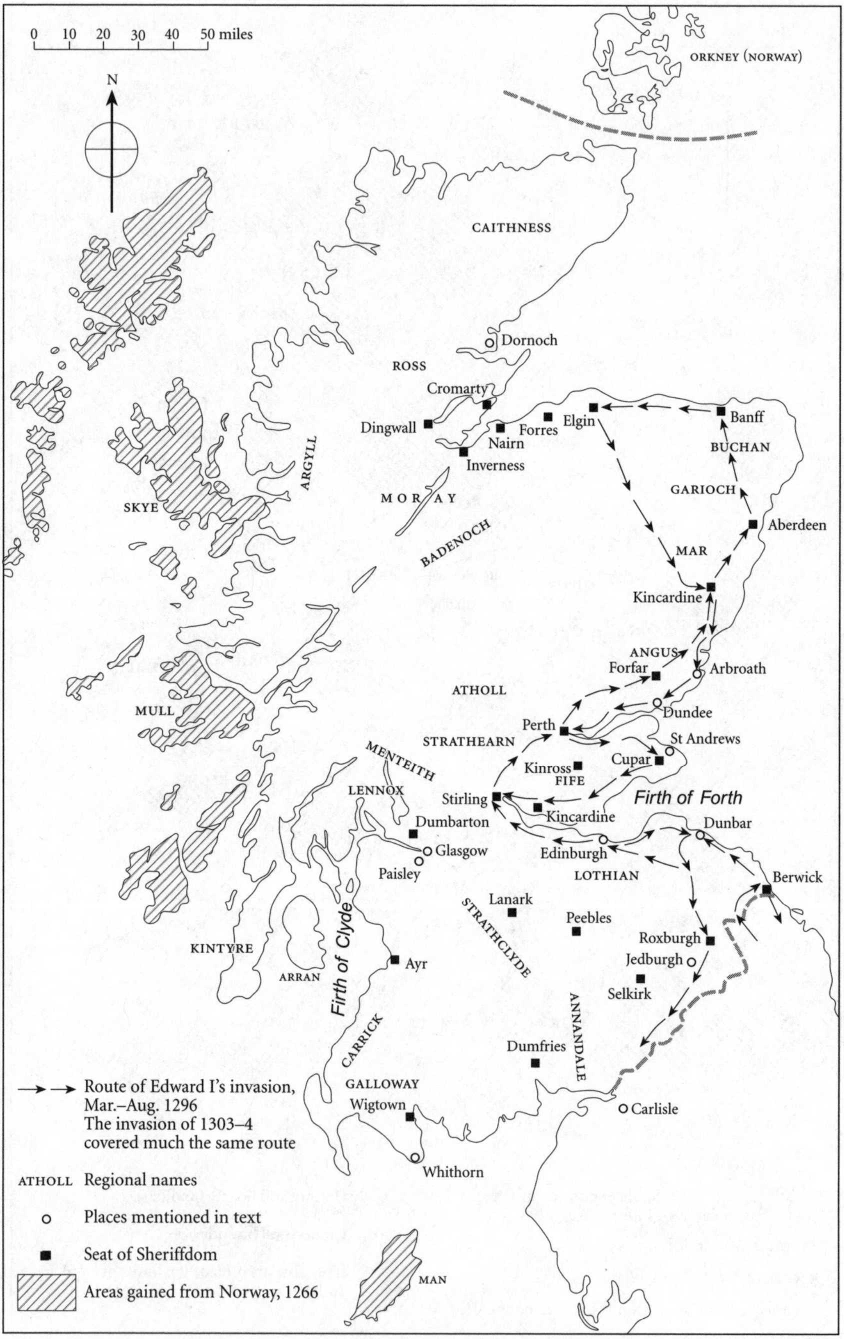

Map 6. Scotland in the late thirteenth century

Wales and the kingdom of Scotland were in effect disbanded. Alongside the lordship of Ireland they now constituted the dominions of the king of England in the British Isles. The king of England was already lord of Ireland; he was soon to bestow the title of the prince of Wales on his son; the kingship of Scotland was suspended indefinitely. There was now but one kingdom in the British Isles; all the other countries were simply referred to as 'lands' (*terrae*) in English parlance; their subjects were required to swear fealty to the king of England in huge public ceremonies; and the symbols of their distinctive nationhood were carted off to Westminster. Some of the governmental and administrative features of a centrally directed unitary polity were beginning to be put into place—be it by legislative ordinance (of which the Statute of Wales 1284 and the Ordinance for the governance of Scotland 1305 are the great exemplars), by tightening the lines of administrative responsibility, especially in financial matters, to the English exchequer, and by designating Westminster as the centre to which petitions and grievances from all parts of the king of England's dominions were addressed. The British Isles were a more thoroughly integrated entity in the late thirteenth century than they had hitherto ever been in their history: troops, supplies, and money from Ireland were critical in the conquest and settlement of Wales and in the English campaigns in Scotland, but equally Welsh levies played a notable role in the maintenance of English authority in Ireland; officials, royal and seignorial, took the whole of the British Isles as the stage on which they played out their careers; while great magnates moved easily from one country to another, as did Gilbert de Clare, earl of Gloucester—the greatest of English magnates and now the son-in-law of Edward I—as he travelled through his estates in Wales to preside at a dramatic council in Dublin in April 1294.

The day of a single British Isles orbit of power, so it would seem, had arrived by the summer of 1296. That is what persuaded the chronicler to announce that the former monarchy of the whole of Britain, for so long fragmented and truncated, had been reconstituted.[89] But he was mistaken. The power which Edward I exercised in 1296 was *not* that of monarch of the whole of Britain, either in name or in substance, but rather that of the king of England who had brought the four countries of the British Isles more or less under his power. The consequences of that fact, and of the way in which the power bloc had been assembled, cast their shadow over the history of the British Isles for generations, indeed centuries, to come. Three consequences in particular may be itemized. First, in a power bloc constructed from England

[89] See the excerpts from the chronicle of Bury St Edmunds (*s.a.* 1296) and Pierre Langtoft (*s.a.* 1305) quoted above, Ch. 2, n. 8, n. 37.

outwards, the status of the other countries and peoples of the British Isles was likely to be at best problematic, at worst inferior. Second, since the ideology and mythology of English power and success remained defined in exclusively English terms, little real attempt was made to create a pluralistic pan-British mythology or to explain English dominance other than in terms of right and of power, English right and English power. Finally, English domination of the British Isles was grounded in the political structures, the economic and social formations and the cultural norms and values of an English world—not only in what we have increasingly come to know as the English 'state', but also in the English communities in Wales and Ireland and in the increasingly English look-alike polity and society which had developed in parts of eastern and southern Scotland. How, and indeed whether, such a view of the world and the ordering of human affairs could come to terms with the very different norms and habits—political, cultural, economic, social—of the outer zones of the British Isles was now the great challenge. It is to these issues that we now turn.

4
POLITICAL HEARTLANDS AND POLITICAL BACKWATERS

Rotherfield Peppard is a pretty village near the Thames valley to the west of Henley. On 30 June 1294, fortified by the company of some of his neighbours, the lord of Rotherfield Peppard, Sir Ralph Pipard, came to a momentous decision.[1] He and his family were part of the bedrock of English landed, political, and county society. They had been tenants of the honour of Wallingford (of which Rotherfield Peppard was a member) from soon after the Norman conquest; they held estates in southern England from Gloucestershire through to Suffolk; they were particularly attached to the manor of Great Linford in Buckinghamshire and to its splendid deer park; they had served as stewards of Wallingford and sheriffs in Gloucestershire and Herefordshire; and Sir Ralph himself was to win the ultimate accolade of an individual summons to the councils and parliaments of the later years of Edward I. He was indeed the English county knight incarnate.[2]

But there was another dimension to Ralph Pipard's life. His ancestors had jumped aboard the band-wagon which we term the English conquest of Ireland in the late twelfth century. Three, or possibly four, Pipard brothers crossed to Ireland with Prince John in 1185 and were soon muscling in on the opportunities presented to them.[3] One rose to be justiciar of Ireland; the descendant of another became steward of Ulster. More secure and permanent than office were lands, and these the Pipards secured in abundance, partly in

[1] *CDI*, V, no. 149.

[2] For the Pipards in general, see G. E. Cokayne et al. (eds.), *The Complete Peerage* (1910–59), X, 526–34; their estates, *Calendar of Inquisitions Post Mortem*, V, no. 191; Great Linford: *Calendar of Patent Rolls 1281–92*, 103; Ralph Pipard: C. Moor, *Knights of Edward I* (Harleian Society, 1929–32), III, 72–3.

[3] In a later deposition Roger Pipard is referred to as 'a conqueror at the first conquest of Ireland' who secured land near Ardee 'vacant at his conquest': *Calendar of Justiciary Rolls, Ireland, 1295–1303* (Dublin, 1905), 281–2. Around 1190 John as lord of Ireland confirmed to Peter Pipard 'his conquest in Uriel': *Calendar of Ormond Deeds*, ed. E. Curtis (Dublin, 1932–43), I, no. 863. The world in which the Pipards moved is re-created in Brendan Smith, 'Tenure and Locality in North Leinster in the Early Thirteenth Century', in *Colony and Frontier in Medieval Ireland*, ed. Terry Barry et al. (1995), 29–40.

Leinster and West Meath but principally in Uriel.[4] It was a very different world from that of the Thames Valley. The Pipards may have felt fairly at ease and secure in the immediate neighbourhood of their chief town at Ardee (between Drogheda and Dundalk), for it had many features with which they were familiar at home—a strong castle, a thriving borough, manors, a well-established English settler community, an English-style pattern of local administration and justice. The Pipards had indeed signalled their affection for the area by founding two religious houses there, one of them a Carmelite friary established by Ralph Pipard himself.[5] But to travel the few miles from the relatively familiar security of Ardee to the family's castle at Donaughmoyne or to its outlying manor at Dysarth in West Meath was to cross as profound a cultural chasm—in the broadest sense of the word culture—as any in Europe.[6]

Ralph Pipard had doubtless crossed that divide more than once in his youth, for he appears to have spent considerable time in Ireland in the 1270s. To do so required him not only to visit an unfamiliar terrain but also to engage with utterly different structures and mechanisms of political power and to master a totally new idiom of social and cultural values. We may identify in particular two lessons that he had to learn. The first related to what the English called war. Ralph Pipard, like other good English knights of his day, was doubtless proud of his military record: he had served in Wales in the 1282–3 campaign and, in late middle age, was summoned to show his skills in Flanders and Scotland. This was well-organized, carefully planned military duty in the name and at the behest of the king. Military realities in Uriel were very different. This was, in the contemporary phrase, a land of war, where (in the words of a jury) Pipard's lands were 'so close to the Irish of Leinster and Meath that no English or peaceful man' (the equation of the two categories is significant) 'remains among them'.[7] Here warfare was a way of life, a means for an impoverished society and its leaders to replenish its stocks of food,

[4] For discussion and map, see Otway-Ruthven, *Medieval Ireland*, 70–2. Also idem, 'The Partition of the de Verdon lands in Ireland in 1332', *Proceedings of the Royal Irish Academy* 66 (1967–8), C, 401–55.

[5] G. H. Orpen, *Ireland under the Normans*, II, 122–4; A. Gwynn and R. N. Hadcock, *Medieval Religious Houses. Ireland* (1970), 210, 286; Brendan Smith, 'A County Community in Early Fourteenth-Century Ireland: The Case of Louth', *English Historical Review* 108 (1993), 561–88.

[6] *CDI*, V, no. 167; Brendan Smith, 'The Concept of the March in Medieval Ireland: The Case of Uriel', *Proceedings of the Royal Irish Academy* 88 (1988), C, 257–69; idem, 'The Medieval Border. Anglo-Irish and Gaelic Irish in Late Thirteenth- and Early Fourteenth-century Uriel', in *The Borderland. Essays on the History of the Ulster–Leinster Border*, ed. R. Gillespie and H. O'Sullivan (Belfast, 1989), 41–53; idem, *Colonisation and Conquest in Medieval Ireland. The English in Louth* (Cambridge, 1999). For similar sharp geographical and cultural contrasts in Leinster, see Alfred P. Smyth, *Celtic Leinster* (Dublin, 1982).

[7] *CDI*, V no. 167 (p. 66).

cattle, and booty. It was war fought on a different rhythm, by different rules, for different reasons, and by different means from those familiar to the gentry of the English shires.[8] English administrators, and in their wake modern historians, bewailed its destructiveness, assessed its damages in detailed calculations, and drew lines on the map—eventually represented physically in a ditch around the Pale—to indicate the flow and ebb of the tide of war.[9] These were, and are, ultimately exercises in misunderstanding. War in the borderlands of Uriel, as elsewhere in Ireland and to some extent in Wales and Scotland, or at least parts of them, was not an occasional diversion or a means of resolving disputes when diplomacy between 'sovereign' rulers had failed; it was the norm, crucial to the power and prestige of the leaders of native Irish society and their followers. Ralph Pipard had to learn as much and had to learn to wage war in the Irish way if he was to survive, let alone flourish, in this world.

He had also to learn a second, arguably more difficult, lesson. The Irish leaders, whom the Pipards and their like had alternately bludgeoned and cajoled, constructed the world of political power on utterly different assumptions and in an utterly different vocabulary from those of the English political communities in England and Ireland. Bridging the gap between these two worlds proved well nigh impossible; Ralph Pipard was one of those who attempted it. At some stage in the 1280s or 1290s he struck an accord with one of his northern Irish neighbours, Aonghus MacMahon.[10] Outwardly the form of the document is not unfamiliar: it is written in Latin and speaks of Pipard as lord, of the rent due to him, and of the land held from him. But beneath such conventional formulae the accord opened a window on to a very different world—one in which MacMahon claimed and was accorded regality (*regalitas*), acknowledged that he would accept the overkingship (*superior regalitas*) of the local Irish dynasty of the O Hanlons, and promised to throw his weight behind one claimant to the headship of the O Hanlon dynasty at

[8] The classic studies are K. Simms, 'Warfare in the Medieval Gaelic Lordships', *Irish Sword* 12 (1975–6), 98–108, and R. Frame, 'War and Peace in the Medieval Lordship of Ireland', republished in idem, *Ireland and Britain*, ch. 12 and idem, 'The Defence of the English Lordship, 1250–1450', in *A Military History of Ireland*, ed. T. Bartlett and K. Jeffery (Cambridge, 1996), 76–98.

[9] Note, for example, the recurrent comments in the extent of Pipard's manor of Dysarth (*CDI*, V, no. 167): 'ought to be worth in time of peace 8*d*. an acre; but for the last ten years no profit has come from it'; 'the land is warlike among the Irish'; 'this land is totally in the march of warlike land.'

[10] *Calendar of Ormond Deeds*, I, no. 268. There is an outstanding discussion of Irish kingship in the area in K. Simms, 'The O Hanlons, the O Neills and the Anglo-Normans in Thirteenth-century Armagh', *Seanchas Ardmhacha* 9 (1978–9), 70–94, esp. pp. 86–7; idem, 'Relations with the Irish', *Law and Disorder in Thirteenth-Century Ireland. The Dublin Parliament of 1297*, ed. James Lydon (Dublin, 1997), 66–86.

the expense of another. MacMahon also promised to help Ralph Pipard in military emergencies and underwrote the agreement by surrendering hostages and paying a tribute in cattle. This was the world of Irish politics, a world of multiple and hierarchical regalities, segmentary divisions within ruling dynasties, hostages, cattle tribute, and so forth. It was a world and a vocabulary with which Ralph Pipard had to engage if he was to exercise power in Uriel. By 30 June 1294, the day of the meeting at Rotherfield Peppard, Ralph Pipard had decided, for whatever reason, that the effort was not worth it. He began the process of disengaging himself, and eventually his family, from Ireland; by 1302 the process was complete.[11]

The story of the Pipards and their estates in Uriel is a study in miniature of the frontier lands of political cultures in the British Isles in the Middle Ages. There were scores of such frontier lands, their boundaries changing over time and cutting across the national and state divisions within which we have imprisoned so much of our historiography. One would traverse such frontier lands were one to travel in Ireland from Dublin into the Wicklow Hills or from the lowland manors of Tipperary to the northern half of the country, in Wales from Chepstow and Caerleon into inland Gwent or from lowland to upland Glamorgan, from Dumfries or Ayr into Galloway proper or from the lowlands of Fife into the earldom of Strathearn. But equally one would encounter the institutions and vocabulary of a broadly English-type political culture well beyond the administrative and jurisdictional boundaries of the English 'state'. Much of lowland Scotland belonged to a world which, though different in the focus of its loyalty and in the form and intensity of its institutions, shared a good deal of the same basic political culture, values, and processes as those of lowland England. Even the Anglicized lowlands of the coastal plains and river valleys of southern Wales and Ireland likewise aped the same political culture; their leaders were desperately anxious to keep in touch with English habits and to be included, however peripherally, in England's political rounds and patronage routines.

The story of the Pipards and their eventual withdrawal from Ireland also brings into focus the essential incommensurability of the idiom, habits, and practices of the English political world and those of native Ireland. Henley was metaphorically too far from Uriel for both to be contained within a single world. Pipard's problems were in that respect a reflection of those of the expanding English 'state' in general. It had secured, to a greater or lesser

[11] *Calendar of Patent Rolls 1301–7*, 78; *Calendar of Close Rolls 1296–1302*, 569; *1302–7*, 32–3, 87.

extent, an overkingship over much of the British Isles; but beyond England and the English-settled and Anglicized parts of these islands, it seemed incapable of establishing—or, alternatively, unwilling to establish—an inclusive political culture and the institutions and habits to sustain and operate it. Putting it rather baldly, the kingship of the English did not convert itself into the monarchy of the British Isles, or perhaps would not, or could not, do so.

What, then, were the distinctive features of English political culture which could be exported into, and assimilated by, the English or Anglicized communities in Ireland, Wales, and Scotland but, equally, could not apparently be grafted onto, or even successfully imposed upon, the native societies of those countries? Likewise, what was it about the political culture of those native societies which cast them, literally and metaphorically, outside the pale of an English and Anglicized political culture? Any answer to these questions will involve the construction of simplified paradigms of the political cultures of either set of societies, paradigms which of their very nature cannot do justice to the complexity and nuances of those cultures or, above all, to their evolving character. Yet it is of the essence of a political culture that it refers not only to the institutions and processes of governance but also to the values, assumptions, habits, etiquette, rhetoric, and language within which individual societies construe and justify the exercise of power. In other words, it constructs an image of the political world it has created for itself; it also, at least by implication, defines the image of a political culture to be compared and, more likely, contrasted with its own. So it was that, when Ralph Pipard travelled from Henley to the borders of his lands in Uriel, he brought with him a set of political expectations and habits, and was confronted by what he could only have seen as profound political and cultural surprises.

The first of those surprises related to what one might call the scale and stage of political activity. Pipard's experience was that of a unitary and, to a remarkable degree, a uniform kingdom, with clearly defined external and internal boundaries. Royal authority within this kingdom was ubiquitous and, on its own terms, exclusive; taxes, justice, governance, coinage, and law were more or less universal; political power was ultimately court-centred and political competition was factional within this court context; a single assembly—the great council or parliament (of both of which Ralph Pipard had been a member)—represented a national, unitary conclave of the political nation with its king. The unity and integrity of the kingdom and the kingship were the cornerstones of this whole political edifice. They were recognized ideologically and historiographically as making England what it was. So it was that Athelstan was remembered as the king 'who by the grace of God ruled all of

England singly which prior to him many kings had shared between them';[12] so it was likewise that the remarkable school of historians of the early twelfth century—notably William of Malmesbury and Henry of Huntingdon—constructed their histories around the theme of the unification of England and arranged their chronologies around the reigns of its kings—as have their successors ever since;[13] so it was again that characters as different as Geoffrey of Monmouth and Gerald of Wales advocated unitary rule as the only road to political salvation, and disunity and civil war as an inevitable prelude to chaos.[14] In its essence this paradigm of the good political life was increasingly shared by the political classes of the Scottish kingdom or at least of southern and eastern Scotland. There likewise a unitary kingship, the creation and acceptance of a large and stable unit of political authority, the introduction of the English-type shire as the unit of governance, and the claims of a 'common law' of Scotland brought much of Scotland—for all its differences in institutional forms and practice—increasingly closer into alignment with the political culture of England. Ralph Pipard could have travelled into lowland Scotland without undue fear of finding himself in a totally alien political environment.

The same was not true of much of Ireland, Wales, and western and northern Scotland. Here plurality, rather than unity, reigned supreme.[15] 'In Ireland,' said the author of *The Song of Dermot and the Earl*, 'there were several kings as elsewhere there were earls,' and so he proceeded to itemize its kingdoms and regions.[16] William of Newburgh made the same point, but added an insightful chronological dimension to his comparison by saying that a plurality of kingdoms had once been the norm in England likewise.[17] Not only were the units of power plural, they were also chronically unstable. They

[12] Quoted by M. Wood, 'The Making of King Aethelstan's Empire: An English Charlemagne?', in *Ideal and Reality in Frankish and Anglo-Saxon Society* (as cited above, Ch. 1, n. 16). Note that the charge against Eadwig (955–9) was that 'he divided this kingdom and parted its unity': quoted by James Campbell in *Uniting the Kingdom?*, ed. Grant and Stringer, 39–40.

[13] James Campbell, 'Some Twelfth-Century Views of the Anglo-Saxon past', in idem, *Essays in Anglo-Saxon History*, ch. 13; Rees Davies, *The Matter of Britain and the Matter of England* (Oxford, 1996), esp. pp. 14–16.

[14] For example, *HRB*, cc. 184–7; Gerald of Wales, *Opera*, VI, 204, 226 (Descriptio Kambrie, I, ch. 18; II, ch. 10).

[15] This remained the view in the sixteenth century. In a famous report on the state of Ireland *c*.1515 it was noted that it was divided into 'sixty countries called regions, some as big as a shire, some half a shire where sixty chief captains, called kings, princes, dukes' and so forth reigned: *State Papers of King Henry VIII* (1834), II, 1.

[16] *Song*, ll. 2191–2.

[17] William of Newburgh, *Historia Rerum Anglicarum*, in *Chronicles of Reigns of Stephen etc.*, I, 167. This theme has been pursued in many recent works, e.g. *The Origins of the Anglo-Saxon Kingdoms*, ed. S. Bassett (Leicester, 1989).

(unlike the regions and countries (Irish *tuatha*, Welsh *cantrefi*, *cymydau*) of which they were composed) had no fixed boundaries; they expanded and contracted according to the swing of the military and political pendulum; hegemonies were at best loose if impressive federations of power, threatened in their stability by dynastic segmentation and by the creation, and subsequent disassembling, of sub- and joint-kingships.[18] This was a defiantly and gloriously fragmented world: instead of the rhetoric of unity and answerability which came so readily to the lips of English observers, the language was that of fierce local independence, bordering on anarchy. As one Irish king was reported to have commented to Brian O'Neill when the latter claimed the high kingship in 1260: 'every man should have his own world.'[19] The orbit of each little world was small and suffocatingly intimate; each little world was vulnerable to its neighbours and easily destabilized. Such a political culture knew parliaments, but they were very different from the unitary parliaments of England, Scotland, or English Ireland. Here parliaments were literally parleys, discussions held at the boundaries of the little worlds of Ireland and Wales to sort out problems, to work out the rules of coexistence (*cydfodau*, as the Welsh called them), in short, to construct 'international' accords in a profoundly fragmented political universe.[20] Such a political society must have sorely tried the patience and, what is more, taxed the imagination of Ralph Pipard and his like, just as its confusing and kaleidoscopic plurality has defeated the historiographical (and cartographical) skills of those brought up on the neatly streamlined unity of English political history. That is why the Statutes of Kilkenny in 1366 talked disparagingly of the problems caused by what it called, rather genteelly, 'diversity of government' and the absence of 'one peace and one war'.[21] Even native rulers recognized that if they were to survive they must somehow break out of the constraints of this political culture. So it was that the letters of the first and last native prince of Wales, Llywelyn ap Gruffudd,

[18] For Ireland, the two classic discussions of Gaelic polities are Kenneth Nicholls, *Gaelic and Gaelicised Ireland in the Middle Ages* (Dublin, 1972) and Katharine Simms, *From Kings to Warlords. The Changing Political Structure of Gaelic Ireland in the Later Middle Ages* (Woodbridge, 1987). Irish historians have been at pains in the last few generations to downplay the fragmentation of pre-conquest Ireland and to play up what they characterize as 'feudalizing' and aggregative elements within its polities. On a long-term view their claims may be persuasive; but they seem to me to protest too much. Kenneth Nicholls's claim that 'native Irish society' was characterized by 'extreme political instability . . . and endemic disorder' (*NHI*, II, 398) seems difficult to gainsay, at least in comparison with England and Scotland.

[19] Orpen, *Ireland under the Normans*, III, 274.

[20] R. R. Davies, *Lordship and Society in the March of Wales*, ch. 11; idem, 'Frontier Arrangements in Fragmented Societies: Ireland and Wales', in *Medieval Frontier Societies*, ed. R. Bartlett and A. Mackay (Oxford, 1987), 77–101; J. B. Smith, 'Cydfodau o'r Bymthegfed Ganrif', *Bulletin of the Board of Celtic Studies* 21 (1966), 309–24; 25 (1973), 128–34.

[21] Berry, *Statutes*, 434–5, 450–1.

resonate with calls for unity (*unitas*) and for 'one peace, one war' or 'one war, one counsel, one aid', and why Llywelyn did his best to make Wales into a coherent, hierarchical political unit.[22] Had that happened, native Wales would have been salvaged by adopting the norms of English political culture.

Llywelyn's plans included the assumption, and eventually the acknowledgement, of the novel title 'prince of Wales'. That, like his other plans, involved a bid to approximate his title and powers as prince to those of an English king—as supreme and sole ruler of a unitary principality. It had not always been so. Kingship in Wales and Ireland and in parts of Scotland was a very different and indeed highly variable institution compared with that familiar to Ralph Pipard in England and to his contemporaries in Scotland. The similarity of the terminology of kingship only confuses in this respect.[23] Different as were the kingships of the English and the Scots in many respects, they shared a great deal in common, the more so as the twelfth and thirteenth centuries progressed and, in particular, as the Scottish monarchy institutionally, though not mythologically, distanced itself from its Gaelic past and reconstructed its power and language on an Anglo-French model. Both were fiercely unitary monarchies which claimed supreme power over all their peoples: *rex Anglorum*, *rex Scottorum*; both claimed and exercised 'the tremendous authority of royal majesty' and used the most fulsome language to proclaim it;[24] both forged a custom of unitary succession out of the various crises they faced; both ruled out claims by or descent through illegitimate members of the royal dynasty; both showed their resilience, and singleness of purpose, by riding out the problems posed by minor heirs (in Scotland in 1153, 1214, 1249, and 1286, and in England in 1216) or by the absence of the heir to the throne (in England in 1272); both deliberately promoted their status by securing the

[22] *Littere Wallie*, ed. J. G. Edwards, 79, 104, 138; Davies, *Conquest*, 317–20; Smith, *Llywelyn ap Gruffudd*, ch. 6.

[23] To that extent Edward James's comment (*The Origins of the Anglo-Saxon Kingdoms*, ed. Bassett, 43) that 'our one English word "king" may translate at least two, and perhaps several, different concepts of kingship and different levels of royal rule among the barbarian kingdoms' has much more general, and later, applicability. This is certainly true of the Gaelic word *ri* (cf. J. Bannerman in idem and K. A. Steer, *Late Medieval Monumental Sculpture in the West Highlands* (Edinburgh, 1977), Appendix II, 201) and of the Welsh term *tywysog* (as a close reading of the Welsh original of the *Brut* shows). See also the seminal essay by T. M. Charles-Edwards, 'Early Medieval Kingships in the British Isles', in *The Origins of Anglo-Saxon Kingdoms*, ed. Steven Bassett (1989), 28–40.

[24] For the phrase 'tremendous authority of royal majesty', *Leges Henrici Primi*, ed. L. J. Downer (Oxford, 1972), 96 (para. 6.2a). It is paralleled in Scotland by emphasis on *regia auctoritas* and *potestas regalis* (*Regesta Regum Scottorum*, I, nos. 131, 288) and by William of Newburgh's comment on Malcolm IV (known to historians as Malcolm the Maiden) that he 'was the greatest terror to bold and wicked men because of his royal authority and severity' (*Historia Rerum Anglicarum* (as cited above, n. 18), 76–7). For this and associated themes see G. W. S. Barrow, *Scotland and its Neighbours*, ch. 2 and idem (ed.), *R.R.S.*, I, 27.

canonization of members of their dynasties[25] and by cultivating a mythology of almost immemorial unitary descent.[26] The political cultures and societies of England and Scotland were to a remarkable degree king-centred and king-dominated.

Kingship elsewhere in the British Isles was also important; but it was a profoundly different kind of kingship. Contemporaries sometimes said so. Lowland commentators could hardly conceal their contemptuous amusement at what passed for kingship in the western British Isles. They referred dismissively to the 'many kinglets' of Ireland and taunted someone who was puffed up beyond his status as 'thinking himself equal to a Welsh king'.[27] Irish annalists for their part showed how their perception of the world differed from that of their English and Scottish colleagues by conferring the title 'king' on all and sundry:[28] so it was that the mormaer or earl of Moray was promoted to the status of 'a king of Scotland' (*ri Alban*) and Hugh de Lacy, lord of Meath and tenant-in-chief of Henry II, was memorialized as nothing less than 'king of Midhe and Breifne and Airghaill'.[29] No wonder that Henry II began to entertain suspicions about Lacy's ambitions or that the ascription of the title 'prince of the kingdom of Ulster' to John de Courcy created consternation in the Angevin court.[30] There was more, much more to this than a culpable looseness of terminology (as the English saw it); it bespoke a very different concept of kingship and power. Here in the western British Isles was a land of a multiplicity of kings, some claiming authority over sizeable districts such as

[25] Edward the Confessor (d.1066) was canonized in 1161; Margaret, queen of Scots (d.1093) in 1250.

[26] Thus in England, Henry of Huntingdon (*Historia Anglorum*, ed. Greenway, 254–5, cf. 333–7) announced with joy and relief that England had arrived at a unitary monarchy (*cum jam ad monarchiam Anglie pervenimus*). The classic statement of Scottish unitary regal descent, doubtless drawing on long-established traditions, was the thumping assertion in the Declaration of Arbroath (1320) that 113 kings of the royal stock had reigned in succession, 'the line unbroken by a single foreigner'.

[27] See, for example, *Chronicon de Lanercost* (Maitland Club, 1839), 230 ('multi reguli ibi regnant'); Roger of Wendover, *Chronica*, ed. H. O. Coxe, 4 vols. (English Historical Society, 1841–4), II, 56–7. Cf. the dismissive references to the petty kings (*reguli*) of Galloway and their quarrels: Walter Daniel, *Life of Ailred of Rievaulx*, ed. F. M. Powicke (1950), 45. 'Thinking himself equal to a Welsh king': *Jordan Fantosme's Chronicle*, ed. R. C. Johnston (Oxford, 1981), 14–15.

[28] Thus nine kings are mentioned on a single printed page of *The Annals of Tigernach s.a.* 1167 (p. 419). Cf. for Wales, for example, the references to 'co-princes' (*conprincipes*) and 'brother-princes' (*fratres principes*) in Keith Williams-Jones, 'Llywelyn's Charter to Cymer Abbey in 1209', *Journal of the Merionethshire Historical and Record Society* 3 (1957–78) at p. 54.

[29] *Annals of Ulster s.a.* 1020; *Annals of Loch Cé*, ed. W. M. Hennessy, 2 vols. (R.S., 1871), I, 173. Cf. the reference to Reginald son of Somerled 'who called himself king of the Isles' (*qui se regem Insularum nominavit*); *Registrum Magni Sigilii Regum Scottorum*, ed. J. M. Thomson et al. (Edinburgh, 1882–1914), II, no. 3170.

[30] Roger Howden, *Chronica*, IV, 25. For John de Courcy, *NHI*, II, 135 and the outstanding study by Sean Duffy in *Colony and Frontier in Medieval Ireland*, ed. Barry et al., 1–27.

Galloway, Gwynedd, Leinster, or the Isles but others no more than lords of Lilliputian kingdoms—such as the king of the cantref of Arwystli in upland mid-Wales or the king of Oirrthir in north-east Ireland.[31] Nor within this mosaic of kingships were all kings equal, let alone sovereign. Far from it. Some were indeed powerful, nor should we underrate their abilities: such was Turlough O'Connor of Connacht (1106–56) who built castles and bridges, created artificial lakes, commanded a huge fleet, and made and unmade kings across almost the whole of Ireland,[32] or the two Llywelyns who forged a principality of Wales out of the disparate units of power in the country.[33] But others were, in the dismissive phrase of a Welsh source, little kings (*brenhinoedd bychain*)—client kings, sub- or vassal-kings, or heads of discard segments of royal dynasties.[34] But all in their own eyes were kings or princes. There was much else that an English observer would have found disconcerting about the kingship of the west: there was, in spite of the ponderous learning of the native jurists, no clear practice of succession;[35] kings were regularly made and unmade by over-kings and, equally, by the men of their own communities; claimants whom the Church and even their own families might regard as illegitimate could certainly throw their hats into the ring, as happened in Galloway in 1234 and Gwynedd in 1240; there was little that was consistent, let alone majestic, about the titles of these men, in so far as they used titles; and above all there was a profound instability about such power as they exercised since it was recurrently challenged by excluded members of their own families (such as brothers and nephews) or by alternative segments of the royal dynasty, as well as by other dynasties fighting for a place in

[31] For the kings of Arwystli, Davies, *Conquest*, 56–7; Huw Pryce, 'The Church of Trefeglwys and the End of the "Celtic" Charter Tradition in Twelfth-Century Wales', *Cambridge Medieval Celtic Studies*, 25 (1993), 15–54; for the kings of Oirrthir, *Dowdall Deeds*, ed. Charles McNeill and A. J. Otway Ruthven (Dublin, 1960), 52–3; K. Simms in *Seanchas Ardmhacha* 9 (1978–9), 70–94.

[32] For Turlough O'Connor, see John Ryan, *Toirdelbach Ó Conchobair 1088–1156* (Dublin, 1966); *NHI*, II, 28–34; *Annals of Tigernach*, esp. *s.a.* 1120, 1124, 1139, 1140, etc. For the power of Irish regional and high kingships, Ó Corráin, 'Nationality and Kingship in Pre-Norman Ireland', *Historical Studies* 11 (1978), 1–35, esp. pp. 28–35; M. T. Flanagan, *Irish Society, Anglo-Norman Settlers, Angevin Kingship*, esp. ch. 3. There is an interesting study of the changing character of native Irish kingship in Helen Perros, 'Crossing the Shannon Frontier. Connacht and the Anglo-Normans 1170–1224', *Colony and Frontier in Medieval Ireland*, 117–39.

[33] Davies, *Conquest*, chs. 8, 9, 12; Smith, *Llywelyn ap Gruffudd*, chs. 3, 6.

[34] 'Other minor kings came to his court to seek his protection and secure his aid and advice': *Historia Gruffudd vab Kenan*, ed. D. Simon Evans (Cardiff, 1971), 31. For this whole theme, Davies, *Conquest*, 74–6. The kinds of gavottes of power danced by these princelings or kinglets is neatly illustrated by the career of Uchdryd ab Edwin, who was given Meirionnydd and Cyfeiliog by Cadwgan ap Bleddyn of Powys, but later lost them for trying to assert his independence: *Brut*, *s.a.* 1116 (p. 46).

[35] The theoretical case, and its possible implications, are fully explored in J. B. Smith, 'Dynastic Succession in Medieval Wales', *Bulletin of the Board of Celtic Studies* 33 (1982), 199–232.

the political sun in a desperately overcrowded political countryside.[36] As one English observer in the reign of Henry I was said to have commented mordantly, 'they were all killing one another.'[37]

Such observers, like Ralph Pipard later, would not only have found the political landscape in the western British Isles unfamiliar; they would also have found its political assumptions deeply disconcerting. They came from tightly regimented and disciplined polities; they were familiar with a world where the king was, or should be, the undoubted political ringmaster, and his court the crucial hub of the political process, a world in which the aristocracy, great and small, was locked into a tenurial relationship and patronage network ultimately controlled by the king. They inhabited a world where obedience was deemed to be axiomatic, where the king covered himself in the language, symbols, and rituals of apartness and exclusiveness, where the distance between the king and the greatest of his earls (an earl of Gloucester or Fife) was profound and unbridgeable (as the earl of Gloucester found to his great cost in the 1290s), and where, in Ralph Pipard's own day, the monarchy was arrogating a new rhetoric as it proclaimed its role as the interpreter of the common utility and the guardian of the public good.[38]

To leave this well-ordered, rather authoritarian world for the jungle that was political life in the west must have been a traumatic experience. Contemporaries vouched as much: 'there is no public authority among the Irish,' was Ralph of Diss's tart comment; 'the Welsh,' said another observer even more dismissively, 'are incapable of obeying anyone'; while Froissart put his usual chivalric spin on the same viewpoint by noting about the Irish that 'although they are governed by kings, of which there are several in the country, they have no experience of noble or civilized behaviour (*gentilesse*).'[39] The comments, as usual, said as much about the observers as the observed, but

[36] All these points can be well illustrated from almost any page of the contemporary Irish annals or from the Welsh *Brut*.

[37] *Brut*, 20. Similar observations were made by William of Newburgh in his *History* (I, 186–7), where he talks of 'barbarians fighting against barbarians', or by Ailred of Rievaulx in his *Eulogium* on David I of Scotland (*Pinkerton's Lives of the Scottish Saints*, ed. W. M. Metcalfe, 2 vols. (Paisley, 1889), II, 271), where he refers to 'mutual slaughter and woundings', just as Walter Daniel in his *Life of Ailred* (46) speaks of 'mutual hatred, rancour and tyranny' as characteristic of life in Galloway. See also the perceptive studies of this theme by John Gillingham: 'Conquering the Barbarians' (as cited above, Ch. I, n. 24) and 'Killing and Mutilating Political Enemies in the British Isles from the Late Twelfth to the Early Fourteenth Century: a Comparative Study', in *Britain and Ireland 900–1300. Insular Responses to Medieval European Change*, ed. Brendan Smith (Cambridge, 1998), 114–35.

[38] F. M. Powicke, *The Thirteenth Century 1216–1307* (Oxford, 1953), 520–8; T. F. T. Plucknett, *Legislation of Edward I* (Oxford, 1949), 4–5; Davies, *Lordship and Society*, 258–65.

[39] Ralph de Diceto, *Opera Historica*, ed. W. Stubbs, 2 vols. (R.S., 1876), I, 350; Glanmor Williams, *The Welsh Church from Conquest to Reformation* (2nd edn., Cardiff, 1976), 398; Jean Froissart, *Oeuvres*, ed. Kervyn de Lettenhove (Brussels, 1867–77), XV, 170.

they also highlighted the chasm between them. Others took a more charitable view. Gerald of Wales, who was better placed than most, noted the passionate delight of the Welsh in liberty (*libertatis hilaritas*) and contrasted it strikingly with the way the English were weighed down with servile exactions and seignorial demands. He also proceeded to observe that the Welsh, from the highest to the lowest, spoke their minds freely 'even in the presence of their princes and chieftains'.[40]

There is little doubt that at least at the level of the noble and the free-born (and the two were largely synonymous in the western British Isles), these societies were (as compared with England) remarkably non-deferential and even non-hierarchical. They had, of course, as with most societies, developed their mechanisms and etiquette of dependence and submission—such as the ceremonies of entering the house of another, paying him tribute and receiving his gifts.[41] But not only were such submissions conditional and often short-lived; they were also seen as negotiating ploys which did not necessarily trench on a man's status. So it was that when Aongus MacMahon struck his bargain with Ralph Pipard, he nevertheless salvaged his regality, as did the O'Neills when they submitted to the earls of Ulster; so it was, as a later English observer noted, that the native rulers of Ireland 'obey no other temporal person but only to himself that is strong'.[42] Moreover, these were societies where aristocracies, as they might be called elsewhere, were exceptionally strong and status-conscious, often deriving their power from their position as leaders of kin-groups. The Welsh sources, for example, have a rich and varied vocabulary to describe these men[43] and the privileges (*breiniau*) which they so jealously cherished;[44] Gerald likewise notes that they 'were often rebellious

[40] Gerald of Wales, *Opera*, VI, 180, 192–3, 221–2, 226 (Description of Wales I, c. 8, c. 15; II, c. 8, c. 10). Cf. Robert Bartlett, *Gerald of Wales*, 198–200.

[41] For Ireland, see the excellent general discussions in M. T. Flanagan, *Irish Society etc.*, 175–99, and K. Simms, *From Kings to Warlords*, ch. 7. For Wales, T. M. Charles-Edwards, 'Honour and Status in some Irish and Welsh Prose Tales', *Erin* 29 (1978), 123–421; Davies, *Conquest*, ch. 3. The etiquette and sensitivities of the ceremonies of gift-giving are well illustrated in a story recounted in *Caithréim Thoirdhealbhaigh or The Triumphs of Turlough*, ed. S. H. O'Grady, 2 vols. (Irish Texts Society, 1929), II, 3: O'Neil was outraged when O'Briain sent him 100 horses, since to accept such a gift would have been to admit dependence. He therefore sent back to O'Briain 200 horses 'wearing gold-adorned, white-edged bridles'.

[42] Aongus MacMahon: above, n. 10; O'Neill: *Report on the Mss. of Lord De L'Isle and Dudley* (Historical Manuscripts Commission, 1925), I, 31–2; *State Papers, Henry VIII*, II, 1.

[43] The terms in Latin include *optimates*, *seniores*, *nobiles*; in Welsh, *pendefigion*, *penaduriaid*, *penaethau*, *tywysogyon* (all terms indicating pre-eminence and leadership), *uchelwyr*, *goreugwyr*, *gwyrda*, *boneddigion* (terms which emphasize high status, moral excellence, and noble lineage). Cf. the reference in an Irish deed to 'honorabilibus viris . . . et omnibus nobilibus patrie': *Irish Monastic and Episcopal Deeds*, ed. N. B. White (Dublin, 1936), xii.

[44] Two of the key texts on aristocratic privileges are (i) The Privileges of the Men of Powys (*Breintiau Gwŷr Powys*, the subject of a memorable ode by the twelfth-century poet, Cynddelw

to their lords and impatient of control'.[45] Much the same was true of Ireland and western Scotland. Kings were often made, controlled, and deposed by such aristocracies; indeed, on occasion a king appears to be little more than a chairman, often a temporary chairman, of a federation of kindreds.

This was indeed a very different pattern and practice of political power from that familiar in England and lowland Scotland. There there was a broadly uniform pattern of governance, an interpenetration between central authority and the localities which worked to the bonding of both, a symbiotic relationship between a unitary monarchy and a local, non-professional, governing class and with it a hierarchy of power with the king clearly unchallenged at its apex. In Ireland, on the contrary, as an English observer put it, 'divers petty captains make war and peace without licence of the chief captain.'[46] The challenge to the English, and for that matter to the Scots, in the western British Isles was whether they could introduce or impose the values and practices of their own political culture in the area, or whether they would be required to adopt the idiom and forms of native political culture and play the power game by its rules. On the outcome would depend the chances of converting the English state into a credible British Isles monarchy.

But the challenge was more than political or institutional. Political cultures are ultimately grounded in social customs and mental attitudes. It was here that the English state faced its greatest challenge in the west. Let us start with war and peace. At a technological level the English were not in doubt about their huge superiority, nor had they reason to be.[47] Their contempt bordered on pity when they commented on the military backwardness of the Welsh, the Irish, the Galwegians, and their like;[48] and the natives returned the compliment, remarking in awe, for example, on the 'terrible mail-clad cavalry' of the English or on 'the castle of dressed stone' built by Thomas de Clare at Bunratty, 'girt with thick outer wall, containing a roofed impregnable donjon

Brydydd Mawr: *Gwaith Cynddelw Brydydd Mawr*, ed. Nerys A. Jones and Ann P. Owen, 2 vols. (Cardiff, 1991–5), I, nos. 10–11) and (ii) The Privileges of Arfon (*Breintiau Arfon*, in *Ancient Laws and Institutes of Wales*, ed. A. Owen (1841), I, 107–8). There is a valuable discussion in J. Beverley Smith, 'Gwlad ac Arglwydd', *Beirdd a Thywysogion. Barddoniaeth Llys yng Nghymru, Iwerddon a'r Alban*, ed. B. F. Roberts and Morfydd E. Owen (Aberystwyth, 1996), 237–57.

45 *Opera*, 166 (Description of Wales, I, ch. 2).

46 *State Papers of Henry VIII*, II, 5.

47 Note, for example, the speech attributed to Ralph, bishop of Orkneys, by Henry of Huntingdon, *Historia Anglorum*, ed. D. Greenway, 715: 'There is among them [sc. the Scots] no knowledge of military matters, experience in battle, or regard for discipline.'

48 See generally R. Bartlett, 'Technique militaire et pouvoir politique, 900–1300', *Annales: Economies, Sociétés, Civilisations* 41 (1986), 1135–59; and Matthew Strickland, *War and Chivalry* (as cited above, Ch. 1, n. 24), ch. 11.

and having capacious limewashed appurtenances'.[49] But it was not in technology so much as in mentality that the most profound difference lay. We may not regard medieval England and lowland Scotland as epitomes of peaceful societies, but such, relatively speaking, they considered themselves to be, both in aspiration and achievement.[50] When Gaimar idealized Edgar as a second Arthur, part of the case was that Edgar 'had peace everywhere, there was no war'.[51] The kings of England and Scotland had in theory, and very considerably in practice, reserved the right to make war to themselves, had effectively demilitarized most of free society other than in the service of the king, and had harnessed the military resources of the warrior class to their own ends. What they found in the west of the British Isles was, of course, the antithesis of this situation. Here was a proudly, defiantly, and exultingly militarized and militarist society; war here was a way of life and one of the few routes to fortune and to political power; the key position after that of the king, and sometimes indeed ahead of him, was that of the captain of the bodyguard or royal army;[52] the sharing of plunder and the billeting of troops were among the most taxing tasks of kingship. The English were suitably appalled by the results: 'mutual slaughter', 'universal discord', brutal and bestial behaviour, and the flouting of the conventions of warfare as they knew them.[53] They

[49] For the 'terrible mail clad cavalry, *Annals of Loch Cé, s.a.* 1249. There is a remarkably vivid description of Anglo-Norman military equipment and tactics as seen through the eyes of a native observer in *Brut* 43 (where the 'rashness' of the Welsh 'like a furious rabble without a ruler' is contrasted with 'the French', their 'mailed knights' and their 'diligence and circumspection'). For Bunratty castle: *Caithréim* (as cited in n. 42 above); II, 8.

[50] The relationship between peace, prosperity, and 'state formation' is explored in James Campbell, 'Was it Infancy in England? Some Questions of Comparison', in *England and her Neighbours 1066–1453. Essays in Honour of Pierre Chaplais*, ed. M. Jones and M. Vale (1989), 1–18, esp. pp. 2–8, and Edmund King, 'Economic Development in the Early Twelfth Century', in *Progress and Problems in Medieval England. Essays in Honour of Edward Miller*, ed. R. Britnell and J. Hatcher (Cambridge, 1996), 1–23.

[51] Gaimar, *Estoire des Engleis*, ed. A. Bell, l. 3564.

[52] Militarized society: e.g. Gerald of Wales, *Opera*, VI, 179 (Description of Wales, I, ch. 18); captain of the bodyguard: e.g. for Ireland, *Annals of Tigernach, s.a.* 1143; *Annals of Connacht, s.a.* 1326; for Wales, Davies, *Conquest*, 67.

[53] Cf. above, n. 37. Also Ralph of Diceto, *Opera*, II, 350 and the letter of Alexander III to Henry II (*Celebri fama*) with its reference to 'internecine slaughter': J. A. Watt, *The Church in Medieval Ireland* (Dublin, 1972), 37. On the ferocity of native rulers, see Davies, *Conquest*, 75–6. A striking Irish parallel is provided by the obituary notice of Cathal Crovderg O'Connor of Connacht (d.1224): 'the king who was the fiercest and harshest towards his enemies that ever lived; the king who most blinded, killed and mutilated rebellious and disaffected subjects' (*Annals of Connacht, s.a.*). Nor did the obit exaggerate (see Helen Perros as cited above, n. 33, p. 135). Nor was he alone: Dermot MacMurrough was alleged to have gnawed the severed head of one of his enemies, while Rory O'Connor drove a nail through the severed hand of a victim: Gerald of Wales, *Expugnatio Hibernica*, 37; *Annals of Tigernach, s.a.* 1173. The contrast with Anglo-Norman practice is explored in John Gillingham, '1066 and the Introduction of Chivalry into England', *Law and Government in Medieval England and Normandy. Essays in Honour of Sir James Holt*, ed. George Garnett and John Hudson (Cambridge, 1994), 31–56.

were equally concerned that their own men in these frontier lands would 'go native': Ralph Pipard himself would have been acutely aware of the terrible dressing-down that Edward I gave to the earls of Hereford and Gloucester in 1291–2 for daring to wage a private war in the March of Wales against his specific prohibition.[54] It was a challenge to the king's personal authority; it was also a challenge to the very premisses of English political culture as they had been shaped over the last few generations.

We could trace contrasts in political cultures in other directions. English and, increasingly, 'modernized' Scottish lowland political society grounded its power in land. It was from its lands and the men who lived on those lands that the political nation drew most of its wealth and prestige; royal and aristocratic estates were the nodal points of authority and patronage as well as of income; the bond of tenure, and the incidents of control that came in its wake, were one of the most effective cements of political power and territorial authority. To talk of tenure is, of course, to broach the issue of feudalism, and to talk of feudalism is to introduce a measure of excitability and controversy which is bad for historians' blood pressure. There are those who would reify feudalism and talk of it lovingly as 'a finished article';[55] there are others who claim that it is a historiographical phantom invented by over-cerebral lawyers. Be that as it may, what is beyond doubt—and what has never been attempted—is that a map of the feudal geography of the British Isles in the twelfth and thirteenth centuries would be one of the most revealing guides to the extent and penetration of English and Anglicized tenurial norms within these islands. It would take in much of lowland southern and eastern Scotland, and the coastal plains and river valleys of south Wales and Ireland. It would serve to highlight the contrast between the small knights' fees of Lothian, Pembroke, and parts of Leinster, as well as of southern England on the one hand and the much larger fiefs of Strathclyde, Cumbria, and much of the Welsh March and Ireland on the other.[56] It would allow comparisons to be made between great honours or lordships such as those of Trim in Ireland, Brecon in Wales, Garioch and Buchan in north-east Scotland, and Pontefract in northern England, and

[54] *Calendar of Chancery Rolls. Various 1277–1326* (1912), 334–49; J. E. Morris, *The Welsh Wars of Edward I* (Oxford, 1901), 220–39; Davies, *Lordship and Society*, ch. 12.

[55] G. W. S. Barrow, *Kingship and Unity*, 44.

[56] For general studies of feudal tenure, see for Scotland: Duncan, *Scotland*, ch. 15; Barrow, *Kingship and Unity*, ch. 3; idem, *The Anglo-Norman Era*; for Ireland: Orpen, *Ireland under the Normans* I, ch. 11; II, ch. 15; A. J. Otway-Ruthven, 'Knight Service in Ireland', *Journal of the Royal Society of the Antiquaries of Ireland* 89 (1959), 1–15; idem, *Medieval Ireland*, ch. 3; E. St J. Brooks, *Knights' Fees in counties Wexford, Carlow and Kilkenny* (Dublin, 1950). The feudal 'settlement' of Wales is an understudied subject; see briefly R. R. Davies, 'Kings, Lords and Liberties in the March of Wales, 1066–1272', *Transactions of the Royal Historical Society*, 5th ser., 29 (1979), 41–61.

would allow us to compare the pattern of subinfeudation followed by, say, Earl David of Huntingdon in Scotland and Hubert Walter in Tipperary.[57] Above all, for our present purposes, it would enable us to see how far the feudal template had to be recast to take account of the existing social and economic structure and, most crucially, what were the limits of its applicability.

Such a map would show that the feudal pattern had to be adjusted as it reached the outer limits of what I have characterized as the English and Anglicized political culture zone. It would show, for example, how an attempt was made to include the O'Kennedys in the feudal network centred on Nenagh in northern county Tipperary, or how a grant of land was made to an Irishman in the Vale of Dublin, to be held by the service of a knight's fee and two otter skins, or how knight service and the payment of *cain* (a tribute in food and produce) were combined in Galloway, or how Welsh knights' fees (so called) appeared in south-east and south-west Wales, combining feudal obligations and Welsh laws of partibility.[58] Native princes might even grant land on what appear to be feudal military terms.[59] But the most striking message that would be conveyed by such a map is how much of upland and western British Isles was totally innocent of the experience of feudal tenure. It was partly that these areas had not been substantially penetrated—other than in isolated pockets—by English or Anglicized settlers; it was even more the fact that land and power, and power over land, were very differently organized in these zones. Land was important; but title to land and to rights over land was embedded in kin-groups, not in lords; dues were collected in respect of membership

[57] Trim: R. Bartlett, 'Colonial Aristocracies in the High Middle Ages', in *Medieval Frontier Societies*, ed. Bartlett and Mackay, 23–47, esp. pp. 30–41; Brecon: W. Rees, 'The Medieval Lordship of Brecon', *Transactions of the Honourable Society of Cymmrodorion* (1915–16), 165–244; D. G. Walker, 'The "honours" of the Earls of Hereford in the Twelfth Century', *Transactions of the Bristol and Gloucestershire Archaeological Society* 79 (1960), 174–211; Garioch: K. J. Stringer, *Earl David of Huntingdon*, 81–91; Buchan: Alan Young, 'The Earls and Earldom of Buchan in the Thirteenth Century', in *Medieval Scotland. Crown, Lordship and Community*, ed. Grant and Stringer, 174–202; Pontefract: *The Lacy Family in England and Normandy 1066–1194* (Oxford, 1966), esp. chs. 1 and 6; Hubert Walter: C. A. Empey, 'The Norman Period, 1185–1500', in *Tipperary: History and Society. Interdisciplinary Essays on the History of an Irish County*, ed. W. Nolan (Dublin, 1985), 71–91; idem., 'Conquest and Settlement: Patterns of Anglo-Norman Settlement in North Munster and South Leinster', *Irish Economic and Social History* 13 (1986), 5–31; idem, 'The Anglo-Norman Settlement in the Cantred of Eliogarty', in *Settlement and Society in Medieval Ireland. Studies presented to F. X. Martin O.S.A.*, ed. J. Bradley (Kilkenny, 1988), 207–28.

[58] Nenagh: *Calendar of Inquisitions Post Mortem*, VIII, no. 184 (p. 127); Vale of Dublin: *CDI*, I, no. 356 (1207); Galloway: K. J. Stringer, 'Acts of Lordship: The Records of the Lords of Galloway to 1234' (as cited above, Ch. 3, n. 25); Welsh knights' fees: Davies, *Lordship and Society*, 76 (and the references cited there).

[59] An example is the grant of land in Landimôr by Llywelyn ap Iorwerth, prince of North Wales, to Morgan Gam (of the Welsh family of Afan) for the service of one knight *c.*1215 × 17: *Cartae et alia munimenta . . . de Glamorgan*, ed. G. T. Clark (2nd edn., Cardiff, 1910), III, no. 900. Plas Baglan may be a native Welsh castle associated with Morgan Gam: Royal Commission on Ancient and Historical Monuments in Wales. *Glamorgan. III, Part 1a. The Early Castles from the Norman Conquest to 1217* (1991), 149–52.

of those kin-groups; and there was no right of permanent land alienation whereby estates could be assembled. Dues payable to lords were tributes of recognition, support, and hospitality rather than rents in respect of land.[60] As one English commentator in Ireland put it, with barely concealed surprise, 'all that is owed for land to the chief captain is service and certain custom in meat and drink at Christmas and Easter and as often as great strangers come to the captain.'[61] His view was echoed by the surveyor of a Welsh estate who was at pains to explain that the renders payable in Oswestry were 'not properly rent issueinge out of land but only a some of money annexed as a Royaltie to my Lordes person'.[62] Feudal tenure and territorial lordship—the very essence of royal and seignorial power in so much of England and Scotland—could not easily put down roots in such a society. Where that was so, the achievements and penetration of the English state and of English-type institutions would be very limited.

Here in the north and west, lordship was essentially personal; it was lordship over men. So it was that the greatest compliment that could be paid to a ruler was to say that his subjects multiplied and his greatest achievement was to carry away the men and movables of his enemies, the most valuable assets in a society where land was relatively abundant but men to work it scarce.[63] So it was likewise that when a Highland chief was asked about the value of his lordship, he replied curtly 'five hundred men',[64] or that a ruler in Ireland would increasingly describe himself as the captain of his nation, or in Carrick as 'head of his whole kin-group' (*capud tocius progenies, kenkynnol*), or in Wales might flaunt the title of lineage chief (*pencenedl*).[65] This was a world of

[60] See generally Davies, *Lordship and Society*, esp. chs. 6 and 16; K. Nicholls, *Gaelic and Gaelicized Ireland*, esp. pp. 8–12, 57–67; idem, *Land, Law and Society in Sixteenth-century Ireland* (Dublin, 1978); K. Simms, 'Guesting and Feasting in Gaelic Ireland', *Journal of the Royal Society of Antiquaries of Ireland* 108 (1978), 67–100; J. E. A. Jolliffe, 'Northumbrian Institutions', *English Historical Review* 41 (1926), 1–43; G. W. S. Barrow, 'Northern English Society in the Twelfth and Thirteenth Centuries', *Northern History* 4 (1969), 1–28.

[61] *State Papers. Henry VIII*, II, 5.

[62] *The Lordship of Oswestry 1393–1607*, ed. W. J. Slack (Shrewsbury, 1951), 15.

[63] Davies, *Conquest*, 74 (and the examples cited); Nicholls, *Land, Law and Society*, 9–10. This also helps to explain the prominence of advowry tenants—men who had entered into the lord's protection—in both Ireland and Wales: Davies, *Lordship and Society*, 138–9.

[64] Quoted in M. Bloch, *French Rural Society* (1966), 72. When Bower recorded the arrest of Highland chiefs in 1429, he indicated the number of men each of them led, e.g. Angus Dubh, *dux* of 4,000: Walter Bower, *Scotichronicon*, ed. D. E. R. Watt et al. (Aberdeen, 1987–98), VIII, 260–1.

[65] Katherine Simms, *From Kings to Warlords*, esp. pp. 36–40; J. Bannerman, 'The Scots Language and the Kin-based Society', *Proceedings of the Second International Conference on the Languages of Scotland*, ed. D. S. Thomson (Glasgow, 1990), 1–19; Hector L. MacQueen, 'The Kin of Kennedy, "Kenkynnol" and the Common Law', in *Medieval Scotland. Crown, Lordship and Community*, ed. Grant and Stringer, 274–96. There are occasional references to the status of *pencenedl* in the Welsh evidence, e.g. *Littere Wallie*, 132 (1271); *Calendar of Ancient Petitions relating to Wales*, ed. W. Rees (Cardiff, 1975), 84, no. 2873; *Calendar of Chancery Rolls, Various*, 179.

tributes, renders, hospitality, and billeting dues often consumed in kind, on the spot, and on circuit: 'when I myself come there staying and consuming my cain', as a Scottish charter put it.[66] The more we know about the complexity of these tributes and renders and the sophisticated mechanisms by which they were assessed and collected, the less likely are we to dismiss them as backward and primitive and the more likely we are to recognize in them the vestiges of a royal tribute system which had once extended across much of the British Isles.[67] But equally, once we compare them with the system of manorial exactions and fiscal demands which had developed in England and to some degree in Scotland by the thirteenth century, and note the way royal and seignorial power in those areas was promoting, regulating, and exploiting a developed economy or economies to its own ends, we are surely struck by the profundity of the political and cultural gap which had opened up in the British Isles. The commentator who observed that Ireland was now at a stage which England had once been at under the Heptarchy was making a shrewd comment and one of general applicability.

We can apply it briefly and finally to one other area of political culture, that of law. By the thirteenth century English law was regarded as one of the distinctive hallmarks of Englishness and as an integral part of English political culture. We can see as much in the way that from at least John's reign the law of England was the only law which was to prevail in English Ireland.[68] Nor was this merely a matter of royal fiat: the English communities in Wales were likewise anxious to avail themselves of the concepts and methods of English law, even though they had no normal access to England's courts, while the law of Scotland, or at least of royal and lowland Scotland, was substantially reshaped on the English model from the mid-twelfth century onwards.[69] Thereby a goodly part of the British Isles had been brought within the ambit

[66] *Early Scottish Charters prior to A.D. 1153*, ed. A. C. Lawrie (Glasgow, 1905), no. 125. One of the dues owed to the prince of Gwynedd was food (butter, bread, fish, and cheese) for his retinue of 300 men when he came on his annual visit to the commote of Penllyn: *Calendar of Inquisitions Miscellaneous 1219–1307*, no. 1357.

[67] Among many studies see, for Scotland, G. W. S. Barrow, *The Kingdom of the Scots* (1973), esp. ch. 1; J. Bannerman, *Studies in the History of Dalriada* (Edinburgh, 1974), 142–6; A. Grant, 'Thanes and Thanages from the Eleventh to the Fourteenth Centuries', in *Medieval Scotland*, ed. Grant and Stringer, 39–81; for Wales and Ireland, T. M. Charles-Edwards, *Early Irish and Welsh Kingship* (Oxford, 1993), esp. ch. 9; *Survey of the Honour of Denbigh 1334*, ed. P. Vinogradoff and F. Morgan (1914); K. Simms, *From Kings to Warlords*, ch. 9; G. R. J. Jones,'The Model for Organisation in *Llyfr Iorwerth* and *Llyfr Cyfnerth*', *Bulletin of the Board of Celtic Studies* 39 (1992), 95–119.

[68] G. J. Hand, 'English Law in Ireland, 1172–1351', *Northern Ireland Legal Quarterly* 23 (1972), 393–422.

[69] English law in Wales: R. R. Davies, 'The Law of the March', *Welsh History Review* 5 (1970–1), 1–30, esp. pp. 12–23; law of Scotland: W. D. H. Sellar, 'The Common Law of Scotland and the Common Law of England', in *The British Isles 1100–1500*, ed. Davies, 82–100; MacQueen, *Common Law and Feudal Society in Medieval Scotland*, ch. 1.

of what we may loosely call English legal custom, specifically the custom emanating from and controlled by the royal court. It was a rapidly evolving and increasingly professionally codified and dispensed body of custom. Part of its strength lay in its mechanisms and methods, such as the returnable and replicable writ and the extensive use of a jury; part of it in its concepts of property, contract, and crime; and part of it in its assertion of the accessibility of the royal courts to all men, at least free men, and in its proclamation of the king as ultimately the sole source of jurisdiction in his realm. Ralph Pipard himself would doubtless have taken note of the great statutes issued by Edward I and of his *quo warranto* inquiries; he might well have heard royal lawyers and commentators declare with thumping assurance that 'we will that our jurisdiction be superior to all jurisdictions in our realm.'[70] Had he crossed into Scotland, he would have found a royal judicial system which was a great deal more intimate, less professional, more decentralized, and, by English standards, whimsically old-fashioned; but recognizable as a country cousin nonetheless.

In Ireland and in Wales, beyond the areas of English settlement, it would have been otherwise. Here were lands of professional and often hereditary jurists,[71] where legal obligations were sustained by an elaborate surety system[72] and that, as the English noted to their surprise, without writing;[73] where there was but a limited notion of a king's peace and of the pleas of the crown; where the collective responsibility of the kindred and what English lawyers might term 'private indictment' were central;[74] where blood-feud compensation

[70] *Britton*, ed. F. M. Nichols, 2 vols. (Oxford, 1865), I, 3.

[71] Wales: R. R. Davies, 'The Administration of Law in Medieval Wales: The Role of the *Ynad Cwmwd* (*Judex Patrie*)', in *Lawyers and Laymen*, ed. T. M. Charles-Edwards et al. (Cardiff, 1986), 258–73; Ireland: K. Simms, 'The Brehons of Later Medieval Ireland', in *Brehons, Serjeants and Attorneys*, ed. D. Hogan and W. N. Osborough (Blackrock, 1990), 51–76; Scotland: G. W. S. Barrow, 'The judex', in idem, *Kingdom of the Scots*, ch. 2.

[72] See the outstanding study by Robin Chapman Stacey, *The Road to Judgment. From Custom to Court in Medieval Ireland and Wales* (Philadelphia, 1994).

[73] Llinos Beverly Smith, 'Inkhorn and Spectacles: the Impact of Literacy in late Medieval Wales', in *Literacy in Medieval Celtic Societies*, ed. Huw Pryce (Cambridge, 1998), 202–22, esp. pp. 214–15. For the conclusion of contracts 'absque scripto' in Wales, see Davies, 'Law of the March' (as in n. 69), p. 17, n. 63. In a case in Dyffryn Clwyd (Ruthin) in 1315 it was argued 'that a contract was made between them (the litigating parties) by the testimony of pledges and other proven men which is as valid in those parts as is a document in England' (Public Record Office, Court Rolls (S.C.2/215/74 m.6). The contrast between the old oral and the newfangled literate worlds is likewise vividly evoked in the attack of a MacDonald poet on the Campbells: 'The sharp stroke of short pens protects Argyll [for the Campbells]. . . . The broad sword's charter is the birthright of that bold people [the Macdonalds]; often without seal's impression do they impose tax or tribute' (quoted in A. Grant, *Independence and Nationhood. Scotland 1306–1469* (1984), 212). For similar views in Ireland, Simms, *From Kings to Warlords*, 1.

[74] For the case for early English developments in these areas, see the two outstanding papers by Patrick Wormald, '"Inter Cetera Bona . . . Genti Suae": Law-Making and Peace-Keeping in the Earliest English Kingdoms' and 'Giving God and King their due: Conflict and its Regulation in the Early English State', *Settimane di Studio del Centro italiano di studi sull'alto medioevo* 42 (1995), 963–96 and 44 (1997), 549–90.

systems and honour payments were still fundamental;[75] and where a great deal of dispute settlement took place extra-curially through what was called the agreement of the parties.[76] Ralph Pipard and his like would have found such a system—in so far as they could engage with it at all—inexplicable where it was not reprehensible (even though several of the features had not been unknown once in England).[77] They might dismiss it out of hand, as Edward I did with Irish law in 1277, as 'detestable to God and so contrary to all laws that they ought not to be called laws', or they might take a more selectively tolerant view of aspects of it, as he did with Welsh law in 1284.[78] Over and above such specific rulings lay the assumption that here indeed lay one of the great psychological fault-lines of the British Isles: on the one side of it lay those who shared what Lord Chancellor Gerard termed 'this instincte of Englishe nature, generally to feare justice', on the other lay those who had not learnt the habit of obedience to laws and whose life, to borrow one of Gerald of Wales's favourite phrases, lacked norm and form.[79] Here truly was one of the frontier lands of English and Anglicized political culture, a *ne ultra plus* line which could not be crossed until a fundamental process of re-education or social engineering or long-term acculturation, or all three, had been achieved.

It might well be objected that the image of two broad political culture zones within the British Isles which is presented here, the worlds of Henley-on-Thames and Uriel, is schematized, simplified, and static. The objection has much force. The very format of our sources may mislead us—be it the stark contrast between the rhetoric and purpose of, say, the Irish annals and those of the records of the English royal chancery or the *acta* of Scottish kings, or the seductive appeal of the generalized theories of external observers from

[75] Davies, *Conquest*, 116–17, 124–5; idem, 'The Survival of the Blood Feud in Medieval Wales', *History* 54 (1964), 338–57.

[76] T. Jones Pierce, *Medieval Welsh Society*, ed. J. B. Smith (Cardiff, 1972), 369–91. The Statute of Wales (1284) allowed that in land pleas in Wales 'the truth may be inquired into by good and law-worthy men of the neighbourhood chosen with the agreement of the parties.'

[77] In spite of heaping abuse on the Welsh (and the Irish) for their faithlessness, Gerald of Wales had to concede that 'they have laws which have stood the test of time, in which a man's plighted word is held sacred, truth is revered, honest dealing is highly thought of, the accused is given the benefit of the doubt, the accuser is allowed no advantage, and the onus of proving a case lies with the man who brings it': *Opera*, VI, 206–7 (Description of Wales, II, ch. 1). These comments make for interesting reading when set side by side with the concessions made to the Welsh by Edward I in cases of debt, contract, surety, covenant trespass, and movable property in the Statute of 1284.

[78] *CDI*, II, no. 1408; Llinos B. Smith, 'The Statute of Wales, 1284', *Welsh History Review* 10 (1980–1), 127–54; R. R. Davies, 'The Twilight of Welsh Law 1284–1536', *History* 51 (1966), 143–64.

[79] 'Lord Chancellor Gerard's Notes of his Report on Ireland . . . 1577–8', *Analecta Hibernica* 2 (1931), 93–291 at p. 96; Gerald of Wales, *Expugnatio Hibernica*, 105 (*in formam omnino redigere*), 230 (*in formam simul et normam redacta*).

Gerald of Wales to Sir John Davies.[80] Images, furthermore, are static, whereas the more we know of the polities and political cultures of the western British Isles, the more aware we are of the far-reaching changes which transformed them—and were often deliberately accelerated by their more enterprising rulers—between 1093 and 1343. It has also to be recognized that political cultures and patterns of political authority are substantially shaped by the geographical, social, and economic structures which underpin them. Thus in a lowland arable area characterized by relatively dense settlement, a developed pattern of economic and commercial networks, and a differentiated structure of wealth, an intensive format of authority with clearly articulated and detailed lines of power and exploitation is likely to be established, as compared with an upland and a maritime zone where poor land is abundant and men scarce, and where kindred bonds and a veneer of extensive lordship are more likely to be the order of the day. In a properly balanced overview of the medieval British Isles, the force of such considerations, and others, would need to be taken on board; but the significance of the broad contrast in political cultures would still stand. Men after all do not construe the world on the basis of balanced, scholarly, nuanced descriptions; rather do they live by images, categories, and metaphors. Anyone who reads, for example, the correspondence of English officials about medieval Ireland will be struck by the degree to which their comments are shaped by their experience of the English polity and by their expectations, their pre-packaged images, of what they would find in Ireland.[81] What they found, or believed they found, was that the form and substance, the tariff of values and the codes of practice of political culture and political competition in the two societies were entirely different.

Ralph Pipard would have known as much. As he travelled through the British Isles in the 1290s he would have found a surprisingly large zone which, for all its substantial differences, shared broadly similar political, governmental, and legal institutions and, even more crucially, the same idiom and assumptions of political life. That zone included not only England but much of lowland Scotland in the east and south, the southern coast-lands of Wales, and some of the river valleys and coastal plains of Ireland. It was a land of counties and sheriffs, manors and market towns, feudal tenurial custom, and an ultimately crown-centred polity or, rather, polities. Beyond it lay a very different zone, a world of fragmented and fluid polities, of intermittent warfare

[80] For comparative comments on Gerald and Sir John Davies, R. R. Davies, *Historical Perception: Celts and Saxons* (Cardiff, 1979).

[81] This is a point which has been very effectively explored in the writings of Robin Frame, esp. *English Lordship in Ireland 1318–1361* (Oxford, 1982), and *Ireland and Britain*, esp. chs. 1, 8, and 11.

and apparent indiscipline, of Welshries and Irishries and even no-go areas. In this world ethnic categorization was a shorthand for a profound political, legal, and cultural separation (in the way, for example, that the Dublin Chronicler or Friar John Clyn at Kilkenny categorized the players on the Irish political and military stage into 'English', even 'our English', and 'Irish' or 'mere Irish'):[82] here one's assumptions about normal human behaviour were defeated—just as one's military methods failed—because, as an exasperated and seasoned official put it in 1296, 'the Welsh, you know, are Welsh.'[83]

The boundaries of the two zones were not, of course, unchanging over time. The area of Anglicized political culture expanded across the twelfth and thirteenth centuries as English or English-type power extended its ambit through military might, governmental penetration, and, above all, settlement. So it was that southern Cumbria—which in the twelfth century was still largely Brythonic-speaking and lacked such features as a normal hundredal organization, view of frankpledge, and a sheriff's tourn—was increasingly absorbed into the polity and society of medieval England.[84] So it was likewise that Galloway—for all its tradition of fierce political and ecclesiastical independence, its separate laws, its kin-centred institutions, and its western orientation—was being drawn increasingly into the effective political orbit of the Scottish kingdom, as was exemplified in the fact that its lord Alan (d.1234) was also constable of Scotland.[85] But equally, areas in Ireland in districts such as counties Kildare, Tipperary, and Kilkenny, which had once, perhaps a little presumptuously, regarded themselves as part of an English world, were by 1300 Irish or at least profoundly Gaelicized in their customs and institutions. As an Irish prose tale commented on the de Burghs, they may have been 'of English origin' but were 'now Irish-natured'.[86]

As these examples suggest, between these two political culture zones there lay a large intermediate area where the practices and assumptions of both overlapped and where a form of *modus vivendi* had to be worked out. One

[82] For examples: *Chartularies of St Mary's Abbey, Dublin*, ed. J. T. Gilbert, 2 vols. (R.S., 1884), II, 333, 335, 359, 374–7, 389, etc.; *The Annals of Ireland by Friar John Clyn and Thady Dowling*, ed. R. Butler (Dublin, 1849), *s.a.* 1274, 1316, 1318, 1325, 1331, 1336, etc.

[83] J. G. Edwards, 'Edward I's Castle-Building in Wales', *Proceedings of the British Academy* 33 (1950), 15–81, at pp. 80–1.

[84] *VCH Cumberland*, I, 310–11; Summerson, *Carlisle*, 67.

[85] *Galloway. Land and Lordship*, ed. R. D. Oram and G. P. Stell (Edinburgh, 1991) (especially the essays by Oram and MacQueen); K. J. Stringer, 'Periphery and Core in Thirteenth-Century Scotland: Alan son of Roland Lord of Galloway and Constable of Scotland', in *Medieval Scotland*, ed. Grant and Stringer, 82–114.

[86] For the quotation, see *Caithreim* (as cited above, n. 42), II, 60. For the process of 'Hibernicization', see the chapters by J. A. Watt and Kenneth Nicholls in *NHI*, II, esp. pp. 308–10, 324–9, 421–4. There is a fine local study of the process by Kenneth Nichols in *Cork. History and Society*, ed. P. O'Flanagan and C. G. Buttimer (Dublin, 1993), 157–211.

would find such districts, great and small, in almost every region of the British Isles—in Glamorgan as one moved from the manorialized and feudalized world of the shire fee of the coastal plains through the great intermediate mesne lordships, such as Coety and Talyfan, to the thoroughly Welsh commotes of the uplands, in greater Galloway as one travelled from east to west, and likewise in Moray, or in Louth or the earldom of Ormond as one moved from islands of English settlement in a few miles to thoroughly Irish districts.[87] These were districts of the great aristocratic supremacies which are so characteristic of the western British Isles and were as often condemned by English-trained observers as they have been misunderstood by English-trained historians.[88] It was here likewise that the accommodations and compromises, which so frequently characterize zones where two cultures and societies meet, prompted officials steeped in English traditions and assumptions to bewail what they called degeneracy, the corrupting and diluting of English political culture by the values and assumptions of a different society.

The charge of degeneracy—which first figures officially in the legislation of the Irish parliament of 1297[89]—not only confirms the deep ethno-cultural divide within the British Isles but also directs our attention to the essential Englishness of English political culture. By the thirteenth century the English state as a construct was so set in its mould in terms of institutions, mechanisms, ideology, idiom, and assumptions, and so centralized in its format, that it was unable to cope with societies which could not be readily integrated into its political and governmental configuration. It either established an English-style government or Englishries for its colonists (as it did in Ireland and south and north-east Wales respectively), or created the veneer of English institutional rule while reserving all major offices to Englishmen (as it did in native Wales after 1277–84), or treated the conquered or semi-conquered areas of Wales and Ireland as annexes or protectorates without assimilating, or feeling that it could assimilate, their indigenous leaders into its own political

[87] Glamorgan: *Glamorgan County History*, III, ed. T. B. Pugh (Cardiff, 1971), esp. chs. 1, 2, 5, 6; Galloway: as in n. 85; Moray: *Moray: Province and People*, ed. W. D. H. Sellar (Edinburgh, 1993); Richard Oram: *Moray and Badenoch, A Historical Guide* (Edinburgh, 1996), 69–102. Louth: Brendan Smith as cited above, nn. 5–6; earldom of Ormond: C. A. Empey's studies, as cited above, n. 57, and idem, 'The Butler Lordship', *Journal of the Butler Society* I, no. 3 (1970–1), 174–87.

[88] For Ireland: Kenneth Nicholls in *NHI*, II, 422–3; Frame, *English Lordship in Ireland 1318–61*, esp. ch. 1; idem, *Ireland and Britain 1170–1450*, ch. 11 ('Power and Society in the Lordship of Ireland 1272–1377'); Wales: Davies, *Lordship and Society*; A. Grant, *Independence and Nationhood*, ch. 5. Important work is being published on late medieval aristocratic power in Scotland by Michael Brown and Steven Boardman.

[89] James Lydon, 'The Middle Nation', in *The English in Medieval Ireland*, ed. James Lydon (Dublin, 1984), 1–27; Seán Duffy, 'The Problem of Degeneracy', in *Law and Disorder in Thirteenth-century Ireland*, ed. James Lydon, 87–106.

processes and habits. There is an instructive degree of contrast here with Scotland. Scottish kingship and political society shared many of the assumptions and practices of the English and Anglicized political culture; but theirs was a far less uniform and centralized polity than that of England, much more federative and loose-limbed in character. This enabled it, in spite of growing tensions between Highlanders and Lowlanders, to avoid the ethnic stereotyping which opened such a chasm between the English on the one hand and the Welsh and the Irish on the other, and to bring large tracts of the north, west, and south-west of Scotland within the formal ambit of the Scottish kingdom, but on a very loose, and thereby tolerable and tolerant, rein.

The English did make an occasional attempt to build bridges across the political cultural divide—bestowing the belt of knighthood on a handful of Irish and Welsh leaders,[90] acceding to their request to hold land on feudal terms,[91] involving them in the king's military campaigns.[92] But such attempts at political and social inclusiveness were rare and were ultimately on the king of England's terms. As Llywelyn ap Gruffudd and John Balliol were both reminded, directly or indirectly, their political survival depended on their accepting that they should come to '*our* parliaments *in England* . . . like others *of our realm*'.[93] There was ultimately room on this view for only one body politic in the British Isles: political Anglicization was the price of political inclusion. There was no meeting of minds: as Froissart commented shrewdly on an English governor of Ireland: 'he never succeeded in learning the lie of the country or in understanding the mind-set of the Irish.'[94] So long as that remained the case, the British Isles would be a land of two political cultures, and there was little hope of the kingship of England being converted into a meaningful monarchy of the British Isles.

[90] Thus in 1210 Donough O'Brien of Thomond was knighted by King John (*NHI*, II, 130); Dafydd ap Llywelyn of Gwynedd may likewise have been knighted in 1241 (*Annales Monastici*, ed. H. R. Luard, I, 115). The Welsh and the Irish saw knighting as an alien practice. It was commented that when Dafydd ap Llywelyn was knighted it was 'contrary to the custom of his people' (*contra morem gentis suae*); *Eulogium Historiarum*, ed. F. S. Haydon, 3 vols. (R.S., 1858–63), III, 144). The observation of the author of the *Caithreim* (as cited above, n. 41) was even more tart (p. 78): 'The baron [Richard de Clare] . . . conferred the degree of knighthood, according to foreign use, upon members of the pale English.'

[91] The O'Connors of Connacht are the classic case: James Lydon, 'Lordship and Crown: Llywelyn of Wales and O'Connor of Connacht', in *The British Isles 1100–1500*, ed. R. R. Davies, 48–63.

[92] A striking example is the individual summons to the Irish kings to join Henry III's proposed expedition to Scotland in 1244: *Close Rolls* 1242–7, 254–5.

[93] *Littere Wallie*, 104; *Anglo-Scottish Relations*, ed. Stones, 210–11.

[94] Froissart, *Oeuvres* (as above, n. 39), XV, 170 ('ne les a sceu tant guerrorier que il puist aprendre la condition du pays, ne la manière des Yrlandois').

5

'SWEET CIVILITY' AND 'BARBAROUS RUDENESS'

During the 1530s there was a lively debate among the circles of Henry VIII's advisers whether the Welsh were sufficiently mature to be admitted to the full privileges and responsibilities of English citizenship. Rowland Lee, bishop of Lichfield (1534–43), president of the Council of Wales and the Marches and arch-exponent of the virtues of terror as the means to obedience, had no doubt that the Welsh failed the litmus test of political maturity. 'There are very few Welsh in Wales above Brecknock,' he declared in a famous comment, 'who have £10 in land, and their discretion is less than their land.'[1] Leaving discretion aside, what is striking about his observation is its assumption that wealth, preferably landed wealth, is a *sine qua non* for political maturity and responsibility, specifically for service as a magistrate, justice of the peace, or member of parliament, and for the measure of self-governance in the king's name which such posts implied. The English state, in other words, was not merely an institutional and political artefact; like all other states, it made assumptions, all the more fundamental for being unwritten, about the nature and distribution of wealth and its relationship to political power and responsibility. It had long been so. Soon after the last major Welsh revolt of the thirteenth century, that of 1294–5, English chroniclers observed with satisfaction that the Welsh were at last beginning to master the most basic political equation, namely that wealth accumulation equals peace equals political stability and so, eventually, social and political maturity. 'The Welsh,' noted the St Albans chronicle, 'began after the English fashion (*more anglicorum*)'—the phrase is very significant—'to accumulate wealth and henceforth lived in fear of losses to their goods.'[2] A truly suburban, insurance broker's view of the good life, but one which opened the door eventually to membership of English society and the English polity. 'Why,' asked Ranulf Higden rhetorically, 'do the Welsh live more

[1] *Letters and Papers, Foreign and Domestic, of the Reign of Henry VIII* (1862–1932), X, 453. See generally Glanmor Williams, *Recovery, Reorientation, and Reformation. Wales c.1415–1642* (Oxford, 1987), ch. 11, esp. pp. 263–5.

[2] William Rishanger, *Chronica et Annales* . . . ed. H. T. Riley (R.S., 1865), 148.

peacefully now? Because they are richer. Fear of loss of their goods keeps them obedient.' It was, appropriately enough, the desire to persuade the Welsh to 'grow and rise to more wealth and prosperity' which Henry VIII was to cite in 1543 as the reason for the final assimilation of Wales into England politically and institutionally.[3]

Apart from mastering the skills of wealth accumulation, there was another stumbling-block which the Welsh would have to overcome if they were to qualify for membership of the English state, that of learning the arts of what Edmund Spenser called 'sweet civility'. Bishop William Barlow of St David's (1536–48) took a rather more generous view of Welsh potential in this respect than did Rowland Lee, but even so he had no doubt that a period of cultural and educational re-orientation was necessary. If provision were made, he suggested, 'for learning as well as in grammar as in other sciences and knowledge of the Scripture, the Welsh rudeness would soon be framed to *English* civility and their corrupt capacities easily reformed into godly intelligence' (my italics).[4] Barlow's recipe for civilizing the Welsh was in no way novel. It had, for example, been much more amply laid out by Archbishop John Pecham (1279–92) in the wake of Edward I's conquest of the country. Indeed, Pecham's programme had involved not only ecclesiastical and moral reform but also ideological cleansing (to wean the Welsh from their fantasies about descent from the Trojans), economic indoctrination, particularly regarding the virtues of hard work, and deliberate resettlement in towns (just as the Romans had resettled the Burgundians), so that, in the archbishop's words, the Welsh could be brought 'to the knowledge of unity with *English* lordship and the *English* people' (my italics)—a pregnant and suggestive phrase indeed.[5]

The comments of Bishops Lee and Barlow, or of the St Albans chronicler and Archbishop Pecham about the economic lifestyle and social customs of the Welsh, are in fact the veriest commonplaces of the observations made about the peoples of the western British Isles—Wales,[6] the north of England

[3] Ranulf Higden, *Polychronicon*, ed. C. Babington and J. R. Lumby (R.S., 1865–86), I, 410–11; 34 & 35 Henry VIII c. 26 preamble (spelling modernized).

[4] Quoted in P. R. Roberts, 'The Welsh Language, English Law and Tudor Legislation', *Transactions of the Cymmrodorion Society* (1989), 19–75 at p. 41 (spelling modernized).

[5] *Registrum Epistolarum Johannis Peckham*, ed. C. T. Martin (R.S., 1882–5), II, 741–2 (ad unitatis studium cum dominio et populo anglicano); III, 776–7.

[6] For typical examples of the term 'barbarian' as applied to the Welsh, see William Malmesbury, *G.R.*, I, 29, 237 (omnemque illam barbariem), ed. Mynors et al. (Oxford, 1998), 351; Orderic Vitalis, *Historia Ecclesiastica*, ed. M. Chibnall, IV, 138; VI, 518, 540 (Welsh and outcasts bracketed together); *Gesta Stephani*, ed. Potter and Davis, 172, 194. For this whole theme, W. R. Jones, 'The Image of the Barbarian in Medieval Europe', *Comparative Studies in Society and History* 13 (1971), 376–407; Robert Bartlett, *Gerald of Wales 1146–1223* (Oxford, 1982), chs. 6–7; and John Gillingham, 'The Context and Purposes of Geoffrey of Monmouth's *History of the Kings of Britain*', *Anglo-Norman Studies* 13 (1991), 99–118, esp. pp. 105–10; idem, 'The Beginnings of English Imperialism', *Journal of Historical Sociology* 5 (1992), 392–410.

(as it now is),[7] Galloway,[8] Scotland[9] especially and increasingly the Highlands and the Isles,[10] and Ireland—from 1100 to 1600, and indeed often well beyond that date. Sometimes the comments are abusively short: 'those stubborn, rude and most barbarous people' is a common formula.[11] At other times—notably from the writings of Gerald of Wales in the late twelfth century to the full-blown treatises of men such as William Gerrard, Edmund Spenser, and John Davies in Tudor and Stuart times[12]—they blossom into elaborate, interlocking, quasi-anthropological field reports. We need, of course, to approach such comments and commentaries with circumspection and to supplement and correct them by the evidence, especially from within the societies they claim to describe; but equally and more importantly for present purposes, we need to appreciate them as images created by contemporaries—and often perpetuated by reiteration—of the world as they understood it. Images in that respect were, and are, reality. Furthermore, in describing other societies and cultures which were not commensurate with, or could not be assimilated into, their own, they were, by refraction as it were, identifying some of the distinctive characteristics of their own society.

It was during the course of the twelfth and thirteenth centuries that the great socio-cultural divide within the British Isles came into clear focus. The reasons are manifold. It was then for the first time that an aggressive and

[7] When Thurstan of Bayeux became archbishop of York in 1114, he was praised for going 'to shed light by your behaviour in the darkness of the barbarian nation over whom you are placed': Donald Nicholl, *Thurstan Archbishop of York (1114–1140)* (York, 1964), 41.

[8] Walter Daniel, *Life of Ailred of Rievaulx*, ed. F. M. Powicke, 45–6, 74 ('It is a wild country where the inhabitants are like beasts and it is altogether barbarous'). When an estate in Galloway was transferred to Melrose Abbey, the pretext given was that it was 'on account of the absence of law and order and by reason of the insidious attack of a barbarous people': *Liber Sancte Marie de Melros* (Bannatyne Club, 1837), no. 195.

[9] Ralph of Diceto, *Opera Historica*, ed. W. Stubbs, 2 vols. (R.S., 1876), II, 8. Cf. the compliment paid to King David (1124–53) that 'he tempered the fierceness of his barbarous nation'; Symeon of Durham, *Opera Omnia*, ed. T. Arnold (R.S., 1882–5), II, 330–1. Likewise William of Malmesbury (*G.R.*, 726–7) commented that David 'had rubbed off all tarnish of Scottish barbarity by his companionship and familiarity with us [the English] from his youth'.

[10] John of Fordun's well-known views (*Chronicle of the Scottish Nation*, ed. W. F. Skene, 2 vols. (Edinburgh, 1872), I, 38) of the Highlanders were uncompromising: 'a savage and untamed nation, rude and independent, given to rapine, ease-loving . . . unsightly in dress . . . and exceedingly cruel'.

[11] The phrase is from Edmund Tremayne's 'Causes why Ireland is not reformed' (1571), cited by Nicholas Canny, 'Revising the Revisionist', *Irish Historical Studies*, 30 (1996), 242–54, at p. 248.

[12] The key works drawn upon are Sir William Gerard (d.1581), 'Lord Chancellor Gerrard's Notes in his Report in Ireland', ed. C. MacNeill, *Analecta Hibernica* 2 (1931), 93–291; Edmund Spenser (d.1599), *A View of the State of Ireland . . . in 1596* (first published in 1633), ed. W. L. Renwick (Oxford, 1970); and Sir John Davies (d.1626), *A Discovery of the True Causes why Ireland was never entirely subdued* . . . (1612), ed. John Barry (1969). For comment on these works, see especially H. S. Paulisch, *Sir John Davies and the Conquest of Ireland: A Study in Legal Imperialism* (1985), and C. Brady, 'Spenser's Irish Crisis: Humanism and Experience in the 1590s', *Past and Present* no. 111 (1986), 17–49.

expansionist English or, if you will, Anglo-Norman society engaged in a regular and sustained fashion with some of the peoples of the outer regions of these islands, not only in military campaigns but also in an extensive process of settlement, initially in Wales and northern England, then in Scotland, and finally in Ireland. Simultaneously, and particularly during the turmoil of Stephen's reign, Welsh and Scottish (especially Galwegian) troops brought parts of English society to the knowledge, profoundly disturbing as it turned out to be, of the behaviour and customs of a different and, as it must have appeared, barbaric world.[13] Finally, and from the point of view of the historian crucially, it was during this period that a towering group of historians—most notably, of course, William of Malmesbury and Henry of Huntingdon—defined the essence and trajectory of what one may call political and social Englishness;[14] while some two generations later Gerald of Wales, whose massively pioneering achievement should not be concealed beneath the cultivation of his even more massive ego, provided one of the first sustained and coherent characterizations of a primitive people, the Welsh and the Irish.[15] Gerald's work, especially on Ireland, was profoundly important not only on account of its undoubted novelty but also because it became an almost canonical text of English views of the Irish for the better part of five centuries.

The image of 'sweet civility' was, as with so much about the early English state, a view of the world as seen from southern and midland England, albeit that one of its most voluble exponents came from Pembrokeshire, little England beyond Wales. It thereby inevitably reflected the values and priorities of a lowland, arable society, a relatively developed and monetized economy, and a region of intensive and exacting lordship and powerfully penetrative kingship. Given the political and economic orientation of southern England at this period, the image came also to be shaped by the aristocratic and cultural values of northern France. The reverberations of the French model reached to the extremities of the British Isles: that was why the modernizing kings of Scotland in the twelfth century were said to 'regard themselves as Frenchmen by race, manners, habit and speech' and to 'retain only Frenchmen in their

[13] Matthew Strickland, *War and Chivalry*, ch. 11; John Gillingham, 'Conquering the Barbarians' (both cited above, Ch. 1, n. 24). Orderic Vitalis (*Historia Ecclesiastica*, VI, 518) talked of the Scots 'invading England with the utmost brutality; giving full rein to their barbarity they treated the peoples of the borders with bestial cruelty.'

[14] Rees Davies, *The Matter of Britain and the Matter of England*; John Gillingham, 'Henry of Huntingdon and the Twelfth-century Revival of the English Nation', *Concepts of National Identity in the Middle Ages*, ed. L. Johnson and A. Murray (Leeds, 1995), 75–101.

[15] Robert Bartlett, *Gerald of Wales 1146–1223* for a general, and highly perceptive, introduction. For Gerald and Wales, see especially Huw Pryce, 'In Search of a Medieval Society: Deheubarth in the Writings of Gerald of Wales', *Welsh History Review* 13 (1986–7), 265–81.

service'.[16] That is likewise the explanation of the outburst that a native Irish ecclesiastic directed at the reforming and French-influenced St Malachy: 'Who do you think you are? A Frenchman? Don't you know that we build in wood, not stone?'[17] Needless to say, it was St Malachy and the French who prevailed: the churches of Ireland were henceforth built in stone, whilst French remained alongside English as the language of public discourse in English Ireland into the fourteenth century.[18]

The image-makers of 'sweet civility' drew on other sources also. As befitted their classical education, they were inevitably influenced by classical models of the good life. We should not dismiss such models as mere bookish analogies; topoi, after all, retain their plausibility only so long as they bear some relationship to contemporary practice and aspiration. So it was that when Geoffrey of Monmouth, fresh from reading his classical texts, explained why the Saxons had historically prevailed over the Britons, he provided simultaneously a revealing check-list of what were seen as the distinctly 'English' virtues of his own day: the promotion of peace and unity, the cultivation of fields, the building of cities and towns, the appointment of magistrates and lords, and the imposition of laws.[19] What was lacking in Geoffrey's check-list, as in his work in general, was morality and the Church; but others more than amply made good the deficiency. The model of 'sweet civility' was, after all, being shaped during the very period when the Church was codifying its laws and extending its jurisdiction, defining and enforcing in detail what Pope Alexander III called 'the established practice of the Christian faith' in terms of the behaviour of laymen and clerics alike.[20] 'Sweet civility' thereby became not merely a matter of refined manners and economic entrepreneurship; it also acquired a strong moral and moral-reforming dimension, and with it the

[16] *Memoriale Fratris Walteri de Coventria*, ed. W. Stubbs, II, 206. Likewise Jordan Fantosme commented that William the Lion of Scotland (1165–1214) 'cherished, loved and held dear people from abroad. He never had much affection for those of his own country': *Chronicle*, ed. R. C. Johnston, 48–9.

[17] *St Bernard of Clairvaux's Life of St. Malachy of Armagh*, ed. H. J. Lawlor (1920), 108–10 (paraphrased). The comment was a fair one in as much as the common material for the building of churches in Ireland (as in Wales) before the eleventh or twelfth century was wood: Nancy Edwards, *The Archaeology of Early Medieval Ireland* (1990), 124; H. Pryce in *The Early Church in Wales and the West*, ed. N. Edwards and A. Lane (Oxford, 1992), 26.

[18] On this subject, see briefly *NHI*, II, 710–14, to which other contemporary examples could be added. Cf. the famous crushing comment of Abbot Stephen of Lexington in 1228: 'No man can love the cloister and learning if he knows only Irish,' quoted in J. A. Watt, *The Church and the Two Nations in Medieval Ireland* (Cambridge, 1970), 96.

[19] Conflating the accounts in *HRB*, c. 207, with the additions and amendments in *Historia Regum Britannie II. The First Variant Version*, ed. N. Wright (1988), c. 204.

[20] The phrase is quoted from the pope's letter of September 1172 to the Irish bishops. It is conveniently translated in *Irish Historical Documents 1172–1922*, ed. E. Curtis and R. B. McDowell (1943), 19–20.

censoriousness and self-serving sanctimoniousness which often come in the wake of such an attitude.

Finally, there was among the more intelligent and sensitive of the image-makers—notably William of Malmesbury and Gerald of Wales—a recognition that there was a historical dimension to the cultural divide that had come to prevail in the British Isles. Gerald, 'avid student of natural history' that he proclaimed himself to be, perceived it most acutely. 'Mankind,' he pronounced with all the dogmatism of the social evolutionist, 'progressed in the common course of things from the forest to the field, from the field to the town and to the social conditions of townsmen.' This general formula provided the explanation, especially when sheer geographical inaccessibility was added thereunto, for the customs of the Irish and, by implication though to a lesser degree, the Welsh: 'they have not progressed at all from the primitive habits of pastoral living.'[21] William of Malmesbury may not have been so explicit and determinist in his social evolutionism; but in his *Gesta Regum Anglorum*, alongside the overriding theme of the political unification of England, there surfaces an awareness that an improvement in manners, morals, and governance—often under the influence of France—was equally important in the transformation of the country and thereby in distancing it from its backward British neighbours.[22] The importance of this time dimension in the cultural analysis of peoples was considerable. It helped, or could have helped, to move the argument away from mere censoriousness and condemnation. It introduced a comparative historical dimension into an issue which too often, contemporaneously and historically, has been imprisoned by the unilinealism of national historiography. It is worth noticing in this context that one of the most exciting developments in current early medieval historical scholarship is the growing awareness that, in broad terms, much of the British Isles may once have shared a common pattern in the organization of lordship and power;[23] it was, arguably, only from about the ninth century that southern and midland England began to move rapidly its own way.[24] It was at the very time that this process of differentiation was accelerating that the cultural

[21] *Expugnatio Hibernica*, 228–9 (naturalis historie diligens perscrutator); *The History and Topography of Ireland*, ed. and trans. J. J. O'Meara (1982), 101–2 (*Opera*, V, 151). For Ireland's remoteness, ibid., 31 (*Opera*, V, 20).

[22] *G.R.*, 152–3.

[23] The various writings of J. E. A. Jolliffe, G. W. S. Barrow, G. R. J. Jones, T. M. Charles-Edwards, and Patrick Wormald have been particularly seminal in this respect. Most recently Rosamond Faith, *The English Peasantry and the Growth of Lordship* (1997) has contributed a major and highly original view of the whole subject.

[24] This seems to me a broad conclusion one might deduce from various recent studies including Pauline Stafford, *The East Midlands in the Early Middle* Ages (1985); John Blair, *Early Medieval Surrey: Landholding, Church and Settlement before 1300* (1991); and idem, *Anglo-Saxon Oxfordshire* (1994).

divide within the British Isles became increasingly obvious and virtually unbridgeable. Gerald and William had the sensitivity to recognize that the divide was historically shaped. They also in effect perceived that while the cultural, social, and economic patterns of the outer British Isles were so far out of alignment with those of southern England and its Anglicized annexes, there could be no prospect of any real political union.

The cultural divide was a very real one: it was the distinction between what contemporaries occasionally called a *regio composita* and a *regio barbara*.[25] We see it, it is true, largely though not exclusively through English eyes. It is one of the distorting prerogatives of a hegemonic culture, especially a written one, that history is largely written on its terms and using its categories. It is thereby difficult, and in some degree impossible, to recover the culture, and the rationale of the culture, it displaces or relegates to the status of the barbarous. Thus, the culture and society of Gaelic Scotland is almost completely hidden from us by the absence of surviving evidence.[26] Nevertheless, the dimensions of the cultural divide are not in doubt. Contemporaries registered the depth of the chasm, as in the report of a Shropshire monk dispatched from a dug-out oak tree in Dunbrody (Co. Wexford) on 'the desolation of the place, the sterility of the soil and the wildness and ferociousness of the natives', or in the pathetic protest of the tax-collector that he would not return to Ireland even if his allowance were doubled or indeed even if he were threatened with imprisonment.[27] The natives, of course, learnt to play to the gallery of these images. One Irishman prefaced his petition by describing himself as 'a resident at the end of the world in the Irish parts'. A Welsh cleric was even more wily: asked to accompany one of Henry II's knights on a reconnaissance of a part of south-west Wales, he resorted to eating grass and roots, thereby ensuring that a report was duly sent back to the king that this was indeed a God-forsaken country fit only for a bestial race of people.[28]

[25] Gerald of Wales uses these contrasting phrases: *Opera*, I, 302; VIII, lviii. Likewise Ailred of Rievaulx saw it as David of Scotland's achievement to have introduced well-ordered and civilized customs (ad mores *compositos* et edomitos illicere satagebat): 'Eulogium Davidis', in *Pinkerton's Lives of the Scottish Saints*, ed. W. M. Metcalfe (Paisley, 1889), II, 273; cf. ibid., 271, 279.

[26] Among important studies are W. D. H. Sellar, 'Celtic Law and Scots Law: Survival and Integration', *Scottish Studies* 29 (1989), 1–27; G. W. S. Barrow, 'The Lost Gaidhealtachd', reprinted in idem, *Scotland and its Neighbours* (1992), 105–26; Dauvit Broun, *The Charters of Gaelic Scotland and Ireland in the Early and Central Middle Ages* (Cambridge, 1995), and *Literacy in Medieval Celtic Societies*, ed. Huw Pryce (Cambridge, 1998).

[27] *Chartularies of St Mary's Abbey, Dublin*, ed. J. T. Gilbert, 2 vols. (R.S., 1884), I, 354–5; *Royal and other Historical Letters illustrative of the Reign of Henry III*, ed. W. W. Shirley, 2 vols. (R.S. 1862–6), II, 119.

[28] *Documents illustrative of English History in the Thirteenth and Fourteenth Centuries*, ed. H. Cole (1844), 69 (cf. Gerald of Wales, *Topography of Ireland*, 31); Gerald of Wales, Itinerary through Wales, book I, ch. 10 (*Opera*, VI, 81–2).

What, then, was it that consigned these people to the category of the bestial and the barbarous? We may begin with those tests of economic competence (in all senses of that word) which Bishop Rowland Lee had decreed to be a minimum qualification for full membership of the English state. Those tests were ultimately constructed from an image of what was deemed to be normal, though not of course necessarily universal or uniform, features of economic activity in lowland England and the Anglicized parts of the British Isles. Already by the twelfth and thirteenth centuries, if not indeed earlier, we might in very general terms itemize the following as some of those features: a well-populated, village-centred country; a cereal-based agriculture; a world of manors and open and common fields; a dependent landed peasantry more or less firmly locked into an intensive system of seignorial exploitation; a powerful lay and ecclesiastical aristocracy and, arguably, an even more significant class of country gentry; an extensive and overlapping network of towns, markets, and fairs and thereby the opportunities for some measure of specialization and surplus production; a single coinage and a rapidly increasing volume of coins in circulation; a well differentiated social structure; some measure of social mobility and an active land market, even among peasants; and finally an economic, as well as a political, order in which a unitary monarchy played a pivotal part in providing peace, founding towns, monopolizing the mints, levying taxation (direct and indirect), and fostering trade. There is, of course, much that can be added to, and qualified about, such a simplified model; but its main features, if not its terminology, would surely be recognizable to Sir Ralph Pipard, the squire of Rotherfield Peppard in the 1280s and 1290s who figured in the previous chapter. By then—though not in the late eleventh century—many of its features were, in a greater or lesser degree, replicated in a great swathe of the British Isles from the Moray Firth through eastern and southern Scotland, across the coastal lowlands and river valleys of south Wales, and throughout the towns and manors of English Ireland.

Elsewhere in the British Isles it was different. Even the very aspect of the countryside was different: that is why 'wild' (*silvestris*) was the word which came most readily to the pen of observers, and from being applied to the landscape was almost instantly transferred to its inhabitants. It was partly a matter of distance and impenetrability: the Welsh, commented John of Salisbury flaunting his experience of European travel, live in their Alps and sub-Alps; Archbishop Pecham was even more dismissive, showing his talent for turning every comment into an insult: 'you live in your little corner in the far end of the world. . . . The rest of the world scarcely knows that you exist as a people'; while Gerald sought to explain some of the idiosyncrasies of the Irish by observing that Ireland 'was separated from the rest of the known world and in some ways is to be distinguished as another world'.[29] Once one had overcome the fatigue of travel to such inaccessible places, the very aspect of the countryside was disturbingly different to those accustomed to the well-manicured arable plains of southern England. 'Wales,' said the author of the *Gesta Stephani*, 'is a country of woodland and pasture . . . abounding in deer and fish, milk and herds . . . a country breeding men of a bestial type.' The image became a literary topos: the Welsh, said Chrétien of Troyes crushingly, 'are by nature more uncouth than the beasts in the fields'. The national character was, as it were, ecologically determined; both were repulsive.[30] The same was true of Ireland. Thus what struck the author of *The Song of Dermot and the Earl* in the thirteenth century about the country was its wastes, woodlands, lakes, and 'flowery moor'. Much in the same vein—and now almost stereotypical—was Jean Froissart's description of it as 'abounding in deep forests and in lakes and bogs'.[31]

Stilted such comments may sound; but their emphasis on forests and water was amply echoed in contemporary Irish annals and poetry. The very structures of social life and political power in Wales, Ireland, and western Scotland were shaped by the still untamed forces of nature. One's mental geography had to adjust to the aspect and exigencies of the landscape.[32] We can see as much in contemporary analyses: a *Description of England* composed *c.*1140[33] proceeds by itemizing the shires and towns of a well-ordered, well-settled country; but when Gerald of Wales came to present his *Description of Wales* he constructed his account around mountains, rivers, and tidal estuaries. The values of these two worlds were bound to be different. Which English annalist would record years of good crops of acorns and beech-mast, as Irish annals regularly do, or which English poet would exult in the greenness of grass and the thickness of nut-sweet woods, as the Irish poet did?[34] Forests in England may have been appropriate venues for outlaws, knightly quests, and royal hunts; in Ireland and Wales they were often central to the livelihood

[29] *The Letters of John of Salisbury*, ed. W. J. Millor et al., 2 vols. (1955–79), I, 52; *Register . . . John Peckham* (as above, n. 5), II, 476; Gerald of Wales, *Opera*, V, 23. (This passage is omitted from the translation of *Topography of Ireland*.)

[30] *Gesta Stephani*, ed. Potter and Davis, 14–15; Chrétien of Troyes, *The Story of the Grail or Perceval*, ed. R. T. Pickens, trans. W. W. Kibley (1990), ll. 242–3.

[31] *Song*, lines 26, 669, 1217, etc.; Jean Froissart, *Chronicles*, ed. and trans. J. Jolliffe (1967), 363 (ed. Kervyn de Lettenhove, XV, 169).

[32] For pioneering studies, see E. Estyn Evans, *The Personality of Ireland: Habitat, Heritage and History* (Cambridge, 1973) and Alfred P. Smyth, *Celtic Leinster: Towards an Historical Geography of Early Irish Civilization A.D. 500–1600* (1982).

[33] Lesley Johnson and Alexander Bell, 'The Anglo-Norman Description of England', *Anglo-Norman Anniversary Studies*, ed. Ian Short (Anglo-Norman Text Society, 1993), 11–47.

[34] *Annals of Tigernach*, *s.a.* 1168; Osbern Bergin, *Irish Bardic Poetry*, ed. D. Greene and F. Kelly (Dublin, 1970), poem no. 5.

of the population. It is, for example, 'in the middle of an oak wood surrounded by his womenfolk and cattle' that we catch a glimpse of an Irish leader, while the men of north-east Wales could likewise claim that 'the greater part of their sustenance is derived from the woods.'[35]

Weather added to the sense that these were indeed foreign countries. 'When elsewhere it is summer,' said an English chronicler sourly, 'in Wales it is winter.' The north of England was similarly handicapped: 'Spring and summer never come here. The north wind is always blowing, and brings with it cold or snow, or storms in which the wind tosses the salt sea-foam in masses over our buildings. . . . See to it, dear brother, that you do not come to so comfortless a place.'[36] Exaggerated and stereotypical such comments about the northern and western British Isles might be, but they were more than amply matched by the experiences of English soldiers and administrators. Henry II's military ambitions and dignity were swept away in torrential rain in the Welsh uplands in 1165, and Henry IV suffered a like fate in 1402.[37] It comes as no surprise that one of the earliest accounts of the misery of rain-sodden and exhausted troops comes from an Englishman serving in Degannwy in north Wales in 1245; nor is it surprising that the Black Prince's officials were given a special allowance of winter clothing when they were sent on a tour of duty to Wales.[38] The wildness of the geography and peoples of this western world seemed to be matched by the foulness of its weather.

Within this alien countryside the settlement pattern was also disconcertingly unfamiliar to southern English eyes. Three features in particular caught their attention and were the occasion of recurrent comment. First, these people, notably in Ireland and Wales, lived in a dispersed habitat, not in neat, well-organized villages—*sparsim* not *vicatim*, as John Leland was to express it pithily.[39] Secondly, their houses were shoddy and impermanent: Walter

[35] *Annals of Connacht*, *s.a.* 1225; *Calendar of Ancient Petitions relating to Wales*, ed. W. Rees (Cardiff, 1975), 74. For the importance of the forest economy in Wales, see W. Rees, *South Wales and the March 1284–1415* (Oxford, 1924), 109–28; R. R. Davies, *Lordship and Society*, 120–7.

[36] *The Chronicle of Pierre de Langtoft*, II, 177; monk of Tynemouth quoted by K. J. Stringer, 'Identities in Thirteenth-Century England: Frontier Society in the Far North', in *Social and Political Identities in Western History*, ed. Claus Bjørn et al. (Copenhagen, 1994), 28–67 at pp. 30–1.

[37] Paul Latimer, 'Henry II's Campaign against the Welsh in 1165', *Welsh History Review* 14 (1988–9), 523–52, esp. pp. 535–6; R. R. Davies, *The Revolt of Owain Glyn Dŵr* (Oxford, 1995), 109, 232.

[38] Matthew Paris, *Chronica Majora*, IV, 481–4; *The Register of Edward the Black Prince* (1930–3), I, 28.

[39] John Leland, *The Itinerary in Wales*, ed. L. T. Smith (1906), 93. For discussion of settlement and habitat patterns in Ireland, see esp. *NHI*, II, 225–6, 404; K. W. Nicholls, *Land, Law and Society in Sixteenth-century Ireland* (Dublin, 1978); T. B. Barry, '"The People of the Country . . . dwell scattered": The Pattern of Rural Settlement in Ireland in the Later Middle Ages', in *Settlement and Society in Medieval Ireland: Studies presented to F. X. Martin*, ed. J. Bradley

Daniel, for example condemned the men of Galloway for living in huts and mean hovels rather than in houses and four-square buildings.[40] The subtext of such a comment, of course, was that only householders disciplined by the cares and demands of permanent homes could qualify for membership of civic and civilized society. Thirdly, the population of the western British Isles was to some degree mobile and unstable, be it because of the demands of pastoral agriculture, or because of the impact of periodic partition and reallocation of lands in a kin-based society and the purely contractual nature of Gaelic tenancy, or because native princes and lords regularly viewed their men and animals as movable commodities to be taken whither they willed. As late as 1596 a commentator could, no doubt with exaggeration, observe that 'the tenants continue not past three years in a place, but run roving about the country like wild men, fleeing from one place to another.'[41] The prevalence of such practices varied hugely over time and place; they were already largely a thing of the past in Wales by the thirteenth century, but survived much longer in parts of Gaelic Ireland. But it is not difficult to see why they were an impediment to the inclusion of such societies within English political culture, predicated as it was on a stable population, on precisely defined units of territorial measurement and the obligations attached to them, and on the discipline, regimentation, and communal responsibilities of a well-organized and submissive village and shire life.

The economic practices and priorities of these western British Isles communities likewise increasingly distanced them from their neighbours to the south and east. Well into the twelfth century in Wales, and far beyond then in Ireland and the Isles, the plunder of goods and the capture of people—a virtual form of slavery—were the normal, almost annual, coin of political competition and wealth accumulation. When we learn, for example, that Owain Gwynedd (d.1170), a prince who was after all extolled for his 'infinite prudence', led his host to Arwystli in 1162 'and carried away vast spoil', we understand why the Welsh law-texts are so particular in their details about the division of plunder. Likewise, the centrality of the control of men, women, and cattle to political power in these societies is a recurrent feature of the native sources, as in the report of the Welsh chronicle of a Welsh princeling

(Kilkenny, 1988), 345–60. For contemporary comments on the dispersed nature of Welsh settlement, see, for example, *Register of John Peckham*, III, 176; *Record of Caernarvon*, ed. H. Ellis (1838), 212 (cum ville Walenses sint disperse).

[40] Walter Daniel, *Life of Ailred of Rievaulx*, 74. Many similar comments were made on Irish and Welsh housing: *NHI*, II, 403; Gerald of Wales, Description of Wales, book 1, ch. 17 (*Opera*, VI, 201).

[41] *Calendar of State Papers, Ireland, 1596–7*, 19. For this subject see K. Simms, 'Nomadry in Medieval Ireland: The Origins of the Creaght or *Caorigheacht*', *Peritia* 5 (1986), 379–91.

ravaging Tegeingl in north-east Wales in 1165 and taking 'all its people and all their chattels with him' into a nearby district.[42] The Irish annals resonate to the lowing of herds being driven hither and thither.[43] English settlers quickly picked up the idiom and practice of this pillage economy, as viciously and deliberately destructive as modern asset-stripping.[44] There was, of course, more, much more to these native economies than plunder and slave-taking; but even that more was disturbingly different. In a world where the advance of bread-grains was much the most dominant feature, these societies appeared to be culpably backward and underdeveloped. William of Newburgh's famous comment on Ireland may speak for many others: 'the soil of Ireland would be fertile if it did not lack the industry of the dedicated farmer; but the country has an uncivilized and barbarous people, almost lacking in laws and discipline, lazy in agriculture, and thereby living more on milk than on bread.'[45]

William's observation is a capacious, interlocking set of value judgements. That it should end, almost in bathos, with the charge that the Irish lived on milk and milk products rather than on grain shows how much an arable-based society—in its rhythms and social organization as much as in its diet—found it difficult to engage with the values and habits of a stock-rearing society. It was a contrast which retained its force for centuries.[46] Exaggerated and oversimplified as the contrast was, there is no doubt that the perceived dominance of cattle (and to a lesser extent horses and pigs) in the economies and value systems of the British Isles—primarily in Ireland but also extensively in Wales, the Lordship of the Isles, the Highlands, Galloway, and Cumbria—set them apart from the arable lowlands.[47] Cattle here were fundamental not only

[42] *Brut*, *s.a.* 1162, 1165, 1170.

[43] See especially K. Simms, 'Warfare in the Medieval Gaelic Lordships', *Irish Sword* 12 (1975–6), 98–108.

[44] References to English settler families in Ireland taking preys in the Irish fashion are legion, e.g. *Chartularies of St Mary's Dublin*, II, 374, 378; *The Annals of Friar John Clyn*, 33 (the sheriff of Kilkenny takes a great prey (magnam predam) on McGillepatrick).

[45] *Chronicles of the Reigns of Stephen, Henry II and Richard I* (R.S.), I, 165–6.

[46] For example, in the late sixteenth century George Owen (*c.*1552–1613) could remark how profoundly different the English and Welsh of Pembrokeshire were in 'maners, diete, buildings and tyllinge of the land' (*The Description of Pembrokeshire*, ed. H. Owen, 4 vols. (Cymmrodorion Record Series, 1902–36), 39, 59–61). Likewise, as late as 1849 a correspondent could observe of Pembrokeshire that 'the superiority of the farming diminishes as it proceeds inland; and above Narberth the Welsh county commences': *Pembrokeshire County History*, IV, 1815–1974, ed. Brian Howells (Haverfordwest, 1990), 82.

[47] The evidence is ubiquitous for Wales and Ireland. For Cumberland, note that the custom of paying noutgeld in cattle lingered until the late twelfth century, partly no doubt because of the shortage of coinage (*V.C.H. Cumberland*, I, 313–14; Richard Fitz Neal, *Dialogus de Scaccario*, ed. C. Johnson (1950), 9). As to Galloway, when the Galwegians came to terms with Henry II in 1174 they offered him 500 cows and 500 swine per annum (as well as a lump sum of 2,000 marks of silver), just as the Lord Rhys of Deheubarth had offered him 300 horses and 4,000 oxen in 1171 (Anderson, *Scottish Annals*, 257; *Brut*, *s.a.* 1171, p. 66). For cattle as the basis of the economy and estimates of worth in the Lordship of the Isles, see J. W. M. Bannerman, 'The Lordship

to diet but to power structures and social relationships. They were the basic surplus product of these societies. They were the units for the measurement of value: so it was that Art Macmurrough's horse was said to have cost him 400 cows.[48] They were also the expression of power and of powerlessness: so it was that the security and acquisition of stocks of cattle were among the basic rules of Irish political power, while to be 'left without kine' was to be stripped of power.[49] They were the prime unit of exchange; and it was in cattle that status and honour was measured,[50] tributes and penalties large and small paid,[51] and bonds of dependence and clientage expressed. As one historian has put it, admittedly with reference to early medieval Ireland: 'It was the circulation of cattle that created a hierarchy of lords and vassals and this is what bound society together.'[52] Nor was this emphasis on cattle merely the prevalence of pastoral over arable agriculture; it shaped the whole code of values and perceptions of authority within society. Equally, it created a set of pejorative assumptions in those societies which did not share its values. So it was that the Bretons, another western people, were criticized because, in William of Poitiers' words, 'they do not engage in the cultivation of fields or of good morals,' as if corn-growing and clean living went together.[53] Edmund Spenser was, as usual, even more dogmatic: countries that live by keeping cattle are both very barbarous and uncivil and also greatly given to war.[54] Tilling and husbandry, he in effect concluded, were the necessary foundations of a

of the Isles', in *Scottish Society in the Fifteenth Century*, ed. Jennifer M. Brown (1977), 209–40 at pp. 220–1. For suggestive comments on the political structures and values of pastoral society, see Christopher Wickham, 'Pastoralism and Underdevelopment', *Settimane di Studio* 31 (1985), 400–51.

48 Jean Creton, 'Histoire du roy d'Angleterre, Richard', ed. J. Webb, *Archaeologia* 20 (1824), 13–243 at pp. 324–5.

49 For the centrality of cattle, see, for example, *Annals of Connacht*, 13, 15, 19, 53, 139, etc.; 'left without kine': *Caithréim Thoirdhealbhaigh*, II, 156.

50 As when the men of Meath gave those of Connacht and Uriel 700 cows as the honour price for a king killed while under the protection of the kings of Connacht and Uriel: *Annals of Tigernach*, *s.a.* 1168.

51 For regular tributes in cattle (*commorth Calan Mai; treth cant eidion*) in Wales, see Davies, *Lordship and Society*, 134, 140–1; in Ireland, for example, *Historical Mss. Commission, Mss. of Lord De L'Isle and Dudley, I* (1925), 31 (Aedh O'Neill acknowledges that he owes the earl of Ulster 3,500 cows); *The Irish Pipe Roll of 14 John, 1211–12*, ed. Oliver Davies and D. B. Quinn (Belfast, 1941), 36–7. In Wales, the normal penalty was a *camlwrw* of three cows. For fines in cattle in Caithness and Ross, see A. A. M. Duncan and A. L. Brown, 'Argyll and the Isles in the Earlier Middle Ages', *Proceedings of the Society of Antiquaries of Scotland* 90 (1956–7), 192–218 at pp. 214–15.

52 C. Doherty, 'Exchange and Trade in Early Medieval Ireland', *Journal of the Royal Society of Antiquaries of Ireland* 110 (1980), 67–89 at p. 72. For an Irish king offering sixty cows as a warranty of dependence and good behaviour to an English settler lord, see *Calendar of Ormond Deeds*, I, no. 268.

53 Quoted in Bartlett, *Gerald of Wales*, 160–1. Cf. Ralph Glaber's view of the Bretons' lifestyle: 'freedom from taxes and an abundance of milk', quoted ibid., 160.

54 *View of the State of Ireland*, 158.

civilized commonwealth. The men of the north and the west for their part had nothing but contempt for those whom they dismissed as 'mere tillers of the soil', 'damned rascals that did nothing but plough the land and sow corn'.[55]

The apartness and backwardness of northern and western British Isles societies were also manifested economically in what they did *not* have. They did not have their own coinage and made little use of money. It was the Welsh of west Wales themselves who declared in 1318 that they were 'never accustomed to have money in the Welshry'; while a French observer noted of the Irish that 'there is little money in the country, so they usually trade in cows.' To societies where money was already a prominent medium of exchange and a source of power—for as William of Malmesbury observed famously, 'money is capable of persuading what it lists'—this was indeed a sign of true backwardness.[56] Towns of any size and significance were also notable by their absence: there was, for example, no burgh in Scotland west of a line from Dumbarton to Dornoch. Trade there was in some degree, but on a very unsystematic, irregular, and non-institutional pattern. Regardless of the exceptions (of which historians have made a great deal) this was, particularly in the twelfth century and away from a few coastal centres, a world very considerably of gift exchange, tribute and reciprocity, of extensive lordship, and of kingships and a military and serviential aristocracy exercising billeting rights and claiming food renders (as once had been the case in much of lowland England).[57] The implications for political power and for claims to membership of the English commonwealth of the virtual absence, or very limited role, of coins, towns, and trade were far-reaching. Each of these features was in its fashion a vital ingredient of effective state-formation, penetrative royal power (ideological as well as political and fiscal), the exchange of large and recurrent surpluses, and capital accumulation. How, as William of Malmesbury might have put it, could one be urbane without an *urbs* or civic and civilized without a *civis*?

Ultimately, as almost all observers agreed, the disqualification *par excellence* of western communities was one not of economic performance but more fundamentally of economic attitude. They simply lacked the spirit of economic enterprise and wealth creation and accumulation. The charges tumble out wherever we look: 'they think,' said Gerald of the Irish, 'that the greatest

[55] J. MacInnes, 'Gaelic Poetry and Historical Tradition', in *The Middle Ages in the Highlands*, ed. L. Maclean (Inverness, 1981) at p. 160; G. W. S. Barrow, *The Kingdom of the Scots*, 368 (quoting James Boswell's report on the response of James Macpherson to Gray's *Elegy*).

[56] *Calendar of Ancient Correspondence concerning Wales*, 19 (1318); Jean Creton as quoted above, n. 48; William of Malmesbury, *G.R.*, I, 734–5.

[57] For an excellent analysis of 'extensive lordship' and full references to the bibliography for England, see Rosamond Faith, *The English Peasantry and the Growth of Lordship*, ch. 1.

pleasure is not to work, and the greatest wealth is to enjoy liberty.' Pecham diagnosed the same culpable shortcoming among the Welsh and branded it as *otium corporale*. In the late fourteenth century, John of Fordun likewise identified it as a feature of the men of the Highlands and Islands of Scotland whom he stigmatized famously as 'a savage and untamed people, rude and independent, given to rapine and ease-loving', compared to the 'home-loving, civilized . . . polite . . . and pacific householders' of the Lowlands.[58] There was, it is true, a recognition that such ease-loving, economically unambitious societies had their virtues—notably a fierce love of liberty, an independence of spirit, a self-denying frugality, and a remarkable etiquette of hospitality.[59] But when the ethic of hard work—'virtuous labour', as Sir Thomas Smith called it[60]—and capital accumulation were ignored and even despised as primary goals, and when economic effort in one generation was often totally undone in the next by the application of the custom of the partibility of lands between male heirs agnatic,[61] there was little prospect indeed of sustained wealth creation or of the emergence of a truly economically differentiated ruling class, comparable with the country gentry of England or the lairds of lowland Scotland. It was for that reason, as we saw earlier, that Bishop Rowland Lee concluded that the Welsh did not qualify for full membership of the English body politic. Where there was no well-calibrated set of social distinctions and no recognized hierarchy of landed competence (whose threshold Bishop Lee set at £10 per annum), there could be no political discretion. Here was a touchstone of political maturity *à l'anglaise*.

It was also in effect a touchstone of civility. The connection between wealth and civility was one which contemporaries made almost unthinkingly. So it was, for example, that an Elizabethan commentator laid out his prescription for the Welsh with admirable succinctness: 'the people of Wales are to

[58] *Topography of Ireland*, 102 (*Opera*, V, 152); *Register of John Peckham*, II, 742; III, 776–7, 796; John of Fordun, as cited in n. 10 above. John Mair (Major) followed Fordun in this respect, contrasting the 'wild Scots' on the one hand with the 'householding', 'domestic', and 'civilized' men of the lowlands on the other: *A History of Greater Britain 1521*, ed. A. Constable (Scottish History Society, 1892), 48–50.

[59] These are recurrent themes in the writings of Gerald of Wales on the Welsh and the Irish, and are the bases of several of Walter Map's stories about the Welsh (*De Nugis Curialium*, ed. M. R. James et al., 100–1, 114–17, 182–5, 194–9). For discussion, see Bartlett, *Gerald of Wales*, 187–200; R. R. Davies, 'Buchedd a Moes y Cymry', *Welsh History Review* 12 (1984–5), 155–79 (with English synopsis); K. Simms, 'Guesting and Feasting in Gaelic Ireland', *Journal of the Royal Society of Antiquaries of Ireland* 108 (1978), 67–100.

[60] 'To keep them [sc. the Irish] in order, in virtuous labour and in justice, and to teach them English laws and civility.' Quoted in C. Brady, *The Chief Governors: The Rise and Fall of Reform Government in Tudor Ireland 1536–1588* (Cambridge, 1988), 253.

[61] For a recent detailed study of the consequences of male partibility, see M. H. Brown, 'Kinship, Land and Law in Fourteenth-Century Wales: The Kindred of Iorwerth ap Cadwgan', *Welsh History Review* 17 (1994–5), 493–520.

be enriched and brought to civility.'[62] Civility—and its Latin counterpart, *mansuetudo*[63]—was, of course, a wonderfully imprecise and catch-all phrase; but its endless repetition in the writings of observers and pundits is a reminder that the cultural fault-line within the British Isles was as much about social mores and codes of values as it was about economic lifestyle and attitudes. Civility implies an image of acceptable behaviour and norms; it also implies an antonym—incivility at best, barbarousness at worst. Without civility, membership of civil or civic society, of the English polity, was out of the question. So what was it about the Welsh which required them, in Bishop William Barlow's view, to undergo a long process of education and indoctrination if they were to attain to what he termed *English* civility or about the Irish which persuaded Edmund Spenser that they would never be able to reach that happy state?

We should not dismiss the physical and the obvious, if only because they proclaimed the profundity of the cultural divide without the need to resort to thought or analysis. The men of the west looked different: the moustaches and hairstyle of the Irish, the bare legs and feet of the Welsh, and the half-naked buttocks of the Scots proclaimed their apartness and their barbarousness.[64] So did their clothes—such as the rough cloth and sinister mantles of the Irish—and their lack of, and indeed indifference, to dress and body cover, civilian or military.[65] 'They pay no attention to outward appearance,' said a fastidious and shocked English observer. To them indeed, such indifference was a cause of pride: 'Little he cares for mantle of gold-embroidered; he has no longing

[62] J. Fisher, 'Wales in the Time of Queen Elizabeth', *Archaeologia Cambrensis*, 6th ser., 15 (1915), 237–48 at p. 244 (spelling modernized).

[63] For example, Walter Map (*De Nugis Curialium*, 146–7) remarked that the Welsh lacked 'habetudo mansuetudinis'. Likewise Ailred of Rievaulx ('Eulogium Davidis', as cited above, n. 25, II, 271, 280) regularly extols King David of Scotland for his *mansuetudo*. For contemporary resonances of the term *mansuetudo*, see J. Gillingham, 'Thegns and Knights in Eleventh-Century England: Who was then the gentleman?', *Transactions of the Royal Historical Society*, 6th ser., 5 (1994), 129–53, esp. pp. 148–52.

[64] For the Welsh as barefoot and barelegged, see, for example, Walter Map, *De Nugis Curialium*, 100–1; *Littere Wallie*, ed. J. G. Edwards, xxviii–xxix; *Eulogium Historiarum* (R.S., 1858–63), III, 388. For the Scots: Ailred of Rievaulx quoted in Anderson, *Scottish Annals*, 197; cf. A. A. M. Duncan, 'The Dress of the Scots', *Scottish Historical Review* 29 (1950), 210–12. Likewise the Irish were said to go 'barefoot and without breeches': *Chronique de la traison et mort de Richard II*, ed. B. Williams (English Historical Society, 1846), 28, 171.

[65] The description in the *Histoire des ducs de Normandie* of the meeting between King John and Cathal O'Connor is revealing: 'The king of Connacht came to his service, one of the richest kings of Ireland, bringing many great men, but all were on foot and very strangely dressed. Even the king was very poorly mounted and dressed in the same manner' (quoted in S. Duffy, 'King John's Expedition to Ireland, 1210: the Evidence Reconsidered', *Irish Historical Studies* 30 (1996), 1–24 at p. 22). Irish hairstyles, moustaches, and mantles figure prominently as ethnic identifiers, as in the legislation of 1297 and 1366 or in the opinions of men such as Edmund Spenser (*A View*, 50, 52, 69, etc.). For the scanty dress of the Welsh, princes included, Gerald of Wales, Itinerary through Wales, book II, ch. 4; Description of Wales, book I, ch. 9 (*Opera*, VI, 119, 182).

for a feather bed or stockings in the English style' was how an Irish poet put it.[66] Their table manners barely existed, not surprisingly so because they had no tables and no sense of the cult of precedence and the snobbery of public eating so familiar in the best Anglo-French circles. That is why the crash course of cultural reorientation devised for four Irish chieftains by an English knight included teaching them how to sit at high table and how to distance themselves from their valets and minstrels.[67] Their manner of riding might also mark them out, most notably the Irish who, as observers regularly noted, used no saddles or stirrups.[68] One should not make light of such differences; they were powerful and visible cultural and ethnic identifiers. Particularly was this so in Ireland, where such differences were legislatively defined as bulwarks of Englishness from the late thirteenth century, and where to become English required one, literally, to change one's hairstyle.[69]

Men who were so uncouth in their appearance could not be expected to be other than loose in their morals. The charges in this respect are broadly similar whether they are directed at the Welsh or the Gallovidians, the Irish or the Highlanders: sexual lasciviousness, pre-nuptial trial marriages, sale and bartering of wives, ease of divorce, equality between legitimate and bastard children, and the practice of fosterage are among the hardy perennials on the list.[70] The charges come, of course, almost exclusively from the pens of reforming ecclesiastics (including, it has to be said, Welsh and Irish clerics) anxious to instil the values and code of practice of a militant Church; as such they have a universal rather than a specifically British application. Yet they are also significant in the construction of cultural stereotypes within the British Isles: churchmen such as Pecham worked hand in hand with the agents of the English state, and the Church's social morality became thereby, as it were, the

[66] Sir Henry Crystede as reported in Froissart, *Chronicles*, ed. Jolliffe, 364 (ed. Kervyn de Lettenhove, XV, 170); Bergin, *Irish Bardic Poetry* (as above, n. 34), no. 9.

[67] Froissart, *Chronicles*, ed. Jolliffe, 366 (ed. Kervyn de Lettenhove, XV, 172–3). Cf. William of Malmesbury's comment that King David of Scotland agreed to give tax concessions to those who 'would live in a more civilized style, dress with more elegance, and learn to eat with more refinement': *G.R.*, 726–7.

[68] See *Histoire des ducs de Normandie* (as cited, n. 65), Froissart (as cited, n. 67), and *Traison et mort* (as cited, n. 64).

[69] Thus in 1333 a Gaelic lord 'had the hair of his *cúlán* cut in order to hold English law': quoted in Robin Frame, '"Les Engleys nées en Irlande": The English Political Identity in Medieval Ireland', *Transactions of the Royal Historical Society*, 6th ser., 3 (1993), 83–103 at p. 93. For the theme in general, Robert Bartlett, 'Symbolic Meanings of Hair in the Middle Ages', ibid., 4 (1994), 43–61.

[70] For Wales, see the references in R. R. Davies, 'Buchedd a Moes' (as cited above, n. 59); *The Welsh Law of Women*, ed. D. Jenkins and M. Owen (Cardiff, 1980), and Llinos Smith, 'Fosterage, Adoption and God-parenthood: Ritual and Fictive Kinship in Medieval Wales', *Welsh History Review* 16 (1992–3), 1–36; for Galloway, Walter Daniel, *Life of Ailred*, 45–6, 74; for Gaelic Scotland, W. H. D. Sellar, 'Marriage, Divorce and Concubinage in Gaelic Scotland', *Transactions of the Gaelic Society of Inverness* 51 (1981), 464–95.

ethical wing of English civility. Take the question of the status of illegitimate sons as an example. When the papacy declared in 1222 that there was an objectionable custom in Wales whereby the son of the handmaiden shared the inheritance with the legitimate child,[71] such a view would have found warm endorsement in English circles (where the government showed its intolerant zeal on the issue in a famous ruling in 1236). It is no surprise, therefore, that at the conquest of Wales in 1284 the ban on the rights of inheritance of illegitimate males (as they were regarded by English law) was legislatively endorsed by Edward I. As such, ecclesiastical morality and English civility marched conveniently together hand in hand.

Morals, dress, and physical appearance were immediately recognizable and easily pilloried features of the broad cultural fault-line within the British Isles; but they were, of course, only the external manifestations of even more profound differences in social values, hierarchies, and organization. Even the sources reflect the profundity of the fault-line. In the western British Isles the most important, if often also the most rebarbative, sources were those produced by hereditary learned classes—jurists, poets, remembrancers, physicians, genealogists, and musicians. They are sources with which the modern document-oriented historiographical mind is barely able to engage, just as the medieval English government dismissed their authors as 'rhymers and wasters'. Yet this professional mandarin class was crucial to the cultural coherence and self-perception of the native societies of western Britain and Ireland.[72] That is why obits of poets and remembrancers figure side by side with those of princes in the native annals,[73] and why more than 2,000 officially composed poems survive in Ireland for the period 1200–1650. These men provided and upheld the framework of memory, mythology, and ideology of their societies; they validated and explained its activities. They took a key part in inaugurating its rulers;[74] their poems were—and were meant to be—

[71] *Calendar of Papal Letters*, I, 87 (discussion in J. B. Smith, *Llywelyn ap Gruffudd*, 12–13).

[72] See generally J. Lloyd-Jones, 'The Court Poets of the Welsh Princes', *Proceedings of the British Academy* 34 (1948), 167–97; J. E. Caerwyn Williams, *The Poets of the Welsh Princes* (Cardiff, 1978); idem, 'The Court Poet in Medieval Ireland', *Proceedings of the British Academy* 57 (1971), 85–135; D. S. Thomson, 'Gaelic Learned Orders and Literati in Medieval Scotland', *Scottish Studies* 12 (1968), 57–75; *Beirdd a Thywysogion. Barddoniaeth Llys yng Nghymru, Iwerddon a'r Alban* (Cardiff, 1996); Osborn Bergin, *Irish Bardic Poetry* (as cited above, n. 34); K. Simms, *From Kings to Warlords*, 4–6.

[73] For example, *Brut*, *s.a.* 1158 ('Morgan ab Owain was slain . . . and along with him, Gwrgant ap Rhys, the best poet that was'); *Annals of Tigernach*, *s.a.* 1160, 1166, 1172, 1177 ('the *olav* of Connacht in poetry'); *Annals of Connacht*, *s.a.* 1226, 1301 ('a master of history and tales and poetry, of the computus, and of many other arts'), 1309, 1328 ('the king of music making').

[74] K. Simms, *From Kings to Warlords*, 23 (inauguration of the kings of Connacht); J. W. M. Bannerman, 'The King's Poet and the Inauguration of Alexander III', *Scottish Historical Review* 68 (1989), 120–49.

resounding affirmations of the traditions, norms, and aspirations of a heroic society. The absence of such a powerful hereditary mandarin class—itself drawn from, and overlapping with, the native aristocracy—is one of the distinctive features of the English and Anglicized polities within the British Isles;[75] there its role was performed by an emergent civil service and judiciary. The difference between the elaborate odes of the great Welsh poet, Cynddelw Brydydd Mawr, and the *Dialogue of the Exchequer* by his contemporary, Richard fitz Neal, is a measure of the cultural chasm within the British Isles.

Cynddelw addressed his eulogies and elegies to the warrior leaders of Wales; his English contemporaries, had they been able to penetrate his recondite archaisms, would have been both surprised and appalled. They would have been surprised that he lauded men who, in the words of Henry of Huntingdon, were as ferocious as beasts and 'ignorant of the science of warfare, of experience in battle'.[76] They would have been appalled because these were men who lived by and for war, and for whom the equation of peace and prosperity was the very reverse of the truth. As Walter Map said of the Welsh: 'They are prodigal of life, greedy of liberty, neglectors of peace, warlike and skilled in arms. . . . Their glory is in plunder and theft, and they are so fond of both that it is a reproach to a son that his father should have died without a wound.'[77] This rampant militarism infected the whole of free society; it was the enemy of the arts of peace and economic effort; and it begat parasitic groups of professional or semi-professional warriors who battened on the rest of society through subsidies, levies (the *commorthau* or aids of Welsh parlance), billeting claims, coyne and livery, and sheer plunder. These men—kern, caterans, galloglasses, *juvenes electi*, and (a significant phrase) idlemen, as they were variously called—offended against all the values of chivalry, good order, and peaceful governance on which the ruling classes of English and Anglicized British Isles based their authority. Here was one of the obvious boundary lines of sweet civility.

But it was not only what were seen as organized thuggery and brutal protection rackets which set the western British Isles outside the pale of civility; so also did their code of social values and the character of their social organization. Most societies have well-articulated codes of honour, punishment,

[75] The phrase 'mandarin class' is used by Ó Corráin, 'Nationality and kingship in pre-Norman Ireland', in *Nationality and the Pursuit of Independence*, ed. T. W. Moody, 1–35 at p. 19. For a cautionary note, see T. Charles-Edwards in *Literacy in Medieval Celtic Societies*, ed. H. Pryce, 70–9.

[76] *Historia Anglorum*, 714–15, 726–7, 734–5. Cf. *Song*, ll. 670–4 ('Most of us are well armed . . . while the traitors are quite naked. They wear neither hauberk nor breastplate').

[77] *De Nugis Curialium*, 182–3, 196–7. Cf. the comment of John Clyn on two Irish chiefs: 'viri bellatores versipelles et pacis et pacificorum impugnatores graves' (*The Annals of . . . Friar John Clyn*, 35).

reparation, and dispute settlement; but they are normally, and sometimes very firmly, controlled within a framework of lordship and state authority. That was so in some and in varying measure in the western British Isles; but what struck all observers was how central and very concrete were concepts of honour and gentility (in the sense of pride in descent),[78] and of shame and vengeance in the value systems of these societies, and how much the personal (as opposed to the public), and the reckless, maintenance and pursuit of these values were central preoccupations of their members.[79] The bonds within society, or at least free society, were as various and as variable as in England. They included rituals of dependence and submission; they also included alliances and blood brotherhoods (as can be seen from both the Irish and the Scottish Gaelic evidence).[80] The centrality, and indeed sanctity, of such bonds explains the sense of moral outrage in native Celtic societies when English settlers ignored the obligations arising from them.[81]

But perhaps the central feature of the societies of the west was the degree to which they were kin-centred, whether it be in male agnatic lineages with their own clan captain—the *pencenedl* of Welsh sources and 'the captain of his nation' in the terminology of English Ireland—or in ego-centred groups of kinsmen. It was in respect of kin-membership that land, mills, churches, and communal easements were inherited and divided, tributes and renders assessed and collected, and warranties of acts and the prosecution of criminals arranged.[82] It was a world whose whole social organization, including the

[78] Gerald's remark (*Expugnatio Hibernica*, 239) that the Irish had 'an inordinate desire to be treated honourably' is echoed in Edmund Spenser's comment (*A View*, 145): 'All the Irish almost boast themselves to be gentlemen, no less than Welshmen.'

[79] See, for example, *Annals of Tigernach*, *s.a.* 1162 (vengeance for dishonour); 1168 (honour price of 700 cows for killing a king). For Wales, see R. R. Davies, 'The Survival of the Blood Feud in Medieval Wales', *History* 54 (1969), 338–57; for Scotland, J. Wormald, 'Bloodfeud, Kindred and Government in Early Medieval Scotland', *Past and Present* 87 (1980), 54–97; and in general T. M. Charles-Edwards, 'Honour and Status in some Irish Prose Tales', *Eriù* 29 (1978), 123–41.

[80] For a description of entry into blood-brotherhood in Galloway, M. Paris, *Chronica Majora*, III, 365. In an agreement between John, Lord of the Isles, and John of Lorn in 1354, both parties agreed to treat each other as 'carnales fratres et compatres': *Acts of the Lords of the Isles 1336–1493*, ed. J. and R. W. Munro (Scottish History Society, 1986), 5–7. For later medieval Irish political structures and relationships in general, see the outstanding study by Katharine Simms, *From Kings to Warlords*.

[81] Note, for example, the outrage at the treachery of the English to those who 'had made gossipry and mixed their blood in one vessel and bound themselves to each other upon the relics of Munster and bells and croziers': *Annals of Connacht*, *s.a.* 1272.

[82] See generally, and more particularly for the early medieval period, T. M. Charles-Edwards, *Early Irish and Welsh Kinship* (Oxford, 1993). One might note the resounding declaration of an Irish law tract: 'Every agricultural partnership, every rent, every sale, every purchase, every exchange, every contract . . . every service is more properly done with a kinsman who is lawful according to the nearness of relationship': quoted in R. C. Stacey, *The Road to Judgment. From Custom to Court in Medieval Ireland and Wales* (Philadelphia, 1994), 56. I hope to return to consider the late medieval evidence for the issues raised here on another occasion.

distribution of wealth and power and the maintenance of social peace, was founded on principles quite different from those of most of England and the Anglicized British Isles, albeit that they were principles which had once been known and practised there. The culture shock experienced on entering such a world registers itself regularly in the documentation: we can see it, for example, in the puzzled marginal entry scrawled on Edward I's report on Welsh laws, *Quid est lex galanas* (blood-feud compensation), or in Archbishop Pecham's outrage at the practice.[83] We can see it equally in the way that the English government had to accept that responsibilities which in England would be discharged by tithings, juries of presentment, and the process of hue and cry had to be placed on kindred groups and their leaders in the western British Isles.[84]

It was ultimately in the sphere of life covered by the catch-all phrase 'law and order' that the political and cultural fault-line within the British Isles was seen at its most unbridgeable. It was not merely or even mainly a matter of procedures, institutions, and jurisprudential principles, even though these were hardening by the generation with the definition and elaboration of the common laws of England and Scotland. Rather was it a matter of attitudes and even psychology. The explanation of the chronic disorder of the western British Isles was seen as a profound character fault;[85] it arose out of the pathological unreliability and inconstancy of the peoples, summed up in the recurrent phrases 'levity', 'lightheadedness', *levitas cervicosa*, 'fickleness', 'excitability'.[86] The consequence was diagnosed as being the same in Galloway

[83] 'Calendar of Welsh Rolls', *Calendar of Chancery Rolls Various 1277–1326*, 199n.; *Register of John Pecham*, I, 135–7.

[84] For the recognition of this practice in Wales, see, for example, *Calendar of Ancient Correspondence concerning Wales*, 234; *The Record of Caernarvon*, 131. For the practice in Ireland, H. G. Richardson and G. O. Sayles, *The Irish Parliament in the Middle Ages* (Philadelphia, 1952), 292; *Chartularies of St Mary's Abbey Dublin*, II, 369. The legal liability of chiefs for the actions of their blood relatives (*cin comfhocuis*) was a central feature of Gaelic legal practice: G. MacNiocaill, 'The Interaction of Laws', in *The English in Medieval Ireland*, ed. J. Lydon (Dublin, 1984), 105–17 at p. 110. It was given legislative blessing by the English authorities in 1351: Berry, *Statutes*, 378–9.

[85] As in the comment of Walter Map (*De Nugis Curialium*, 146–76): 'So strong and as it were innate is the absence of civility to the Welsh, that if in one respect they appear kindly (*modesti*), in most things they show themselves ill-tempered and uncouth (*discoli et silvestres*).'

[86] Examples are legion, e.g. *Gesta Stephani*, 14 (fide semper et locis instabilium); Walter Map, *De Nugis Curialium*, 182–3 (cum omnino sint infideles ad omnes tam adinvicem quam ad alios); Gerald of Wales, *Expugnatio Hibernica*, 134–5, 248–9 on the Irish (gens sola constans inconstancia, sola instabilitate stabilis, sola infidelitate fidelis; gens nec levis minus animo quam corpore); cf. Description of Wales, book II, ch. 9 (*Opera* VI, 23). The Irish legislation of 1297 speaks of the Irish as being 'easily excited (*leves*)' and 'immediately rushing to war' (Berry, *Statutes*, 204–5), and the king's council referred to 'the fickleness of an unconquered people (*indomiti populi levitate*)' (Robin Frame, 'Thomas Rokeby, Sheriff of Yorkshire, Justiciar of Ireland', *Peritia* 10 (1996), 274–96 at p. 284). For the phrase *levitas cervicosa* as applied to the Welsh, E. A. Lewis, 'Historical Documents re Carmarthen Castle', in *West Wales Historical Records*, II (1913–14) at p. 55.

as in Ireland, and among monks as well as laymen: 'unruliness and civil disorder', 'ignorance of law and discipline', or the absence (as Stephen of Lexington said of Cistercian monks in Ireland) of 'a well-ordered mind' and 'ordered habits'.[87] It was little wonder that land transactions in Shropshire could be warranted against everyone except Welshmen; they, like acts of God, were beyond any insurance policy.[88] If sweet civility of the English variety was to make headway in such a benighted world it would ultimately do so only by instilling the values and practice of law, order, and obedience, as these concepts were understood and interpreted by English and Anglicized observers. So it was that the author of the *Gesta Stephani* commented on how 'the Normans imposed law and statutes on the Welsh', that Gerald hailed Hugh de Lacy's greatest achievement as that of 'compelling the Irish to obey and observe laws', and that the supreme accolade given to David I of Scotland was the comment that he had weaned the Scots from 'their natural fierceness and submitted their necks to the laws which royal gentleness dictated'.[89] Law and order, preferably English law and order, always marched hand in hand with civility. Until the victory of the one was assured, the other could not prevail; until both were securely ensconced, the peoples of the western British Isles could not be fully admitted into the political and social world of Englishness. That is why Sir Thomas Smith in the sixteenth century advocated a programme 'to teach [the Irish] English laws and civility', and equally why Sir William Gerrard, writing in 1577, concluded that it was through Henry VIII's dispatch of itinerant justices that 'Wales was brought to know civility.'[90]

The contrast which has been presented here between the economic, social, and cultural zones of the British Isles in the medieval period is, of its very nature, a very simplified intellectual construct; so likewise is the image of the 'barbarous rudeness' (as Edmund Spenser called it) of the societies of the west. In reality and in detail both contrast and image would have to be qualified in many directions. The applicability of the image varied hugely, in part or in whole, both in time and in place across the fragmented and highly individual

[87] *Liber . . . de Melros* (as cited above, n. 8), no. 195; William of Newburgh, *Chronicles of the Reign of Stephen, etc.*, 165–6; Stephen of Lexington, *Letters from Ireland 1228–9*, ed. O'Dwyer, 58, 65.

[88] R. W. Eyton, *Antiquities of Shropshire* (1853–60), X, 367. Alternatively a gift might be warranted 'especially against Welshmen': *Cartae et alia munimenta . . . de Glamorgancia* . . . ed. G. T. Clark (2nd edn., Cardiff, 1910), III, no. 380, IV, no. 814.

[89] *Gesta Stephani*, 14–15; *Expugnatio Hibernica*, 190–1; Anderson, *Scottish Annals*, 232–3.

[90] Quoted in C. Brady, *The Chief Governors*, 253; 'Lord Chancellor Gerrard's Notes' (as cited above, n. 12), *Analecta Hibernica* 2 (1931), 124.

societies of the western British Isles. This is a point that cannot be emphasized too much. Furthermore those societies, it is now recognized, also underwent far-reaching changes within the time-frame covered by this book: the Wales of Llywelyn ap Gruffudd (d.1282) was as different from the Wales of Gruffudd ap Cynan (d.1137) as is the England of Edward I from the realm ruled by Henry I; likewise, recent scholarship has begun to reveal the profound social and political changes that were afoot in Gaelic Ireland and the Lordship of the Isles in the later Middle Ages. Too often these societies have been pickled in a historiographical aspic created from the intensively conservative, even archaic, sources available to the historian—notably the annals, a large corpus of poetry, and perhaps above all an exceptional corpus of legal texts, all of which to a greater or lesser degree convey an image and façade of unchangeability. Furthermore, between the two broad cultural zones (of 'sweet civility' and 'barbarous rudeness'), there were both large and indeed growing regions of cultural overlap (districts such as Galloway, Powys, and the Ormond lordship immediately spring to mind) and even beyond those frontier regions an inevitable process of acculturation, contact, and invitation. When we learn, for example, of the recently discovered hoards of English coins in the Welsh proto-town of Llanfaes in Anglesey, or of the conferral of knighthood and the earldom of Ross on Farquhar Maccintsacairt after he had brought the heads of rebels in Moray to the king of Scots in 1215, or of how in September of the same year Cathal Crobderg O Connor of Connacht (whose table manners had doubtless been refined by spending Christmas in the English justiciar's house in Dublin) agreed to hold his land on English terms and was endowed with sake and soke as if he were an English baron, we recognize that these cultural zones were fully permeable frontier lands of acculturation as much as of confrontation.[91] Finally, and most important of all, the borderline between these broad culture zones changed dramatically between the eleventh and the fourteenth centuries. In many respects the zone of 'sweet civility' barely extended east of Offa's Dyke or north of the River Ribble in 1093; by 1170 it could be said to embrace the north of England and much of southern and eastern Scotland, and to extend sinuously along the major river valleys and coastal plains of south Wales; by a century later it extended in a broad swathe from the Dornoch Firth to the Shannon, taking in a more or less urbanized,

[91] Llanfaes: Edward Besley, 'Short Cross and Other Medieval Coins from Llanfaes, Anglesey', *British Numismatic Journal* 65 (1996), 46–82; earldom of Ross: Chronicle of Melrose in Anderson, *Early Sources*, 404 (cf. R. A. McDonald, *The Kingdom of the Isles*, 82); O'Connor: *Rotuli Chartarum 1199–1216* (1837), 219; for discussion, James Lydon, 'Lordship and Crown: Llywelyn of Wales and O'Connor of Connacht', in *The British Isles 1100–1500*, ed. R. R. Davies, 48–63; for O'Connor's Christmas sojourn with the justiciar, see *Annals of Clonmacnoise*, ed. D. Murphy (Dublin, 1896), 225.

monetized, manorialized, and seignorialized society whose similarities and bonds were ultimately more important than their differences. One of the bonuses of studying the British Isles as a whole, alongside the study of its individual countries and polities, is that it should help us to grasp and characterize the scale and nature of the economic and social changes they experienced across these centuries.

Any division of the medieval British Isles into two broad zones of 'sweet civility' and 'barbarous rudeness' needs, therefore, to be hugely qualified; but the significance of the division surely remains and remains important. It is important because it was itself a contemporary image, a mental package ranging from the crude and abusive to the well-articulated and complex which men at all levels—from government officials to local settlers—deployed to make sense of their world, to bolster their privileges, and to confirm their prejudices. It was also a satisfyingly unchanging image: writing in 1577, for example, Sir William Gerrard held that the Irish of his day 'lived as the Irish lived in all respects before the conquest', some 400 years earlier.[92] Such images became imprisoning categories, and it was in the light of those categories that the ethnic line of separation between the 'pure Welsh' or the 'wild Irish' on the one hand and the English on the other was drawn with increasingly intolerant definition from the thirteenth century onwards, be it in official legislation (such as the legislation of the 1297 parliament or the Statutes of Kilkenny of 1366 in Ireland) or in curial practice.[93] Nor was such ethnic definition merely the mental construct of over-zealous English administrators (though it was certainly that); it was also a recognition that on the frontier lands of the cultural fault-line of the British Isles, English settlers often became the prisoners of the social customs and cultural habits of native society. In much of English Ireland, for example, it had to be conceded that English settlers had frequently deserted the norms of English law in favour of practices such as the taking of preys by way of distraint, concluding redemption fines for homicide, and holding parleys with their enemies *ad modum hibernicorum* (as it was said).[94] In such borderland cultural zones—in northern England and Scotland as much as in Wales or Ireland—the appearance of extended lineages or surnames, as they were called, often bearing sound English names such as Barry, Bermingham,

[92] 'Lord Chancellor Gerrard's Notes', *Analecta Hibernica* 2 (1931), 95.

[93] See generally for Ireland: *NHI*, II, 240–3, 268–74, 306–13, 386–96; Robin Frame, *Colonial Ireland 1169–1369* (Dublin, 1981), 105–10, 130–5; S. Duffy, 'The Problem of Degeneracy', in *Law and Disorder in Thirteenth-Century Ireland*, ed. J. Lydon, 87–107; for Wales, R. R. Davies, 'Race Relations in Post-Conquest Wales: Confrontation and Compromise', *Transactions of the Honourable Society of Cymmrodorion* (1974–5), 32–56; idem, *Lordship and Society in the March of Wales 1284–1400*, ch. 14; idem, *Domination and Conquest*, 116–20.

[94] The letter from Edward III printed in *Historical Manuscripts Commission. Tenth Report*. Appendix, Part V, 260–3; *Calendar of Ormond Deeds*, I, 328. Cf. the comments of K. Nicholls in *NHI*, II, 421–3.

Le Poer, or Archbold, was further confirmation that power structures and social networks took on the colour of their local landscape.[95] Even English officials had no alternative—however distasteful and alien they might find the experience—but to be party to such developments.[96] Or, to take an individual local example, no one who lived at Kilkenny in the fourteenth century could have been in doubt that they lived astride a profound cultural fault-line. The town, with its imposing cathedral of St Canice, was in many respects an epitome of Englishness; its citizens could still be addressed in the fourteenth century by their bishop in both English and French. But the annals compiled in the local Franciscan friary by John Clyn open a window into a very different world—one of 'nations', surnames, kerns, hostages, plunder, war, and a fiercely protected division between Irish and English.[97]

The essential appropriateness of the notion of a cultural fault-line within the British Isles is also vouched for in the scale of the transformation of those societies which moved from one zone to the other within the time-frame of this book, that is, 1093 to 1343—notably northern England, southern and eastern Scotland, lowland south Wales, and southern and eastern Ireland. In none of these areas in 1093, with the possible exception of the Viking towns of Ireland and of proto-urban settlements around major monastic and royal centres, was there any clear sign of truly burghal life. By the end of the twelfth century one might count some forty or fifty boroughs or markets in northern England and forty new burghs (most of them royal foundations) in Scotland; by 1300 one could on a generous definition count some 225 towns (many of them admittedly very small) in Ireland and some 85 in Wales.[98] The same pattern applies broadly to mints and to monetization. In 1093 no coins were struck in

[95] See, for example, *The Red Book of the Earls of Kildare*, ed. G. Mac Niocaill (Dublin, 1964), nos. 45 (Cogans), 152 (Berminghams), 167 (Kildares). For a recent study, see C. Parker, 'Paterfamilias and Parentela: The Le Poer Lineage in Fourteenth-century Waterford', *Proceedings of the Royal Irish Academy* 95 (1995), C, 93–117. For general comments on lineage, *NHI*, II, 297–300; R. Frame, *English Lordship*, 27–38.

[96] In 1350 the justiciar presided at the election of 'English' clan chiefs in Wicklow: E. Curtis, 'The Clan System among English Settlers in Ireland', *English Historical Review* 25 (1910), 116–20.

[97] For the town: *Liber primus Kilkenniensis*, ed. C. MacNeill (Dublin, 1931); for the church: *'A Worthy Foundation': The Cathedral Church of St. Canice, Kilkenny 1285–1985*, ed. C. A. Empey (Mountrath, 1985); for John Clyn: *Chronicle* as cited above, n. 44; for Bishop Ledred's address in English and French: *Proceedings against Alice Kyteler . . . 1324*, ed. T. Wright (Camden Society, 1843), 15.

[98] North of England: Richard Britnell, 'Boroughs, Markets and Trade in Northern England, 1000–1216', in *Progress and Problems in Medieval England*, ed. R. Britnell and J. Hatcher (Cambridge, 1996), 46–67; Scotland: G. W. S. Barrow, *Kingship and Unity*, ch. 4, esp. p. 87; M. R. Spearman, 'Early Scottish Towns: Their Origins and Economy', in *Power and Politics in Early Medieval Britain and Ireland*, ed. S. T. Driscoll and M. R. Nieke (Edinburgh, 1988), 95–110. Ireland: G. H. Martin, 'Plantation Boroughs in Medieval Ireland (with a Handlist of Boroughs to *c.*1500)', *Historical Studies* 13 (1981), 23–53; *NHI*, II, 232–9; Wales: *The Boroughs of Medieval Wales*, ed. R. A. Griffiths (Cardiff, 1978).

these areas (except in Durham) and there is no evidence that the coins in the hoards in the western British Isles were part of a local money economy. By the thirteenth century coins were minted in sixteen centres in Scotland (including western burghs such as Glasgow, Ayr, and Dumfries) and, albeit very intermittently, at up to six centres in Ireland. There was an astonishing growth in the money supply in Scotland in the thirteenth century, so much so that Nicholas Mayhew can speak of it as 'a widely monetized society'. Moreover, there was a remarkable degree of homogeneity and interchangeability about the coins which circulated throughout the lowland British Isles: the zone of 'sweet civility' and a common coinage coincided.[99]

The same transformation with its far-reaching social and political repercussions can be traced in many other directions; it is particularly vivid in southern and eastern Ireland between 1170 and 1220.[100] It is to be seen—and is well documented—in the establishment of manors and common fields, the building of mills, bridges, fords, salt-pans, and lime-kilns, the assarting of waste land and disafforestation, the market-oriented, large-scale, demesne production both of cereals and of sheep, and a more dynamic and exploitative lordship. It is as evident around the new borough of Carlisle as in the lordship of Garioch in north-east Scotland, in the earl of Gloucester's estates in Glamorgan as in the great demesne enterprises of the Marshals and the Lacies in Ireland.[101] What binds it together ultimately is a mind-set: that of an entrepreneurial, exploitative, and profit-making aristocracy. It was not without reason that Gerald of Wales identified *lucrum* (profit) and *cupiditas* (acquisitiveness) as the distinguishing hallmarks of these men and their followers.[102] We get an echo of the same entrepreneurial drive in the commission to inquire how Connacht could be turned to the king's profit, how it should be settled and colonized, what and how many towns and castles ought to be

[99] *Coinage in Medieval Scotland (1100–1600)*, ed. D. M. Metcalf (British Archaeological Reports 45, 1977), esp. essays by Michael Metcalf, Ian Stewart, and Nicholas Mayhew; W. W. Scott, 'The Use of Money in Scotland, 1124–1230', *Scottish Historical Reiew* 58 (1979), 105–31; M. Dolley, *Medieval Anglo-Irish Coins* (London and Belfast, 1972); idem in *NHI* II, ch. 29. Cf. below, p. 162.

[100] See *NHI*, II, ch. 15. The evidence for the agricultural and marketing transformation in Ireland 1170–1250 is relatively abundant; but it has occupied a much lower profile in the historiography than has the story of conquest. It is high time that the issue be given more centrality.

[101] Carlisle and the north: W. E. Kapelle, *The Norman Conquest of the North*, 200–6; H. Summerson, *Medieval Carlisle* (as cited above, Ch. 1, n. 6), 19–22; Garioch: K. J. Stringer, *Earl David of Huntingdon*, esp. ch. 4; Glamorgan: Davies, *Lordship and Society*, 86–7, 116–17; Ireland: *NHI*, II, 459–87 (mainly concentrating on the later evidence).

[102] Description of Wales, book 2, ch. 10 (*Opera*, VI, 226; *cupiditas*); Itinerary in Wales, book 1, ch. 11 (*Opera* VI, 83—*lucrum*, of Flemings); *Expugnatio Hibernica*, 165 (nec lucri nec laudis contemptor, of Hugh de Lacy). For the theme of the profiteering and exploitative mentality, see Edmund King, 'Economic Development in the Early Twelfth Century', in *Progress and Problems in Medieval England*, ed. Britnell and Hatcher, 1–23. Cf. William of Newburgh's comment on Hugh de Lacy (*Historians of the Reigns of Stephen, etc.*, I, 239–40): 'so extended his boundaries and prospered and increased in magnitude of wealth and power that he now became formidable'.

constructed and where, and what demesne should be retained.[103] How far this transformation was shaped and triggered by rising populations, yields, and expectations within native societies and how far by the impetus of the Anglo-Norman diaspora and its habits may be a moot point; but the scale of the transformation is not to be doubted, in spite of the fact that it has not won the historical headlines it deserves. When Ailred of Rievaulx commented that Scotland was 'no longer a beggar from other countries . . . [but is now] adorned with castles and cities and her ports filled with foreign merchandise', he is only sharing in florid language the same sentiment as a modern historian who claims that Ireland in the century or so after 1170 underwent 'a radical social and economic revolution'.[104]

We can take the argument one step further. Just as it is now increasingly recognized that much of southern and midland England was transformed between the mid-ninth and mid-twelfth centuries, and much of the template of its social, economic, and political power for the rest of the Middle Ages established in that period, so the period between 1093 and 1343 witnessed an equally far-reaching transformation in what might be called by way of shorthand the intermediate zone of the English and Anglicized British Isles, the area that lay between and astride the region of 'sweet civility' on the one hand and that of 'barbarous rudeness' on the other. The variations in development within and between this intermediate zone and the original English heartland were, of course, immense. We might recall, for example, that the number of coins circulating in late thirteenth-century England was possibly five times as much as a century earlier and that, impressive as was the advance made in the use of money in Scotland, the coinage in circulation there in the third quarter of the thirteenth century was still only equivalent to 2 or 3 per cent of the coinage in circulation in England.[105] Yet in spite of these disparities, what is surely even more striking is that the advancing tide of Anglicization—in the very widest sense of that term—within the British Isles had made the chasm between England and the Anglicized zone on the one hand and the zone of 'barbarous rudeness' that lay beyond it on the other even starker, both in material terms and mind-set, in 1343 than in 1093. If, for example, one looks

[103] *Close Rolls 1237–42*, 140–1; cf. ibid., *1242–7*, 480.

[104] Scotland: 'Eulogium Davidis', in *Pinkerton's Lives of the Scottish Saints*, II, 279. (For comment, see I. Blanchard, 'Lothian and Beyond: The Economy of the "English empire" of David I', in *Progress and Problems in Medieval England*, 23–45); Ireland: C. A. Empey, 'County Kilkenny in the Anglo-Norman Period', in *Kilkenny: History and Society*, ed. W. Nolan and K. Whelan (Dublin, 1990), 75–95, at p. 80. See also in general idem, 'Conquest and Settlement: Patterns of Anglo-Norman Settlement in North Munster and South Leinster', *Irish Economic and Social History* 13 (1986), 5–31.

[105] J. L. Bolton, 'Inflation, Economics and Politics in Thirteenth-Century England', in *England in the Thirteenth Century*, ed. P. R. Coss and S. D. Lloyd, IV (1992), 1–15, and the literature cited there.

at two documents produced within a couple of years of 1343, the *terminus ad quem* of this study—the rental of the Englishry and Welshry of Hay on the border with England of 1340 and the detailed division of the Multon inheritance in Ireland of 1341—one cannot but be struck by the continuing economic and social fault-line between these two societies.[106] To talk of 'sweet civility' on the one hand and 'barbarous rudeness' on the other was to overlay the fault-line with a value judgement; but that is not to deny that the fault-line existed. It is replicated, in greater or lesser degree, wherever one looks: be it in the contrast between the demesne manors of the earls of Ulster and the cow-based economy of the O'Neills, or in that between the seignorial demesnes of Lisronagh (Co. Tipperary) or Knocktopher (Co. Kilkenny) and their surrounding Irishries, or in a similar contrast between the new-fangled manors and knights' fees of north-east Wales and the world of food renders, circuit dues, and kin-based obligations revealed in the splendid array of post-Edwardian surveys, of which the most magnificent is the Survey of Denbigh of 1334.[107] Furthermore, this fault-line was to persist in some measure for generations, indeed centuries, to come. It is not the least of the handicaps of our modern assumptions and the overwhelmingly English-adjusted character of so much of the documentation that we have consistently underrated it.

The existence of such a fault-line was bound to have profound political repercussions for the British Isles. The social and economic character of the English and Anglicized parts of these islands—be it in England itself or in Scotland, Wales, or Ireland—existed in intimate symbiosis with their political institutions and procedures. Where the one was lacking, the other could scarcely exist or survive. There was, moreover, a further and sinister dimension to the issue, at least in Wales and Ireland. The economic, social, and cultural fault-line coincided very broadly with an ethnic one and came to be defined in ethnic terms. It looked periodically in the late twelfth and early thirteenth centuries as if the high kingship of the British Isles might evolve into a federative, loose-limbed, composite monarchy. That, after all, had been

[106] Richard Morgan, 'An Extent of the Lordship of Hay', *Brycheiniog* 28 (1995–6), 15–21 (for comment, Davies, *Lordship and Society*, 309–10); *Calendar of the Gormanston Register*, ed. J. Mills and M. J. McEnery (Dublin, 1916), 111–16.

[107] The details of the 1333 inquisitions for Ulster are published by G. H. Orpen in *Journal of the Royal Society of Antiquaries of Ireland* 43 (1913), 30–46, 133–43; 44 (1914), 51–66; 45 (1915), 123–42; 50 (1920), 167–77; 51 (1921), 68–76; for discussion, Orpen, *Ireland under the Normans*, IV, 147–9; Lisronagh: E. Curtis, 'Rental of the Manor of Lisronagh', *Proceedings of the Royal Irish Academy* 43 (1935–7), C, 141–76; Knocktopher: C. A. Empey, 'Medieval Knocktopher: A Study in Manorial Settlement', *Old Kilkenny Review*, new ser., 2 (1979–83), 329–42, 441–52. For north-east Wales, Davies, *Lordship and Society in the March of Wales*, *passim*; *Survey of the Honour of Denbigh 1334*, ed. P. Vinogradoff and F. Morgan (1914); D. H. Owen, 'The Englishry of Denbigh: An English Colony in Medieval Wales', *Transactions of the Honourable Society of Cymmrodorion* (1974–5), 57–76.

the character of the so-called Norman and Angevin empires—composite assemblies of peoples and territories under the presidency of a single and multi-titled ruler. But as the Angevin power contracted mainly into the confines of an English state and its annexes, and as the ideology and institutions of that state became more stridently and defiantly English, so the prospect of the kingship of the English converting itself into the monarchy of the British Isles other than on its own terms largely disappeared.[108] Rather were the ethnic lines *vis-à-vis* the Welsh and especially the Irish drawn more clearly and intolerantly than ever before. When Edward I issued his ordinances in 1295, imposing specified restrictions on Welshmen, and when the Irish parliament two years later proclaimed its statutes against degeneracy in an attempt to prevent Englishmen in Ireland from going native, an ethnic line was formally drawn on the sands of the map of political power in the British Isles.[109] The fault-line of cultures, economies, and societies had thereby become the frontier line of political and legal exclusion.

The only possible route across that frontier line lay not only in military power and political control, but also in the acceptance of the social, economic, and cultural norms of the English state and its Anglicized look-alikes. The programme was explained with admirable clarity in the list of requirements that the Chief Governor of Ireland laid out in 1541 to the Irish chiefs: they were to renounce Gaelic titles; to accept, assist, and obey the courts, writs, and laws of the English government; to do military service; to adopt English customs and language; and to encourage tillage, build houses, and generally reorganize their territories on more English lines. It was an updated and expanded version of the agenda that Archbishop Pecham had laid out for the Welsh in 1284.[110] Its ultimate aim was spelt out with his usual bluntness by Edmund Spenser: 'union of manners and conformity of minds, to bring them to be one people [with the English]'.[111] In order to be worthy to enter the portals of the English state, it was essential to travel the path from 'barbarous rudeness' to 'sweet civility'. Until and unless that happened, the kingship of England could not be translated into the monarchy of the British Isles, nor could the peoples of the north and west be admitted into full membership of an England- and English-centred polity.

[108] Cf. Davies, *Domination and Conquest*, esp. chs. 3 and 6.

[109] For the 1295 ordinances, *Record of Caernarvon* (1831), 131–2, and for discussion of the background, Davies, *Conquest*, 385–6. For the Irish statutes of 1297, see esp. *Law and Disorder in Thirteenth Century Ireland. The Dublin Parliament of 1297*, ed. James Lydon (Dublin, 1997).

[110] For Ireland: Steven G. Ellis, *Tudor Ireland. Crown, Community and the Conflict of Cultures 1470–1603* (1985), 137–8; Pecham: as above, n. 5.

[111] Edmund Spenser, *A View*, 153.

6

THE ANGLICIZATION OF THE BRITISH ISLES

The British Isles, so it has been argued in the earlier chapters of this book, did not constitute an integrated entity in the medieval period, other than in periodic, incomplete, and often short-lived assertions of military supremacy and claims to political hegemony. Rather were they divided—however much the line of division might change over time—by a profound fault-line in political norms and attitudes and in economic assumptions and social behaviour.[1] There could be little prospect of meaningful unity, of a single British Isles at a measure of ease with itself, until and unless this fault-line was substantially eroded or at least tolerantly accepted. But there lay an associated, and arguably even more profound, obstacle on such a path. By 1093, and even more so by 1343, the cultural fault-line was overlaid by profound regnal and ethnic fissures. By the end of the thirteenth century those fissures are plain to see in the historical evidence; they have helped to shape the history of the British Isles ever since.

The most prominent regnal fissure by that date was the existence of two well-defined units, the kingdoms of England and Scotland. This fissure alone, it seemed, now stood in the way of achieving a single political hegemony over Britain and Ireland; nor did it seem by 1300 as if that achievement would be long delayed.[2] The ethnic fissure was more complex and could not be disposed of so readily. It was composed of the peoples who now called themselves, and were known to others as, English, Scots, Welsh, and Irish.[3] These ethnic identities did not coincide entirely or adequately with the regnal structures of the British Isles in at least two important respects. First, such native regnal structures as were known in Ireland and Wales were either small-scale and anaemic (by contemporary English or Scottish standards) or had been disbanded to be replaced by annexes of the English polity. To that extent Irish

[1] See above, Chs. 4–5.

[2] See above, pp. 26–9.

[3] This theme is explored in R. R Davies, 'The Peoples of Britain and Ireland 1100–1400', *Transactions of the Royal Historical Society*, 6th ser., 4 (1994), 1–20; 5 (1995), 1–20; 6 (1996), 1–23; 7 (1997), 1–24.

and Welsh cultural and ethnic identity had to find an outlet other than that provided by unitary native regnal structures. Secondly, the very substantial English settlements in Wales and Ireland were proudly and defiantly English; they were most decidedly English and yet they were not of England.

On the ability—or failure—to address the tensions occasioned by these regnal and ethnic fissures would turn very considerably the future of the British Isles. Central to that outcome were the attitude and response of the kingdom of England and of the English people, both those within and those beyond England. This was bound to be so, since the advancing power and influence of the English have been the dominant theme in the history of the British Isles since the *adventus Saxonum*. The story of that advance has certainly not been without its periods of prolonged quiescence and serious setbacks; but on a long-term view of the history of the British Isles, the general direction of the trajectory has not been in doubt. One period of rapid, indeed apparently overwhelming, English advance is that covered by the chronological limits of this volume, the period between the late eleventh and the early fourteenth centuries.

The story of the advance of English power in the British Isles across these centuries—and specifically beyond the boundaries of the country known since the tenth century as England—has frequently been told. But the scale of the achievement has rarely been fully appreciated. This is so in part because the story has been related fragmentarily as episodes within the histories of England, Scotland, Wales, and Ireland, and as such has been absorbed into, and curtailed by, the framework of four separate historiographies. More seriously, the story of English advance in the British Isles has been recounted mainly in terms of domination and conquest, campaigns and castles, political masterfulness and even, occasionally, moral shabbiness.[4] It is a story that can be told well and with considerable precision as such, not least because it can draw on the unparalleled riches—and thereby the perspective—of English documentation. But it is only half, and by most yardsticks the less important half, of the story of English advance.

The other half is the process of what may be called, by way of shorthand, Anglicization—the penetration of English peoples, institutions, norms, and culture (broadly defined) into the outer, non-English parts of the British Isles. In that process few periods, until the last two centuries, were more significant or profoundly transformative as the centuries which are the subject of the present book. Putting it baldly, the British Isles were altogether a much more

[4] For 'moral shabbiness', Barrow, *Bruce*, 52. The charge is echoed by other historians, e.g. *Welsh Assize Roll 1277–84*, ed. J. Conway Davies, 81 ('double dealing').

England-dominated and English-influenced collection of societies in 1300 than they had been two centuries earlier. Such a bald statement requires some degree of explanatory gloss, even qualification, before we consider very briefly some of the evidence which might be adduced to support it. The first relates to the word 'English'. The historiography of medieval England has lived so much under the shadow of the Norman conquest and of its Norman and Angevin royal dynasties and Norman aristocracy that the concept of Englishness has not been much in evidence in writings on the twelfth and, to a much lesser extent, the thirteenth centuries. A hyphenated 'Anglo-Norman' or 'Anglo-French' is the best that can often be managed. There is, of course, much to be said for such a terminology, not least in emphasizing the international and often specifically French character of many of the social and cultural forces which transformed the British Isles, in common with other parts of Europe, across these centuries. Exclusively, narrowly, or even mainly English they certainly were not. It is not without significance that annalists and scribes in Wales, Ireland, and Scotland, at least in the twelfth century, drew clear distinctions between French, Flemings, and English as invaders of, and/or settlers in, their countries.[5] To that extent they were aware that the movement of peoples which was now so profoundly affecting the character of their societies had its roots in north-western Europe generally, as well as in England more particularly. Nevertheless, in the process of colonization and settlement it was the English who were the numerically dominant and critical group, regardless of the role played by non-English personnel in the leadership, momentum, and documentation of the movement. And this became steadily more obvious with the passage of the decades. In the contemporary Annals of Tigernach and in *The Song of Dermot and the Earl*, for example, it was the English, *Saxanach*, *Engleis*, who were singled out for their group identity in the invasion of Ireland; and it was as 'the conquest of the English' that the settlement came to be remembered.[6] The same was true of Wales and, in terms of settlers, Scotland.[7]

[5] See, for example, *Brut, s.a.* 1158, 1159, 1164, etc.; Lawrie, *Early Scottish Charters*, *passim*; Davies, *Domination and Conquest*, 3, 12–15.

[6] *Annals of Tigernach*, *s.a.* 1167, 1172, 1177, etc: *Song*, ll. 467, 510, 545, 573–4, 609, 1960 ('nos Engleys'). For other early references, see *Calendar of Archbishop Alen's Register, c.1172–1534*, ed. C. McNeill (Dublin, 1950), 28 (1202 'before the English came to Ireland'); *The 'Dignitas Decani' of St Patrick's Cathedral Dublin*, ed. N. B. White (Dublin, 1957), 113; *CDI*, II, no. 503 ('the conquest of the English'). For this whole issue, see John Gillingham, 'The English Invasion of Ireland', in *Representing Ireland 1534–1660*, ed. Brendan Bradshaw et al. (Cambridge, 1993), 24–42.

[7] Wales: Davies, *Conquest*, 99–100; George Owen, *The Description of Penbrokeshire*, I, 36–7. Scotland: Barrow, *Anglo-Norman Era*, 82 ('Their speech [that of the majority of immigrant families] was doubtless English, their experience was limited to England, and they would have regarded themselves as English by race.').

Nor is this emphasis on the dominant Englishness of the movement merely a matter of numbers; it helps to explain the increasingly defiant Englishness of the settler communities in the western parts of the British Isles. During the course of the twelfth century, and at an accelerating pace, the sense of a separate Norman or French identity among the ruling elites of England wilted, to be replaced by a single, undifferentiated English identity. That identity became raucously strident during the thirteenth century. Nor was it confined to England. The settler communities in Wales and Ireland likewise protected, fostered, and promoted their English identity vociferously and defiantly.[8] Thus when Edward III declared in 1357 that 'both the English born in Ireland and those born in England and dwelling in Ireland are true English,' he was reaffirming what the English communities in Ireland, and for that matter in Wales likewise, believed to be self-evidently true.[9] Ultimately the quality, extent, and durability of the English impact on the rest of the British Isles would depend very considerably on these communities rather than on the generals and the politically powerful who have so often captured the historical headlines. Their story badly needs to be told.

Let us therefore start with people. The English diaspora within the British Isles is one of the largely untold stories of the twelfth and thirteenth centuries, fully worthy to be set beside the great colonizing movements east of the River Elbe, into the Spain of the *reconquista* or the Crusader states which figure so prominently in our history books. The chronological framework of the story can be fairly precisely delineated. It opened in the two decades or so on either side of 1100, as two well-recorded episodes may testify. In 1092 William Rufus, anxious to proclaim and underpin his title to the southern Brythonic-speaking region of Cumbria, founded a castle at Carlisle, posted a detachment of knights there, and, in the words of the Anglo-Saxon chronicle, 'sent thither a great multitude of lowly folk with women and cattle to dwell and till the land'. Some twenty years or so later Ceredigion in west Wales witnessed a similar scene but with two noteworthy differences—the mastermind behind the operation there was a great aristocrat, Gilbert fitz Richard of Clare in East Anglia (who, in the words of the native chronicler, had long been pestering Henry I for a portion of Wales) and the colonists (again in the words of the chronicle) 'brought in to fill the land' were specifically identified as English, Saxons.[10] The great movement of colonization and Anglicization petered out almost exactly two centuries later. Once again we may choose two episodes to illustrate this epilogue, both from the frontier lands of the English British

[8] Davies, *Domination and Conquest*, 15.
[9] Berry, *Statutes*, 417.
[10] *Anglo-Saxon Chronicle*, *s.a.* 1092; *Brut*, *s.a.* 1110, 1116 (34, 42).

Isles. In 1276 Thomas de Clare, the virtually landless brother of the earl of Gloucester and a descendant of that conqueror of Ceredigion mentioned above, was granted land in the Irish kingdom of Thomond in the far west of Ireland by Edward I and brought thither what a later vernacular Irish source referred to dismissively as 'common' and 'plebeian' English to colonize the area near his castle of Bunratty.[11] During the next decade the final Edwardian conquest of north Wales opened up similar opportunities nearer home. The far north-west of Wales was too remote and mountainous to attract English colonists except into the safety of the castellated boroughs; but the same was not true of the fertile river valleys of the north-east, notably those of the Clwyd and the Dee.[12] It is from the Lacy lordship of Denbigh—granted by Edward I to the earl of Lincoln in 1282—that we can best gauge, through the great Survey of 1334, how the social and ethnic configuration of an area of the British Isles could be transformed dramatically by a deliberate process of English colonization. The pages of the Survey are full of the place-names of Lancashire and Yorkshire whence the earl of Lincoln recruited his English settlers—Pontefract, Sunderland, Skipton, Blackburn, Clitheroe, Castleford, and so forth; at least 10,000 acres of the best arable land in the valleys of the Clwyd and its tributaries were commandeered for their use and occasionally a whole vill was converted into an exclusively English enclave; Welsh peasants were resettled, often in remote vills, to make way for the English newcomers; and the institutional framework—separate officers, courts, rents, inheritance practices, and so forth—was put in place to secure the continued integrity and apartness of the new English settlement. To borrow a contemporary word from the social terminology of medieval Wales, an Englishry had been established.[13]

The Englishry at Denbigh is remarkably well documented; but it is in fact but one, albeit also one of the last, of the scores of Englishries created throughout the British Isles in the twelfth and thirteenth centuries. They were

[11] *Calendar of Charter Rolls 1257–1300*, 198; *Calendar of Patent Rolls 1272–81*, 135; *Caithréim Thoirdhealbhaigh* (as cited above, ch. 4, n. 41), II, 817. For Thomas de Clare's career, M. Altschul, *A Baronial Family in Medieval England. The Clares 1217–1314* (Baltimore, Md., 1965), 187–95.

[12] For the north-west: E. A. Lewis, *The Medieval Boroughs of Snowdonia* (1912); the north-east: Davies, *Lordship and Society*, 319–52; R. I. Jack, 'Welsh and English in the Medieval Lordship of Ruthin', *Transactions of the Denbighshire Historical Society* 18 (1969), 23–49; A. D. M. Barrell and M. H. Brown, 'A Settler Community in Post-Conquest Rural Wales: The English of Dyffryn Clwyd, 1294–1399', *Welsh History Review* 17 (1995), 332–53; Michael Rogers, 'The Welsh Marcher Lordship of Bromfield and Yale 1282–1485' (University of Wales, unpublished Ph.D. thesis, 1992), ch. 8.

[13] *Survey of the Honour of Denbigh, 1334*, ed. Vinogradoff and Morgan; D. H. Owen, 'The Englishry of Denbigh. An English Colony in Medieval Wales', *Transactions of the Honourable Society of Cymmrodorion* (1974–5), 57–76; Davies, *Lordship and Society*, 338–9, 345–7; idem, 'Colonial Wales', *Past and Present* 65 (1974), 3–23 at p. 10.

crucial ingredients in the process of Anglicization. The motive for the establishment of such English colonies was in good part strategic; they were often the deliberate economic arm of a policy of military power and political control. Such was the case, to a greater or lesser degree, in each of the instances so far cited—at Carlisle and in Ceredigion, in Thomond as in Denbigh. Sometimes the security dimensions of the policy were starkly spelt out by official advisers: one, for example, suggested that the Welsh should be removed to the mountains, and the plains of Glamorgan settled with Englishmen for the greater safety of the lands; another advised that 'the peace will be better assured and security improved' if escheated Welsh lands were assigned to English colonists;[14] a colleague in Ireland likewise indicated that English control could only be assured where it was underwritten by extensive colonization by English settlers, while a petitioner could hope to promote his case by asserting that 'it is useful to the lord king that the English should outnumber the Irish.'[15] A process similar to that of *incastellamento*, so vividly described by Pierre Toubert for the Latium, was afoot in the outer parts of the British Isles, with the key difference that the castle was more often than not the focal point for an *English* borough and an *English* rural settlement, so located (to borrow the words of one Irish charter) that the settlers could be conveniently and safely within reach of the castle.[16]

Castles are the instruments of power and lordship. It was under the aegis of lordship, be it that of the king or of his aristocracy, that the Anglicization of the British Isles was undertaken. It was not so much that these lords saw themselves, at least initially, as the agents of an aggressive ethnic resettlement policy; but rather that in terms of their two overriding concerns—namely security of control and a quick economic return—the introduction of English settlers had much to recommend it. The *locus classicus* of the entrepreneurial attitude of the new lords in this respect is the famous comment of the *Song of Dermot and the Earl* on how Hugh de Lacy, one of the premier Anglo-Norman lords involved in the conquest and exploitation of Ireland, 'set out for Meath with many a renowned vassal in order to plant his land' (*pour sa terre herberger*), very much in the fashion of Albert the Bear or Henry the Lion on the eastern frontier lands of Germany and at much the same time.[17] But it

[14] *Calendar of Chancery Warrants 1244–1326*, 448; *Calendar of Close Rolls 1339–41*, 251.

[15] *Documents on the Affairs of Ireland before the King's Council*, ed. G. O. Sayles (Dublin, 1979), 128, 193; *Documents Illustrative of English History in the Thirteenth and Fourteenth Centuries*, ed. H. Cole (1844), 68–9.

[16] *Register of the Abbey of St Thomas, Dublin*, ed. J. T. Gilbert (R.S., 1889), 214.

[17] *Song*, ll. 2940–3. For discussion of the colonization of Meath, Robert Bartlett, 'Colonial Aristocracies of the High Middle Ages', in *Medieval Frontier Societies*, ed. R. Bartlett and A. Mackay (Oxford, 1989), 23–49. For the entrepreneurship of a Scottish aristocrat, see, for example, Alan Young, *Robert Bruce's Rivals: The Comyns, 1212–1314* (East Linton, 1997), 26.

is from a vernacular Irish source, and that a century or so later, that we can perhaps best catch how castle, colonization, and Englishness were linked in the onward march of English power and presence in the British Isles. Thomas de Clare, so *The Triumphs of Turlogh* tells us, 'built a castle of dressed stone' (itself no doubt an object of wonder) at Bunratty 'girt with a thick outer wall, containing a roofed impregnable donjon and having capacious limewashed appurtenances'. He 'proceeded to inhabit the settlement with so many low-born English . . . as by bribes and purchase he was able to retain, having first expelled the ancient dwellers of the soil of Tradree'.[18] Discounting the ethnic venom and social snobbery of the comment, Thomas de Clare in fact encapsulates the spirit of economic entrepreneurship and social engineering, as well as the large military appetites and political ambition, which characterized so many of the lords of the frontier lands of the British Isles. They were regularly given licences to colonize their newly-won lands, sometimes (as in the case of the bishop of Waterford in 1219) specifically with English settlers.[19] And they were quickly exploiting their new estates to maximum effect: the arrival of a ship-load of a thousand crannocks of wheat in London from the Marshal estates in Ireland in 1224 may be taken to symbolize the profiteering, market-oriented mentality of these new English lords.[20]

They were conscious that they were creating a new, more profitable, and more modern world. It was also an English world, conforming in so far as possible to the paradigm of lordship, exploitation, and power prevalent in England and with a complement of English settlers as the agents and exemplars of a new economic order. Two images from north-east Wales from the morrow of the English conquest of 1282–3 may help to particularize the experience. The first is that of the aggressive and greedy new English lord of Dyffryn Clwyd or Ruthin, Reginald de Grey, *primus et conquestor* as he was remembered, dispatching a land surveyor to measure out his new lordship in advance of its settlement and exploitation.[21] The second, even more vivid,

[18] *Caithréim Thoirdhealbaigh*, II, 7–8. It was common to entice settlers to the boroughs of north Wales with an offer of land—two curtilages and two bovates each at Denbigh, sixty acres at Cricieth (J. Williams, *Records of Denbigh and its Lordship* (Wrexham, 1860), 119–24; E. A. Lewis, *Medieval Boroughs of Snowdonia*, 48).

[19] *Rotuli litterarum clausarum*, ed. T. D. Hardy, I, 394 (bishop of Waterford, 1219; English settlers); *CDI*, no. 120 (Hamo de Valognes, 'ad terram suam hospitandam'); no. 1677 (to colonize and build on their lands); no. 2567 (Rosea de Verdon; 'de terra sua hospitanda').

[20] *CDI*, I, no. 459. The degree to which the crown and English magnates were exploiting the agricultural potential of Ireland is obvious in the earliest surviving Irish pipe roll: *The Irish Pipe Roll of 14 John* (as cited above, Ch. 5, n. 51), 21, 32–5, 38–41, 56–7. For discussion, *NHI*, II, 457–62.

[21] 'primus et conquestor': Public Record Office (PRO) Court Rolls (SC2) 218/4, m.21; 218/8, m.4; 219/2, m.29 (1354–65); his acquisitiveness and greed: *Calendar of Ancient*

is that of Grey's neighbour in north-east Wales, Henry Lacy, earl of Lincoln: in his new, vast lordship of Denbigh not only did he create a brand new manor (with a brand new name) for himself from forfeited and other lands, grant out sizable estates for his followers and servants (including his chamberlain and his cook), establish two studs for his horses, and carve out parks for his pleasure and stock them with deer from Cheshire; but he also declared majestically that the new land measurement to be used in Denbigh was to be a perch of twenty-one feet as gauged by the length of his own foot.[22] The new lords were almost literally stamping their authority on the outer reaches of the British Isles, and the imprint of that authority was, increasingly and self-consciously, an English one.

The input of lords—in military power, capital, political favours, and much else—was, of course, central; but without a critical mass of peasant and burghal settlement not only would the long-term future of seignorial control be very uncertain but—crucial for the present argument—a penetrative and potentially transformative Anglicizing dimension would have been lacking. The English diaspora within the British Isles may have been seignorially led, but it was demographically and economically determined. The prospectus that the poet issued through the mouth of Dermot MacMurrough, king of Leinster, must have been replicated scores of times throughout Britain: 'Whoever shall wish for land or pence / . . . Whoever shall wish for soil or sod / Richly shall I enfeoff them.'[23] The offer was taken up—be it out of desperation, hope, or compulsion—by thousands, such as the men from Lincolnshire who migrated to Carlisle, the followers of Walter fitz Alan who travelled with him from Shropshire and elsewhere in England, and indeed from the continent to his new lands in Lothian and Clydesdale, the men from Cornwall, Wales, Berwick, Glastonbury, Wigmore, and other places far afield who sat on the jury on Thomas de Clare's estates at Youghal and Bunratty in Ireland, or the families from Lancashire, Cheshire, and Shropshire who were enticed by the rich pickings offered to them in the Vale of Clwyd.[24] Many of them

Correspondence concerning Wales, 170–1; *Rotuli Parliamentorum*, III, 70a; PRO Ancient Petitions (SC8) 108, no. 5359 (petition of men of Dyffryn Clwyd about Grey); his land surveyor: PRO SC2/215/69, m.11; 217/9, m.4.

[22] *Survey of Denbigh, 1334*, 1: 'After the conquest of Wales lord Henry de Lacy earl of Lincoln made the manor of Kilforn for himself from forfeited lands in the same township and from unforfeited lands which the earl exchanged with the tenants': Davies, *Lordship and Society*, 70, 109, 119–20, 341–2 (and the references cited there). For the perch measured by Henry de Lacy's foot: *Survey of Denbigh*, 2.

[23] *Song*, ll. 431–6.

[24] Carlisle: Summerson, *Medieval Carlisle*, I, 17; followers of Walter fitz Alan: Barrow, *Anglo-Norman Era*, 64–7; Youghal and Bunratty: *CDI*, III, no. 459; Dyffryn Clwyd: Barrell and Brown (as above, n. 12) in *Welsh History Review* 17 (1995), esp. pp. 334–8.

doubtless came in family or neighbourhood groups[25]—as did the four members of the Bloet family who witnessed one of Strongbow's charters 'in Ireland at Waterford', or the three le Gras brothers who hitched their wagon to William Marshal's star, or the Feypo clan from Herefordshire.[26] The Bloets, the Feypos, and the le Gras brothers belonged to the higher, though not the highest, echelons of migrant settlers into Ireland; the great mass of the lesser colonists left few traces in the skimpy records. But those occasional traces do hint at the scale of the movement we are trying to capture—such as the 120 or so colonists, most of them very small-scale farmers, who took over the vill of Lleweni in the Vale of Clwyd, or the 191 English names recorded in Cloncurry in County Kildare in 1304, or the 59 English names, out of a total of 62, which constituted the population of the tiny Tipperary borough of Moyaliff in the next year.[27]

And so the individual examples could be, and have been, multiplied. Given the nature of the evidence, such examples can only be the basis of broad impressions rather than of irrefutable statistical argument. But with that caveat in mind, what can we say about the geography and scale of this English, or largely English, diaspora of the twelfth and thirteenth centuries? Take Scotland. We start with a paradox. What we know as south-east Scotland was already very considerably an Anglian, if not an English, district which had fallen recently into the orbit of the aggressive kings of Scots: it was, in the suggestive phrase of Adam of Dryburgh of *c.*1180, the land of the English in the kingdom of the Scots.[28] There is also evidence that from at least the tenth century Anglian settlers were moving in force into Galloway.[29] In other words, the English element in the make-up of the peoples of the country which we have come to know as Scotland was very considerable at the beginning of the period under discussion here, as the multiple greeting clauses of

[25] Cf. S. Reynolds, *Kingdoms and Communities in Western Europe 900–1300* (2nd edn., 1997), 127: 'Many of the settlers . . . came in fairly homogeneous groups.'

[26] Bloet: *Historical Collections of Staffordshire*, new ser., 5 (1902), 212; D. Crouch, *William Marshal* (1990), 139–40, 198–9; le Gras: 'Charters of Abbey of Duiske', ed. J. H. Bernard and M. C. Butler, *Proceedings of the Royal Irish Academy* 35 (1918–20), 1–189 at pp. 16–17 (cf. pp. 62–3 for Somery family); Feypo: *The Irish Cartularies of Llanthony Prima et Secunda*, ed. E. St John Brooks (Dublin, 1953), 94, 98; R. Bartlett, 'Colonial Aristocracies' (as cited above, n. 17) at pp. 37–9.

[27] Lleweni, *Survey of Denbigh 1334*, 62–80; Cloncurry: A. J. Otway-Ruthven, *Medieval Ireland*, 114; Moyaliff: idem in *Historical Studies* 5 (as cited above, n. 24), 81–2.

[28] Quoted from *Patrologia Cursus Completus, Series Latina*, ed. J. P. Migne, vol. 198, p. 723 in Stringer, 'Reform Monasticism and Celtic Scotland' (see below, n. 84).

[29] Daphne Brook, 'The Northumbrian Settlements in Galloway and Carrick: An Historical Assessment', *Proceedings of the Society of Antiquaries of Scotland* 121 (1991), 295–327; idem, 'Gall-Gaidhil and Galloway', in *Galloway. Land and Lordship*, ed. R. D. Oram and G. P. Stell (Edinburgh, 1991), 97–116. Cf. the comments of W. F. Nicolaisen, *Scottish Place Names: Their Study and Significance* (1976), 111–12.

the earliest Scottish royal writs—addressed as they are to French, English, and Scots—make clear enough.[30] This makes it more difficult to trace, and estimate the dimensions of, English migration into Scotland after 1100; but that it was considerable and transformative hardly admits of doubt.[31] Well-informed contemporaries noted that the burghs of Scotland were inhabited by Englishmen and how vulnerable those English burgesses were when the political atmosphere in Scotland turned sour; likewise, in the native uprising in Galloway in 1174, it was the English and French settlers who were the targets of the wrath of the natives.[32] But the evidence for English colonization is not only to be seen at moments of tension: it is also evident, as Geoffrey Barrow and others have shown, in the English place-names, notably Ingleston (English town), and in the English and English-speaking followers who entered the country from the 1120s in the following of the new Anglo-Norman lords such as Hugh de Morville.[33]

In Wales the tide of English colonization swept along the coastline of the south from Gwent to Pembroke (where the Flemings made their distinctive contribution) and up the river valleys of the Usk and the Wye; along the eastern borderlands it made but a limited impression, nor did it leave much of a mark as yet on the fertile and attractive Severn valley; its final chapter took the form of the intensive colonization of restricted parts of north-east Wales and the establishment of what were conceived as exclusively English urban bridgeheads, with attendant grants of good agricultural land, in north-west and west Wales.[34] The pattern of English colonization was broadly similar in Ireland, but there it did not get under way until the 1170s—when it had already lost much of its momentum in southern Wales—and was largely completed in the next century or so. Speaking broadly, the great impact of the colonization movement was to be seen in the south and east of Ireland, along the coastal plains of Ulster, Meath, and Leinster and even further west to Cork and Limerick, but also well inland up the river valleys into counties Tipperary,

[30] See, for example, Lawrie, *Early Scottish Charters*, nos. 18–22, 35, 54, 65, 72.

[31] Cf. the comments of A. A. M. Duncan in *Why Scottish History Matters*, ed. Rosalind Mitchison (Saltire Society, 1991), 10: 'French influence was brief and probably confined to the most aristocratic of these families. Their dependants . . . were . . . English-speaking and imbued with Romance culture as transmitted into English.'

[32] Anderson, *Scottish Annals*, 255–6.

[33] G. W. S. Barrow, *The Anglo-Norman Era*, 30–5, 74, 82; idem, 'The Anglo-Scottish Border: Growth and Structure in the Middle Ages', *Grenzen und Grenzregionen* (Saarbrücken, 1994), 197–212 (map of Inglestone names p. 212); Duncan, *Scotland*, 436. There was also no doubt much internal migration and colonization: cf. G. W. S. Barrow, 'Popular Courts in Early Medieval Scotland: Some Suggested Place-Name Evidence', *Scottish Studies* 25 (1981), 1–24 at p. 3.

[34] Davies, *Lordship and Society*, 303–6, 319–49; idem, *Conquest*, 97–100, 370–3.

Limerick, and Carlow.[35] Elsewhere—notably in the Wicklow mountains, or in the great boglands of Leix and Offaly, let alone in whole vast areas of the north and west—such settlement as there was was light and often short-lived, though the recent tendency of Irish scholarship has been to emphasize how geographically ambitious was the first phase of English settlement and how it found a new outlet for its enterprise in the north and the west of the island in the second half of the thirteenth century.[36]

What, therefore, was the impact of this English diaspora—with sub-themes of Flemish immigration and also quite extensive Welsh migration to Ireland[37] —on the ethnic map of the British Isles and on the process of Anglicization? The chief feature of such a map (one of the major desiderata of the medieval history of these islands) would be how limited were the strips and isolated pockets of substantial English settlement—generally along the coastal lowlands, up some of the major river valleys and below the 600-foot contour line. Much of the map of the northern and western British Isles would be unaffected in terms of substantial settlements. Even in areas of relatively dense colonization, English settlements seemed often in danger of being overwhelmed by the indigenous population around them. Thus in Ulster and Louth few of the English manors were more than ten miles from the sea; in the barony of Knocktopher in southern Kilkennny, though 90 per cent of the free tenants around Knocktopher itself were of English stock, the majority of the population of the district was undoubtedly Irish.[38] And it should be recalled that the period of intensive colonization of a given district was relatively short:

[35] See in general Otway-Ruthven, 'The Character of Norman Settlement in Ireland' (as cited above, n. 24); the various studies of C. A. Empey (as cited above, Ch. 4, n. 57); *NHI*, II, 221–5.

[36] K. W. Nicholls, 'Anglo-French Ireland and After', *Peritia* 1 (1982), 370–403 at pp. 372–3. For the castle, manor, and town of Ballylahan in county Mayo, founded by Jordan of Exeter in the mid-thirteenth century (and the Dominican friary in nearby Slade), Orpen, *Ireland under the Normans*, III, 197–8.

[37] For Flemish migration to Wales: Lauran Toorians, 'Wizo Flandrensis and the Flemish Settlement in Pembrokeshire', *Cambridge Medieval Celtic Studies* 20 (1990), 99–118; to Scotland: Barrow, *Anglo-Norman Era*, 44–6, 57; L. Toorians, 'Twelfth-Century Flemish Settlements in Scotland', in *Scotland and the Low Countries 1124–1884*, ed. G. G. Simpson (East Linton, 1996), 1–14; to Ireland, *NHI*, II, 444. Welsh settlers in Ireland are commonly greeted in early charters or referred to individually, e.g. *Register of St Thomas Dublin*, 214–15; *Chartularies of St Mary's Dublin*, I, no. 54; *CDI*, I, nos. 673, 1059, 1198, 2487, etc.; *Red Book of Ormond*, ed. N. B. White (Dublin, 1932), nos. 2, 5, 73; *Red Book of the Earls of Kildare*, ed. G. MacNiocaill (Dublin, 1964), no. 183; *Calendar of Justiciary Rolls, Ireland, 1305–7*, 104–5, 135. Stephen of Lexington during his visitation of 1228 was concerned that Welsh was spoken at the Cistercian abbey of Tracton, a daughter-house of Whitland, *Letters from Ireland, 1228–9*, ed. B. W. O'Dyer, no. 98.

[38] Ulster: T. E. McNeill, *Anglo-Norman Ulster*, 33–6; Louth: Brendan Smith, 'A County Community in Early Fourteenth-Century Ireland: The Case of Louth', *English Historical Review* 108 (1993), 561–88; idem, *Colonisation and Conquest in Medieval Ireland. The English in Louth 1170–1330*, esp. ch. 2; Knocktopher: C. A. Empey, 'Medieval Knocktopher: A Study in Manorial Settlement', *Old Kilkenny Review*, new ser., 2 (1979–83), 329–42, 441–52.

some thirty years or so at most in Uriel at the turn of the twelfth century, and a like period in the lowlands of Denbigh a century later.

We must, therefore, assuredly not exaggerate; but, given the assumptions of the historiographies of the British Isles, the greater danger is to underestimate. First, the size of the colonizing impact needs to be gauged in relation to the size of the existing population. That, of course, is to pose an impossible question; but it would not be too wild a guess to conjecture that native populations and land usage in both Wales and Ireland were low. Even the Welsh chronicle conceded that when the English settled in west Wales in the early twelfth century they found a 'land which was before that, as it were, empty'.[39] Secondly, the English and associated settlements were so substantial within their respective regions that they could and did transform utterly the ethnic complexion of those particular districts. That was, for example, self-evidently true of southern Gower, the area to be appropriately known in future as the English county of Gower, *pars Anglicorum* or *Gower Anglicana*, as it was called, and of southern Pembroke where the Flemings, fully Anglicized by the early thirteenth century, 'occupied the whole cantref of Rhos . . . and drove away all the inhabitants from the land', as the Welsh chronicle has it. In both districts there is evidence of major immigration across the sea from south-west England.[40] The same was doubtless true of parts of Ireland, such as around Ross or Waterford, where the 'social and economic structure of the region was transformed'.[41] Indeed, it is an Irish historian who has been brave, or foolhardy, enough to estimate the size of one of these English colonies: Adrian Empey suggests that 2,000 to 4,000 people might have composed the colonial settlement in the Kilkenny district of Gowran.[42] In other words, these communities were too substantial and too entrenched to be overwhelmed.

They were also self-consciously and durably English; in terms of Anglicization, that was crucial. They left their mark deeply on their host countries. It has been calculated, for example, that 8,800 of Ireland's total of 62,000

[39] *Brut*, *s.a.* 1116 (p. 42). For low population density in medieval Ireland, *NHI*, II, 212–13 (Glassock), 408–10 (Nicholls).

[40] *Pars Anglicorum*: *Annales Cambrie*, ed. J. Williams ab Ithel (R.S., 1860), *s.a.* 1257; Pembroke: *Brut*, *s.a.*, 1108; I. W. Rowlands, 'The Making of the March. Aspects of the Norman Settlement of Dyfed', *Proceedings of the Battle Conference of Anglo-Norman Studies*, 3 (1981), 142–57. The English dialect of south Pembrokeshire belongs to the south-western group of English dialects: B. G. Charles, *The English Dialect of South Pembrokeshire* (Pembrokeshire Record Society, 1982).

[41] C. A. Empey, 'County Waterford 1200–1300', in *Waterford. History and Society*, ed. W. Nolan, ch. 6. For some documentary support for these claims, see, for Waterford, *CDI*, II, no. 1912 (p. 425); IV, no. 551 (pp. 259–63), and, for Ross, *Chartularies of St Mary's Dublin*, II, 154–7.

[42] C. A. Empey, 'Conquest and Settlement: Patterns of Anglo-Norman Settlement in North Munster and South Leinster', *Irish Economic and Social History* 13 (1986), 5–31 at p. 26.

townland names are English and belong overwhelmingly to the medieval period; in Wales likewise there are some 350 '-ton' names, again from the medieval period by and large, with Glamorgan and Pembrokeshire appropriately claiming two-thirds of them.[43] When the deed and associated evidence begins to become abundant from the end of the twelfth century, it becomes apparent what deep roots these English colonists had put down in their new homes. Field- and furlong-names were often exclusively English; the customary acres of England were imported into south Wales and doubtless into Ireland;[44] and in both countries the colonists created a world—in terms of farming methods, manorial organization, lifestyle, towns, and so forth—in the image of the one they had left. What is more, they built up cultural, political, and economic connections which bound the Anglicized worlds they had founded in Wales and Ireland to England itself.

And those worlds were, and remained, worlds apart. In Scotland, the English colonists and their Anglo-Norman worlds were eventually, though not always initially, absorbed into the social and political fabric of a unitary kingdom. The absorption was clearly well under way by the 1180s, much at the period when the word Scotland as we know it was coming into common usage and also, interestingly, much at the time when Richard fitz Neal commented that it was difficult to distinguish between Normans and English in England.[45] Henceforth all the various ethnic groups in Scotland were brought under a common umbrella: they were the king's *probi homines*, 'responsible men'.[46] It was quite otherwise in Wales and Ireland. There the substantial English communities—for reasons of security, status, privilege, and ethnic pride—sedulously cultivated their distinctive and exclusive Englishness. They had doubtless stood apart from the natives in language and culture from early days. So it was, for example, that as early as 1126 the earl of Gloucester and the bishop of Llandaff distinguished between their Welshmen on the one hand and their Normans and Englishmen on the other in terms of access to fishing and pasture; likewise, when Archbishop Baldwin came to the same area to preach the crusade in 1188 the English lined up on one side, the Welsh on the other.[47] During the course of the next two centuries this ethnic divide was

[43] Townland names: *NHI*, II, 311; 'ton' names in Wales: B. G. Charles, *Non-Celtic Place-Names in Wales* (1938), esp. pp. xxviii–xxx; G. O. Pierce, *The Place Names of Dinas Powys Hundred* (Cardiff, 1968).

[44] B. E. Howells 'The Distribution of Customary Acres in South Wales', *National Library of Wales Journal* 15 (1967–8), 226–33.

[45] G. W. S. Barrow, *Anglo-Norman Era*, 153–5; Richard fitz Nigel, *The Course of the Exchequer*, ed. C. Johnson (rev. edn., Oxford, 1983), 53.

[46] *RRS*, II, 77.

[47] *Earldom of Gloucester Charters . . . to A.D. 1217*, ed. R. B. Patterson (Oxford, 1973), 109; Giraldus Cambrensis, Itinerary through Wales, book 1, ch. 6 (*Opera*, VI, 67).

institutionalized, legalized, and, arguably, intensified in a variety of ways in both countries, be it in the formal division between Welshries and Englishries which is basic to the administrative, legal, and tenurial geography of so much of late medieval Wales or, more menacingly, in the anti-degeneracy legislation (ranging from the initial act of 1297 to the famous Statutes of Kilkenny of 1366) which sought to protect the purity of the English community in Ireland in marriage, name-forms, law, horse-riding habits, haircuts, and much else.[48]

What has been claimed so far is that the ethnic make-up of the British Isles was profoundly changed by the English diaspora of the twelfth and thirteenth centuries. By 1300, therefore, not only could Edward I—as some contemporaries recognized—lay claim to the effective high kingship of the British Isles, the substantial English communities in the outer zones of these islands were also a powerful force for cultural and economic Anglicization, and in Wales and Ireland, though not in Scotland, were seen, and saw themselves, as moving firmly in the orbit of English political, legal, and institutional power and habits. In short, Englishness was not coextensive with what we increasingly nowadays call the English state; it far exceeded it. It was as evident—and arguably more defiant and triumphalist—in Bunratty or Beaumaris, Kilkenny or Kidwelly, as it was in Westminster or York.

So was the English language, that instrument *par excellence* of Anglicization in our own day. A linguistic map of the British Isles in 1300 would surely reveal what major advances the English language had made in the last two centuries. Indeed, by that date the English tidal wave was beginning to ebb. The demand in the Irish parliament in 1366 that 'every Englishman use the English language and be named by an English name' suggested as much.[49] That retreat continued apace and even greatly accelerated across the next two centuries in both Wales and Ireland, as hitherto English-speaking communities became either bilingual or largely Welsh- or Gaelic-speaking.[50] If the experience of the Flemish-speaking communities established by Henry I in south-west Wales is taken as a guide, then it was unlikely that small and isolated English-speaking communities would be able to retain their linguistic identity beyond three or four generations.[51] 'Small' and 'isolated' are the

[48] Davies, *Lordship and Society*, ch. 14; idem, 'The Peoples of Britain and Ireland. 1. Identities', *Transactions of the Royal Historical Society*, 6th ser., 4 (1994), 1–20.

[49] Berry, *Statutes*, 434–5.

[50] For Wales, Llinos Smith, 'The Welsh Language before 1536', in *The Welsh Language before the Industrial Revolution*, ed. G. H. Jenkins (Cardiff, 1997), 15–44; for the linguistic situation in Ireland, see the essays by James Lydon and Alan Bliss in *The English in Medieval Ireland*, ed. James Lydon; and J. L. Kallen, 'English in Ireland', in *The Cambridge History of the English Language*, V, ed. R. Burchfield (Cambridge, 1994), 148–96.

[51] Flemish was still apparently spoken in Pembrokeshire in the early thirteenth century: *Speculum Duorum*, ed. M. Richter et al. (Cardiff, 1974), 37.

key words here; neither applies to several of the English communities that were established in southern Wales and in southern and eastern Ireland in the twelfth and thirteenth centuries. Rather were they, within admittedly restricted areas, the dominant communities, aggressively imposing their own norms and consciously cultivating their Englishness and their connections with a wider English world. Thus the surviving deed and associated evidence for personal, place-, and field-names along the south Wales coastal lowlands from Chepstow to Pembroke leaves one in no doubt that English was the dominant, if not necessarily the only, language of several of the communities by the thirteenth and fourteenth centuries, and the same was true of parts of the Usk and Wye valleys. The same was likewise true of the urban and some of the rural communities of settlers in Ireland. A society which produced, and presumably found an audience for, two striking Anglo-Norman verse accounts of the thirteenth century—*The Song of Dermot and the Earl* and the remarkable poem about the Walling of New Ross—or the satirical and associated Middle English poems to be found in the manuscript known as the 'Kildare poems' (British Library, Harleian MS 913) is clearly a society at home with the linguistic and cultural norms of an English and indeed Anglo-Norman world.[52] When an exchequer clerk at Dublin in the mid-fourteenth century admitted that Irish names could not easily be transcribed in 'our language' (*in lingua nostra*), it was almost certainly to English that he was referring.[53]

The advance of English in Scotland is arguably even more impressive, for there it was not tied to the coat-tails of an English military and political conquest. Historians of Scottish Gaeldom have, of late, very properly been emphasizing and attempting to recover the extent of a 'lost' Gaelic culture in law, institutions, literacy, and language in parts of Scotland, and pointing out how a newly dominant language of literacy has the capacity to expunge the memory and evidence for the language and culture it eventually displaces—be it Pictish by Gaelic, or Gaelic in turn by Anglo-Norman and English.[54]

[52] *Song*; H. Shields, 'The Walling of New Ross: A Thirteenth-century Poem in French', *Long Room* 12–13 (1975–6), 24–33. For discussion, *NHI*, II, ch. 26. For an address being given in French and English at Kilkenny, see above, Ch. 5, n. 97.

[53] Quoted in James Lydon, 'The Middle Nation', in *The English in Medieval Ireland*, ed. J. Lydon, 1–26 at p. 14 n. 3.

[54] For example, G. W. S. Barrow, 'The Lost Gàidhealtachd', republished in idem, *Scotland and its Neighbours in the Middle Ages* (1992), 105–27; J. Bannerman, 'The King's Poet and the Inauguration of Alexander III'; *Scottish Historical Review* 68 (1989), 120–49; W. D. H. Sellar, 'Celtic Law and Scots Law. Survival and Integration', *Scottish Studies* 29 (1989), 1–27; Dauvit Broun, *The Charters of Gaelic Scotland and Ireland in the Early and Central Middle Ages* (Quiggin Lecture, Cambridge, 1995); idem, 'Gaelic Literacy in Eastern Scotland between 1124 and 1249', in *Literacy in Medieval Celtic Societies*, ed. H. Pryce (Cambridge, 1998), 183–202.

Nevertheless there is little doubt that Gaelic probably reached its maximum area of currency in the early twelfth century; thereafter the story is that of the advance of English and the retreat of Gaelic and Cumbric. English, of course, already had a powerful foothold, since Lothian was already overwhelmingly English-speaking; but it is in the twelfth and thirteenth centuries that the language began to establish itself strongly north of the Firth of Forth in what was the original Scotia.[55] The growth of burghs and trade[56] was an important agency of change; so, no doubt, was an increasingly English-influenced royal administration and law. Settlers from England doubtless played their part; but native society, especially in southern and eastern Scotland, seems also to have been party to a process of acculturation and cultural surrender, abandoning many of the crucial features of Gaelic culture (including classes of hereditary *judices* and poets, and offices such as that of *mair*),[57] contracting mixed marriages, giving Anglo-Norman names to its children,[58] and adopting English terminology for its urban and trading activities. It is not the least of the paradoxes in the history of the British Isles that it was in the kingdom of the Scots—the very area in which English kingship did not directly impose its military and political power and in which English settlers and institutions were absorbed comfortably into the existing society and polity—that the English language and with it English culture arguably made its greatest and most enduring advances in the twelfth and thirteenth centuries.

The same was true of law. We might start with a concession issued by King Robert I, Robert the Bruce, of Scotland in 1324, permitting his men of Galloway to use 'English law', referring possibly to the employment of a jury to determine guilt or otherwise. It is surely an eloquent comment on the penetrative influence of English law that it should be invoked *eo nomine* by a king of Scots for one of the more thoroughly Celtic parts of his kingdom.[59] The grant of 1324 was in fact but the latest eddy of the tide of English or

[55] D. Murison, 'Linguistic Relationships in Medieval Scotland', in *The Scottish Tradition*, ed. G. W. S. Barrow (1974), 71–83. Barrow, *Anglo-Norman Era*, 35, notes the 'unmistakable English ascendancy in a context of four vernaculars' in south-west Scotland. For a recent attempt to represent the linguistic situation cartographically, see *Atlas of Scottish History to 1707*, ed. P. G. B. McNeill and H. L. MacQueen (Edinburgh, 1996), 426–7.

[56] The Laws of the Four Burghs, which were the template for Scottish town governance in the Middle Ages, were, appropriately, largely based on the customs of the English royal borough of Newcastle upon Tyne (just as the customs of Hereford, and thereby of Breteuil in Normandy, became the blueprint for many Welsh boroughs).

[57] G. W. S. Barrow, *The Kingdom of the Scots*, ch. 2 (The *judex*); *The Sheriff Court Book of Fife 1515–22*, ed. W. Croft Dickinson (Scottish History Society, 1928), lxii–lxvii.

[58] D. Murison, 'Linguistic Relationships' (as cited above, n. 55), esp. pp. 71–4.

[59] Barrow, *Robert Bruce*, 298. The grant can be compared with a grant by the earl of Carrick and his wife in 1285 of *lex anglicana* to the tenants of Melrose Abbey: Hector L. MacQueen, 'Scots Law under Alexander III', in *Scotland in the Reign of Alexander III 1249–1286*, ed. Norman H. Reid, 74–102 at p. 95.

Anglo-Norman legal custom as it washed over the distant shores of the British Isles. As the barons, knights, colonists, burgesses, and churchmen made their way from England (and beyond) into Wales and Scotland and later into Ireland, so they naturally took with them, in their baggage, as it were, the institutions, practices, and customs for dispute settlement and judicial and tenurial authority with which they were familiar into their host society.[60] So it was, for example, that Robert Fitz Hamon had established a *comitatus* in his new land of Glamorgan by the opening years of the twelfth century, or that Robert Bruce adopted 'all the customs Ranulf le Meschin ever had in Carlisle' in his new lordship of Annandale in south-west Scotland; so it was likewise that the future David I of Scotland picked up the judicial idiom of the court of his brother-in-law, Henry I, from the years he spent there and on the estates of the honour of Huntingdon with which he had been so munificently endowed, or that Adam de Feypo gave tithes to the church of Skreen in Meath in Ireland 'as freely as any knight gives tithes to his chapel in England or in Normandy'.[61] From about 1180 or so this process of legal, judicial, and administrative acculturation acquired an altogether more aggressive, even proselytizing, and royalist edge; and the scale of its victories was proportionately the greater. It was now a self-consciously and proudly *English* law. The age which may be said to open with Glanvill's summation of English laws (*leges anglicanae*) in the 1180s and close with Magna Carta's reference to the 'law of England' (*lex Anglie*), and which takes in the legal apocrypha of the Laws of Edward the Confessor *en route*, may be claimed to be the era in which the common law became distinctively and self-consciously English. It was then also that it became a written corpus of law, developing its procedures and forms of action and, increasingly, its professional functionaries. Such a law was becoming a litmus test of Englishness, wherever the English were living in the British Isles. So it was, in the words of a later royal letter, that in 1210 'King John brought men learned in the law to Ireland with him; by their advice and at the request of the Irish he ordered the laws of *England* to be observed in Ireland.'[62] It is appropriate and revealing that it was, in effect, for the large English

[60] P. R. Hyams, 'The Common Law and the French Connection', *Proceedings of the Battle Conference of Anglo-Norman Studies*, 4 (1982), 77–93.

[61] Glamorgan: *Cartae de Glamorgan* (cited above, Ch. 4, n. 59), I, no. 51; Annandale: Lawrie, *Early Scottish Charters*, no. 54; David I: G. W. S. Barrow, 'David I of Scotland: The Balance of New and Old', reprinted in *Scotland and its Neighbours in the Middle Ages*, 45–67; Skreen: *Chartularies of St Mary's Dublin*, I, 91 (for discussion A. J. Otway-Ruthven, 'Parochial Development in the Rural Deanery of Skreen', *Journal of the Royal Society of Antiquaries of Ireland* 94 (1964), 111–22).

[62] *Patent Rolls 1225–32*, 96. Roger of Wendover's view (*Flores Historiarum*, ed. H. O. Coxe, III, 233–4) was that John 'established the laws and customs of England (in Ireland), appointing sheriffs and other officers to administer justice'.

community in Ireland that what Paul Brand has termed the first 'official *summa* of the English common law' was prepared.[63] Thereafter, and indeed probably earlier, the orthodoxy was established that 'the land of Ireland ought to be governed by the laws and customs used in the kingdom of England.'[64] In short, the orbit of English common law was already wider than the ambit of the English state.

That orbit already included the extensive English settlements in southern Wales.[65] In 1284 Edward I extended that orbit to include the recently conquered parts of Wales. He did not impose English law unilaterally on Welsh communities other than in respect of crime and criminal procedures; but the register of writs he deposited at Caernarfon castle, and the copy of Chief Justice Hengham's breviate which he despatched to Carmarthen, proclaimed his hope and intention that the Welsh would gradually be weaned from their own laws and habits to the higher wisdom of English common law.[66] He was not to be disappointed. Indeed, powerful as were royal fiat and statute in the promotion of English law in the British Isles, its victory was ultimately that of popular appeal and demand. In Wales, the story of that victory can be documented from different parts of the country—notably in the widespread popularity of jury verdict, in the abandonment of blood-feud compensation procedures, in the growing demand for what was regarded as the English freedom to alienate land, and in the adoption of petty assizes and final concords for terminating land disputes.[67] In Ireland, the request for individual grants of English law to Irishmen is evidence of the same demand; but even more interesting, if ultimately unsuccessful, was the 'big bang' approach adopted

[63] Paul Brand, 'Ireland and the Literature of the Early Common Law', *Irish Jurist*, new ser., 16 (1981), 95–113 at p. 97 (reprinted in idem, *The Making of the Common Law* (1992), ch. 19).

[64] The statement is a commonplace, e.g. *CDI*, I, nos. 985, 1003, 1430, etc.; Berry, *Statutes*, 20, 21, 23–4, etc. In 1328 the justiciar requested that an authenticated copy of all English statutes should be sent to Ireland: J. F. Baldwin, *The King's Council in the Middle Ages* (Oxford, 1913), 475. See in general G. J. Hand, *English Law in Ireland 1290–1324* (Cambridge, 1967); Brand, *The Making of the Common Law* (as in n. 63), chs. 2, 19, 20. For an excellent brief introduction (as to so many other topics broached in this book), Robin Frame, *The Political Development of the British Isles 1100–1400* (new edn., Oxford, 1995), 85–9.

[65] For the early adoption of aspects of English law and procedure in the March of Wales, see, briefly, R. R. Davies, 'The Law of the March', *Welsh History Review* 5 (1970–1), 1–30, esp. pp. 19–22. The question merits fuller treatment.

[66] Statute of Wales, 1284: Llinos Smith in *Welsh History Review* 10 (1980–1), 127–54; Chief Justice Hengham's breviate: E. A. Lewis, 'Account Roll of the Chamberlain of West Wales 1301–3', *Bulletin of the Board of Celtic Studies* 2 (1923–5), 49–86 at p. 82.

[67] See generally, jury: Davies, 'Twilight', *History* 51 (1966), 143–64, esp. p. 148; idem, *Lordship and Society*, 160–1; bloodfeud: idem, 'Survival of Bloodfeud', *History* 54 (1969), 338–57; freedom to alienate land: idem, *Lordship and Society*, 449–56; J. B. Smith, 'Crown and Community in the Principality of North Wales in the Reign of Henry Tudor', *Welsh History Review* 3 (1966–7), 145–71 (of much wider chronological significance than the title might suggest).

by a group of leading Irish ecclesiastics in 1276–80 in an attempt to secure a general extension of English law to the Irish.[68] Neither in Wales nor in Ireland in fact was there an immediate prospect that the indigenous native population would desert their native laws wholesale; they were too closely woven into the structures and mechanisms of native society for that to happen. Nevertheless the attraction of English procedures and growing contacts with the worlds and habits of English settlers were already beginning to prepare the ground for the advance of English law.[69] It was to become one of the most fundamental and far-reaching facets of the process of Anglicization.

Its greatest and most immediate triumph was neither in Wales nor in Ireland, but in Scotland. 'In the thirteenth century,' so asserts one recent authority, 'Scots and English common law could be spoken of as a single entity.'[70] Such a claim may perhaps be oversimplified, underrating Gaelic influences and practices, and not acknowledging sufficiently the regional diversity of law and justice in the Scottish kingdom as a whole.[71] But in terms of what we may term the royal Scotland of the south and east, what was coming to be known as the common law of Scotland was substantially parasitic—albeit sometimes after a lapse of time—on that of its southern neighbour. The writs of the Angevins appeared as the legal brieves of the Scots; William the Lion appears to have borrowed shamelessly from the assizes of Henry II and Hubert Walter; the jury of presentment, the process of indictment, the writ of naifty, and other procedures became well entrenched north of the border.[72] Scottish practice, it is true, diverged from English practice, notably in not developing a central court or a cadre of professional lawyers. But when King Robert I issued major legislation in 1318 his aim in part was still to bring Scots law into line with recent developments in English practice, and when *Regiam*

[68] A. J. Otway-Ruthven, 'The Request of the Irish for English Law', *Irish Historical Studies* 6 (1948–9), 261–70; A. Gwynn, 'Edward I and the Proposed Purchase of English Law for the Irish, *c.*1276–80', *Transactions of the Royal Historical Society*, 5th ser., 10 (1960), 11–27; J. R. S. Phillips, 'David MacCarwell and the Proposal to Purchase English Law *c.*1273–*c.*1280', *Peritia* 10 (1996), 253–73.

[69] For Ireland, see G. MacNiocaill, 'The Interaction of the Laws', in *The English in Medieval Ireland*, ed. J. Lydon, 105–18.

[70] W. David H. Sellar, 'The Common Law of Scotland and the Common Law of England', in *The British Isles 1100–1500*, ed. R. R. Davies, 82–100, 86. Cf. Barrow, *Anglo-Norman Era*, 118. Cf. the comment of F. W. Maitland: 'We may doubt whether a man who crossed the river [Tweed] felt that he had passed from the land of one law to the land of another. . . . The law of Scotland . . . was closely akin to English law' (F. Pollock and F. W. Maitland, *The History of English Law before the time of Edward I* (Cambridge, 1968 edn.), I, 222–3).

[71] W. H. D. Sellar in *Scottish Studies* 29 (1989) (as cited above, n. 54); H. L. MacQueen, 'Scots Law under Alexander III' (as cited above, n. 59), esp. pp. 92–3.

[72] From a large literature, see *RRS*, I, 62; II, 74; Duncan, *Scotland*, 201–6; Barrow, *Kingdom of the Scots*, 112; Hector L. MacQueen, *Common Law and Feudal Society in Medieval Scotland* (Edinburgh, 1993).

Maiestatem, the first treatise on Scots law, was compiled in the 1320s it could be regarded as 'essentially a book of English law, albeit with a Scottish reference'.[73]

All in all, the common law of England by the early fourteenth century was very much more than that. It was also the law of the large English communities in Wales and Ireland; it was the dominant influence in the shaping of the common law of Scotland; and many of its procedures and central ideas were being voluntarily and sometimes enthusiastically adopted by the indigenous communities of the farthest parts of the British Isles. That was indeed a remarkable triumph of Anglicization, all the more impressive and durable for not being ethnically exclusive or always determined by military and political power. This process of Anglicization was at work in other directions. It can be seen, for example, in the forms and instruments of government, central and local—in the borrowing, for instance, of the office of justiciar in Scotland and its introduction by English rulers into Ireland and Wales, albeit that in each country it took on a different form and local colour;[74] in the adoption of the writ-charter as the fundamental instrument of written command;[75] and in the proliferation of the English-type shire and many of its associated features—including the offices of sheriff and coroner, the county court, the tourn—as the basic blocks of local governance (albeit often built on a native infrastructure) in much of the British Isles beyond the English state.[76] The pattern of institutional borrowing was by no means identical, nor did it proceed on a single chronological register. In Wales it was inhibited by the early date of Anglo-Norman penetration and by the survival of an earlier and seigneurial pattern of authority in the March,[77] but it was imposed in a fairly fully-fledged form in the newly conquered districts in the thirteenth century.[78] In Ireland it

[73] MacQueen, *Common Law* (as in n. 72), 148–53; H. G. Richardson, 'Roman Law in the *Regiam Maiestatem*', *Juridical Review* 67 (1955), 155–87 at p. 155.

[74] Scotland: G. W. S. Barrow, *The Kingdom of the Scots*, ch. 3; Ireland: H. G. Richardson and G. O. Sayles, *The Administration of Ireland 1172–1377* (Dublin, 1963); Wales: W. H. Waters, *The Edwardian Settlement of North Wales in its Administrative and Legal Aspects* (Cardiff, 1935), 9–14, 71–5; R. A. Griffiths, *The Principality of Wales in the Later Middle Ages. 1. South Wales 1277–1536* (Cardiff, 1972), 19–23.

[75] G. W. S. Barrow, 'The Scots Charter' in idem, *Scotland and its Neighbours*, ch. 5. Also *RRS*, I, 60–2.

[76] Cf. Duncan, *Scotland*, 162–3. Barrow (*Bruce*, 8) refers to the shrievalty as 'an English import, distinctly scotticized'. See also below, pp. 165–6.

[77] For patterns of governance and their 'feudal' character in the March, see A. J. Otway-Ruthven, 'The Constitutional Position of the Great Lordships of South Wales', *Transactions of the Royal Historical Society*, 5th ser., 8 (1958), 1–20, and R. R. Davies, 'Kings, Lords and Liberties in the March of Wales, 1066–1272', ibid, 29 (1979), 41–61.

[78] See Waters, *Edwardian Settlement* (cited above, n. 74), 9; Griffiths, *The Principality of Wales* (cited above, n. 74). A special reward was given to sheriffs in north Wales in 1284 'by reason of the newness of the office' (Waters, 25, n. 1). Sheriffs there were to be appointed 'according to the custom used in England and Ireland': *Calendar of Ancient Petitions re. Wales*, no. 5455 (1308–9).

was imported more or less ready-made and imposed on English-controlled Ireland, royal land and aristocratic liberties alike.[79] In Scotland it was a case of the enthusiastic but not uncritical adoption of English practice by a kingship, aristocracy, and Church anxious to reshape the pattern of their authority according to the most avant-garde and enterprising methods of its southern neighbour, so much so that in James Campbell's provocative comment, 'it is almost as if there are two Englands and one of them is called Scotland.'[80]

A similar pattern of pervasive English influence and dominance could be readily traced in matters economic, ecclesiastical, and cultural. The British Isles, for example, became an English-dominated monetary zone. It was the English king's coins—Stephen's reign apart—which circulated in Marcher and increasingly in native Wales.[81] As for Ireland, its story especially from John's reign was, as usual, that of being kept firmly in step with England with regard to weights, measures, and coinage. The first coinage issued by the English in Ireland was to be of the same weight, fineness, and standard as English coinage and was to be legal tender on both sides of the Irish Sea. For much of the thirteenth century, in fact, Ireland was no more than a virtual monetary annex of the English kingdom. All dies used in Ireland were returned to England in 1251, and the coinages of the two countries were virtually integrated.[82] Scotland was, of course, an independent kingdom with its own coinage from the time of David I. But that could not conceal its monetary dependence on England: its coinage shadowed that of England in weight, alloy, denominations, and design until the mid-fourteenth century; English coins outnumbered Scottish coins in circulation in Scotland in the thirteenth century, according to the evidence of hoards, by a factor of at least ten to one; and price movements in Scotland closely mimicked those of its southern neighbour.[83] In short, the British Isles was coming to form a single sterling area, and it was the coinage and values of the English crown which were its motor and agents, often in areas well beyond the formal and military reach of the English state.

The same was less true of the Church and of culture. In those spheres many of the truly transformative influences could be said to be European

[79] Otway-Ruthven, *Medieval Ireland*, ch. V.

[80] James Campbell, 'The United Kingdom of England' in *Uniting the Kingdom?*, ed. Grant and Stringer, 31–47 at p. 47.

[81] G. C. Boon, *Welsh Hoards 1979–1881* (Cardiff, 1986); Edward Besley, 'Short Cross and Other Medieval Coins from Llanfaes, Anglesey', *British Numismatic Journal* 65 (1996), 46–82.

[82] Michael Dolley in *NHI*, II, ch. 29. Among early expressions of the total uniformity of Irish with English coinage are *CDI*, no. 353; Roger of Wendover, *Chronica* (as cited above, n. 62), III, 233–4.

[83] *Coinage in Medieval Scotland* (1100–1600), ed. D. M. Metcalf (British Archaeological Reports 45, 1977); N. J. Mayhew, 'Alexander III—A Silver Age?', in *Scotland in the Reign of Alexander III*, ed. N. H. Reid, 53–73; Elizabeth Gemmill and N. J. Mayhew, *Changing Values in Medieval Scotland: A Study of Prices, Money, and Weights and Measures* (Cambridge, 1995).

rather than specifically English. The changes in monastic practice and religious organization were often introduced by native rulers independently, and chronologically often well in advance, of English power and domination. This, for example, is pre-eminently true of the impact of the so-called papal reform movement and of the new monastic orders in Ireland, Scotland, Galloway, and in a measure Wales.[84] Furthermore, Canterbury's vision of a single British or indeed British and Irish Church under its ultimate control—an ecclesiastical vision to match the prospect of a single high kingship—was recurrently thwarted during the twelfth century and had been finally dashed before the century was out.[85]

Yet even in ecclesiastical and religious matters the English were often, as the phrase has it, making the weather. It was partly that political and military clout brought its own ecclesiastical reward. Thus in Ireland the norms of the English Church, *ecclesia anglicana*, were mandatorily and recurrently imposed as those to be followed, so that, in Ralph of Diss's words, 'similar observance should bind one kingdom to the other in all details'; in Scotland the Church was formally made subject to the Church of England between 1174 and 1189; while Wales was brought securely into the jurisdiction of the see of Canterbury from the early twelfth century.[86] More generally, wherever the English penetrated in the British Isles they naturally introduced the ecclesiastical practices and organization, and often with them the personnel, from their home bases, or alternatively their norms and institutions were borrowed by native societies. 'In general,' so Professor Duncan asserts, 'the Scottish church gradually lost its peculiar features and, where the church tolerated variety,

[84] Ireland: Otway-Ruthven, *Medieval Ireland*, 37–40, 126–43; J. A. Watt, *The Church in Medieval Ireland* (Dublin, 1972), ch. 1; Scotland: Duncan, *Scotland*, chs. 10–11; Barrow, *Kingship and Unity*, ch. 4; Galloway: R. A. McDonald, 'Scoto-Norse Kings and the Reformed Religious Orders: Patterns of Monastic Patronage in Twelfth-century Galloway and Argyll', *Albion* 27 (1995), 187–219; K. J. Stringer, 'Reform Monasticism and Celtic Scotland: Galloway, *c.*1140–*c.*1240', in *Alba: Celtic Scotland in the Medieval Era*, ed. E. J. Cowan and R. A. McDonald (East Linton, 2000), 127–65; Wales: Huw Pryce, 'Church and Society in Wales, 1150–1250: An Irish Perspective', in *The British Isles 1100–1500*, ed. R. R. Davies, 27–48. The Cistercian houses of Mellifont in Ireland and Dundrennan in Galloway were both founded by native endowment in 1142.

[85] See above, pp. 11–12.

[86] Ireland: Ralph of Diceto, *Opera Historica* (R.S.), II, 350. Gerald of Wales (*Expugnatio Hibernica*, 100–1) likewise claimed that one of the decisions of the Council of Cashel (1172) was that 'in all parts of the Irish church all matters relating to religion are to be conducted hereafter . . . in line with the observances of the English church (*anglicana ecclesia*).' This doctrine of ecclesiastical conformity with the English Church was regularly reiterated, e.g. *CDI*, III, no. 10; *Affairs of Ireland before King's Council*, 64–6. Scotland: the 'treaty' of Falaise (1174) decreed that 'the church of Scotland shall henceforward owe such subjection to the church of England as it should do' (*Anglo-Scottish Relations*, 5); Duncan, *Scotland*, 264; Wales: see especially J. Conway Davies, *Episcopal Acts re. Welsh Dioceses 1066–1272*, esp. 76 *et seq.*; for very brief summary, Davies, *Conquest*, 188–91.

adopted English ecclesiastical custom'—including organization into parishes and the payment of tithes.[87] Likewise, the coming of the English to Ireland was accompanied by the further creation of parishes, the requirement to pay tithes, and the aggregation of parishes into rural deaneries.[88]

The same was true with respect to monasticism in what was after all the most explosively expansionist period in the history of western monasticism. It may be some indication of the scale of the redrawing of the map of ecclesiastical endowment in the British Isles in these years if we recall that 31 out of the 36 monasteries and priories founded in south Wales between 1066 and 1272 were established by Anglo-Norman and English lords; in Ireland the tally in the century from 1170 rises to 55 monasteries and 37 friaries.[89] Even if we concede that many of the inmates of these houses were drawn from the native populations and that there may well have been more continuities with traditional religious structures and culture than is immediately apparent,[90] it must be evident that such a massive inward ecclesiastical investment of English lords and clerics must have had a transformative effect on the character of monastic and religious life in both countries. Nor should it be overlooked that in terms of religious and monastic practice, and likewise in terms of culture, the Anglo-Normans and the English saw themselves—and, what is more, were often seen by the leaders of cultural and ecclesiastical life in the outer parts of the British Isles—as the purveyors of a higher standard of life, conduct, and religion. So it was, for example, that it was monks from houses in England who were dispatched to establish monastic practice at houses such as Dunfermline or on the Isle of May, or that the constitution of the cathedral chapter of Elgin was specifically based on the usage of Lincoln; so it was likewise that Geoffrey fitz Robert recruited four monks for the house of Kells in Ossory from Bodmin in Cornwall or that a band of thirteen monks from Wenlock (in Shropshire) were dispatched to found the monastery at Paisley; so it was, to cull an example from a different world, that the church of St Canice at Kilkenny—in common with so many of the major stone buildings

[87] Duncan, *Scotland*, 257; cf. *RRS*, I, 66.

[88] Otway-Ruthven, *Medieval Ireland*, 118–20, 126–7; idem, 'Parochial Development' (as cited above, n. 61).

[89] Wales: F. G. Cowley, *The Monastic Order in South Wales 1066–1349* (Cardiff, 1977). Ireland: the figures have been calculated from Aubrey Gwynn and R. N. Hadcock, *Medieval Religious Houses: Ireland* (1970). For a helpful map of new religious foundations in Ireland 1169–1320, see K. Simms, 'Frontiers in the Irish Church—Regional and Cultural', in *Colony and Frontier in Medieval Ireland*, ed. T. Barry et al., 177–200 at p. 185.

[90] Though occasionally it was stipulated that monks should be English: 'The charters of the Cistercian abbey of Duiske', *Proceedings of the Royal Irish Academy*, 35 (1918), at pp. 16, 21, 24 (qui tandem de lingua anglicana sit).

of thirteenth-century Ireland—proclaimed its essential Englishness to all, specifically in its case in its west doorway, which was modelled on that of the cathedral at Wells.[91]

How then might we characterize the impact of the process of Anglicization on the British Isles by about 1300? We could do worse than start with the shire, for the shire with its sheriff and county court was in many respects, both socially and governmentally, the bedrock of the English state. Contemporaries recognized as much: when John Trevisa wanted to demonstrate that Cornwall had become firmly part of England, he did so by noting that 'it is divided into hundreds and is ruled by the law of England and holdeth shire and shire days, as other shires do.'[92] Much the same could now be said about much more remote parts of the British Isles, at least in respect of shire organization. The thirteenth century had been a momentous chapter in that story. By 1307 there were six shires in Wales (exclusive of great Marcher lordships such as Brecon, Glamorgan, Pembroke, and Gower, which had many of the features, including the terminology, of county governance); twelve in Ireland (and a further four liberties, each divided into several shires with a sheriff and county court of its own); and some twenty-six in Scotland. Doubtless many of these outer British shires retained older boundaries and were amalgamated out of native units of assessment and governance;[93] but the paradigm of their organization and operation was now essentially that of the English shire. It is a measure of its impact that the word for shire had already probably been borrowed into Gaelic by the mid-twelfth century.[94] The shire map of the British Isles by the death of Edward I was an eloquent comment on how much their local governance had been reshaped in the last two centuries to conform, voluntarily or otherwise, to an English model—in Scotland in the service of

[91] Dunfermline, Isle of May: I. B. Cowan, *Medieval Religious Houses. Scotland* (2nd edn., 1976), 58–9; Elgin: *Registrum Episcopatus Moraviensis*, ed. C. Innes (Bannatyne Club, 1827), nos. 46–9; Kells in Ossory: *Irish Monastic and Episcopal Deeds 1200–1600*, ed. N. B. White (Dublin, 1936), 311; Paisley: *Registrum Monasterii de Passelet*, ed. C. Innes (Maitland Club, 1832), 1–2; St Canice, Kilkenny: *'A Worthy Foundation'* (as cited above, ch. 5, n. 97), 38. See in general, Roger Stalley, *Architecture and Sculpture in Ireland 1150–1350* (Dublin, 1971); idem, 'Irish Gothic and English Fashion', *The English in Medieval Ireland*, ed. Lydon, 65–85; idem, *The Cistercian Monasteries of Ireland: An Account of the History, Art and Architecture of the White Monks in Ireland from 1142 to 1540* (1987).

[92] Ranulf Higden, *Polychronicon*, II, 91.

[93] Note in particular the comments of Duncan, *Scotland*, 161–3, 596–7. For Ireland, Otway-Ruthven, *Medieval Ireland*, 173–81; idem, 'Anglo-Irish Shire Government in the Thirteenth Century', *Irish Historical Studies* 5 (1946), 1–28. For the evolution of royal shires in west Wales, J. G. Edwards, 'The Early History of the Counties of Carmarthen and Cardigan', *English Historical Review* 31 (1916), 90–8.

[94] *RRS*, I, 41. Duncan (*Scotland*, 160–1) also notes that the earliest Scottish sheriffs seem to have been Anglians or French.

the Scottish monarchy, but in Ireland and in Wales as an arm of English power (and often resented as such by the native societies).[95]

The account for one of these new shires—that for county Tipperary in 1275–6—brings us to another cardinal feature of the process of the Anglicization of the British Isles. The account mentions some 500 or so names, and indicates, as Edmund Curtis pointed out many years ago, that county Tipperary was 'effectively governed by and for the Norman English element' (as he called them).[96] The establishment of substantial English colonies in Wales and Ireland was critical to the process of Anglicization. They were the primary stakeholders of English values and identity in the outer reaches of the British Isles, specifically in Wales and Ireland. How much that was so we may appreciate by pointing out a negative. The assemblage of lands which Edward I ruled included not only the high kingship of the British Isles (as I have termed it) but also the remains of the earlier continental empires of the Norman and Angevin dynasties, notably the Channel Islands and the duchy of Aquitaine. In neither of these were there substantial and privileged English colonies; in both, law, judicial administration, language, and so forth remained indigenous.[97] Part of Edward I's empire they might be; part of the world of Englishness and Anglicization they were not, or at least not in the way that was true of notable parts of Ireland and Wales by the late thirteenth century.

What is surely striking about the British Isles in 1300 compared with the British Isles of 1100 is how much more integrated—though far from unitary—a world they now were, and how central in that integration had been the drive, enterprise, and ambition of the English—peasants, burgesses, and merchants as well as kings, barons, knights, and churchmen. It was a world in which great aristocratic complexes (such as those of the Marshals and the Lacies in the early thirteenth century or those of Clare and Bigod later) and even more modest ones (such as the estates of the Mohun family) straddled effortlessly across England, Wales, and Ireland or, alternatively and occasionally additionally, across the Scottish border (as did the estates of Roger de

[95] Thus one of the charges against Geoffrey de Langley in the newly annexed districts of north-east Wales in the 1250s was that he established shires and hundreds (*Annales Monastici*, II, 20). Likewise, part of the dossier of complaints of Rhys ap Maredudd, the Welsh princeling who led the revolt of 1287, was that he was compelled 'to follow the county and hundred courts' (ibid., III, 338).

[96] Edmund Curtis, 'Sheriff's Accounts for County Tipperary, 1275–6', *Proceedings of the Royal Irish Academy* 42 (1934–5), C, 65–95. The comment is at p. 89.

[97] J. Le Patourel, 'The Plantagenet Dominions', *History* 50 (1965), 289–308, esp. pp. 304–6.

Quincy, earl of Winchester (d.1264)).[98] Kings, magnates, and clerics now played their games of power, patronage, and exploitation in some measure on a pan-British stage. This was also a world in which what was effectively a single currency and an increasingly sophisticated network of markets and trading connections were integrating ever further parts of the British Isles into a wider, and predominantly English, economic and commercial orbit. It was also a world in which common Anglo-French cultural, architectural, and ecclesiastical norms increasingly dominated, and even threatened, indigenous and local traditions.

This was more, much more, than a by-product of English military power and political domination. Indeed, it is clear that even without English conquest and colonization, the native societies of the outer parts of the British Isles would have been brought within the magnetic reach of the demographic, economic, cultural, and religious forces which were transforming the face of north-western Europe from the mid-eleventh century onwards. Momentous developments in Ireland in the first half of the twelfth century, particularly in the ecclesiastical and monastic spheres, but also arguably in the structuring and sinews of political power, clearly suggest as much.[99] So above all does the remarkable transformation of the kingdom of the Scots in the twelfth and thirteenth centuries. But equally, there is surely no doubt that English power and colonization greatly accelerated the process and gave it an intensity, range, character, and durability which it would otherwise have lacked. Nor should the central and catalytic role of the English state, its institutions, and its demands in the process be underestimated, especially in Ireland and Wales.

The accelerating pace of commercial change is a case in point, particularly in Ireland. English commercial enterprise in Ireland could build on the achievements and networks of the five Norse-founded towns of Dublin, Wexford, Waterford, Cork, and Limerick, and on existing trade links, especially with Bristol and Chester. To that extent Gerald of Wales's characterization of the Irish, as of the Welsh, as being without knowledge of towns or commerce is, as so often with Gerald's generalizations, a simplification which borders on

[98] For this theme in general, see esp. J. R. S. Phillips, 'The Anglo-Norman Nobility', in *The English in Medieval Ireland*, ed. J. Lydon, 87–104; R. Frame, 'Aristocracies and the Political Configuration of the British Isles', in *The British Isles 1100–1500*, ed. R. R. Davies, 142–59; K. J. Stringer, *Earl David*, ch. 9. For the Mohun family: *Calendar of Inquisitions Post Mortem*, II, no. 430; for the de Quincy family: Barrow, *Anglo-Norman Era*, 44–6, 111–12; G. G. Simpson, 'The *Familia* of Roger de Quincy, Earl of Winchester and Constable of Scotland', in *Essays on the Nobility of Medieval Scotland*, ed. K. J. Stringer (Edinburgh, 1985), 102–30.

[99] For the Church, see above, n. 84; for political changes, sometimes described as 'the feudalization of Irish society', see *NHI*, II, 4–13; F. J. Byrne, *Irish Kings and High-kings* (1973), 269–74 and D. Ó Corráin in *Historical Studies* 11 (1978), 1–35.

becoming a distortion. Yet there is not a shadow of doubt that in the eighty years after 1170 the volume, scale, and range of trade from, into, and within much of Ireland was utterly transformed, and that it was the coming of the English—with Italian bankers and Flemish merchants in their wake—which was the prime agency of their transformation. Commercial privileges (such as those extended to Dublin at an early date by Henry II) brought the major Irish towns a favoured position in the Angevin trading network. The provision of a stable and internationally acceptable coinage lubricated trade, while the existence of a ready market for Irish produce in England, and also in Wales and western Scotland, served as a major accelerator of economic development. It is appropriate that when the first full customs figures become available—those on wool, wool-fells, and hides imposed by the customs ordinance of 1275—it was New Ross, a new town founded by the English in the late twelfth century, which easily topped the Irish league.[100]

The customs ordinance of 1275 directs us to the role of the English state in this process of transformation, specifically in the exploitation, promotion, and regulation of trade in the outer reaches of the British Isles (except Scotland, other than in the very late thirteenth century). From an early date the customs rates levied on goods exported from Ireland had been consistently kept in line with those of England,[101] thereby making it clear that as in so many other respects—law, coinage, weights and measures—Ireland (or rather English Ireland) was to be regarded as governed as an annexe subject to an England-determined set of rules. The customs ordinance of 1275 was to apply to Ireland and Wales as well as to England; briefly in the late 1290s Scotland was also absorbed into this world of English commercial regulation.[102] To a degree, therefore, it looked by the end of the thirteenth century as if the whole of the British Isles was about to become an integrated, uniform, English-regulated, and state-controlled commercial zone in terms of external trade. That would have been an appropriate commercial counterpart to the high kingship which Edward I seemed on the point of establishing. Nowhere was that more obvious than in the way that the commercial and financial resources of Ireland were ruthlessly exploited, and indeed exhausted, in pursuit of the English state's ambition to secure the submission of Wales and Scotland.

[100] *NHI*, II, 481–7; ch. 17 *passim*; M. D. O'Sullivan, *Old Galway. The History of a Norman Colony in Ireland* (Cambridge, 1942); idem, *Italian Merchant Bankers in Ireland in the Thirteenth Century* (Dublin, 1962). For the 1275–80 customs figures, *CDI*, II, no. 1902.

[101] N. S. B. Gras, *The Early English Customs System* (Cambridge, Mass., 1918), 41, 59, 79 n. 2, 222–3.

[102] The customs figures for Ireland are tabulated in G. Mac Niocaill, *Na buirgéisí xii–xv aois* (Dublin, 1964), II, 523–8; those for Wales in E. A. Lewis, 'A Contribution to the Commercial History of Medieval Wales', *Y Cymmrodor* 24 (1913), 86–188. For Scotland, see above, p. 28.

In 1298, for example, Edward I demanded that Ireland should produce 8,000 quarters of wheat, 11,000 quarters of oats, 2,000 quarters of crushed malt, 1,000 tuns of wine, 500 carcasses of beef, 1,000 pigs, and 20,000 dried fish for his forthcoming campaign to Scotland. The demands of the English war-state were transforming the commercial opportunities of Ireland, but doing so in a fashion which made it clear that Ireland's wealth was now at the beck and call of the English state, to further its own purposes.[103]

Anglicization was, nevertheless, not merely a matter of *force majeure*, state power, or ruthless exploitation. It was also, and perhaps even more so, a matter of mind-sets—of a confident conviction in the superiority of its norms and lifestyle. Three familiar images may convey its flavour and the way that life in the outer reaches of the British Isles was being shaped to follow its norms. The first is the crushing comment of Stephen of Lexington, sent on a visitation to Cistercian monasteries in Ireland in 1228: 'no man,' he commented, 'can love the cloister and learning if he knows only Irish'; he was equally disparaging about so-called Irish kings who dwelt in little huts made of wattle.[104] The second image bespeaks the confident expansiveness of the English monarchy and its aristocracy in the mid-thirteenth century, and their anxiety to build, literally, a new political order based on English standards in Ireland: it is the command issued by Henry III in 1243 for the construction of a massive hall, 120 feet by 80 feet, in Dublin castle, specifically in the style of the hall of Canterbury and decorated with a grand painting beyond the dais of the king and queen seated with the baronage.[105] The third image is as restrained as the hall was to be extravagant, but its telegraphic brevity is thereby all the more powerful. It is the curt comment, echoed time and again in response to requests and petitions from Ireland and Wales to the king of England: *si in Anglia fit, fiat*, 'if it is done in England, let it be so.'[106] This was a world which was being constructed, and reconstructed, in the light of English standards.

[103] *CDI*, III, no. 570; *NHI*, II, 196–202. This is a theme which has been widely explored by J. F. Lydon, esp. 'Irish levies in Scottish Wars, 1296–1302', *Irish Sword* 5 (1962), 207–17; 'Edward I, Ireland and the War in Scotland, 1303–4', in *England and Ireland in the Later Middle Ages*, ed. J. F. Lydon (Dublin, 1981), 43–61.

[104] Stephen of Lexington, *Letters from Ireland 1228–1229*, ed. B. W. O'Dwyer, 68, 210.

[105] *Close Rolls 1242–7*, 23. For comment, Roger Stalley in *The English in Medieval Ireland*, ed. Lydon, 74–5.

[106] Mac Niocaill in 'The Interaction of the Laws', in *The English in Medieval Ireland*, ed. Lydon, at p. 111; Davies, *Domination and Conquest*, 123. For other examples, see *Document of Affairs of Ireland before King's Council*, 12, 34–5 ('Respondetur per consilium secundum quod respondetur illis de Anglia in casu consimilo'). Cf. the replies of Edward I to the petitions of the Irish clergy: 'fiat eis secundum quod sit prelatis in Anglia'; 'other things . . . belong to the king according to the English courts and laws': quoted in J. A. Watt, 'Edward I and the Irish Church', in *Medieval Studies to Aubrey Gwynn*, ed. J. A. Watt et al. (Dublin, 1961), 133–67 at pp. 160, 166.

Political and military domination brings its own forms of cultural obeisance. Those who wield power in any society and in any period have the capacity to construct worlds in their own image and to their own tastes, and to persuade, cajole, or compel others, consciously or otherwise, to inhabit their world and to borrow its idioms, customs, and written formulae.[107] But cultural and economic domination knows no political boundaries or ignores them. The Anglicization of the British Isles was not merely a by-product of the military and political power of the English monarchy and aristocracy or of the entrepreneurship and acquisitiveness of English and other settlers. It was also the triumph of the fashionable, the innovative, the exciting, the technologically more advanced, the wealth-creating, the transformative. Its victories were as much the splendid feast and unheard-of dishes with which Henry II overwhelmed the Irish kings at Dublin in December 1171, or the hoards of English coins circulating in the small and distant outpost of Llanfaes in Anglesey, as the intimidating walls of the castles of Caerphilly or Trim.[108] Its apotheosis may be said to be the gleeful comment of Ranulf Higden at Chester on the Welsh of his day aping civilized English habits such as tilling gardens and fields, inhabiting towns, riding armed, wearing stockings and shoes, and even sleeping under sheets,

> 'So they semeth now in mynde
> More Englische men than Walsche kynd.'[109]

Just as Robert Bartlett can talk about the Europeanization of Europe as the distinctive feature of the centuries 950–1350,[110] so likewise it may not be improper to refer to the Anglicization of the British Isles during the period covered by this book. Indeed Anglicization may be interpreted as the distinctively insular version of this process of Europeanization.

But it was a process which had its limits. Those limits, it could be argued, have shaped the history of the British Isles in a measure ever since. Paradoxically, the most extensively English-settled and Anglicized part of the British Isles was the country which retained its political independence and proved capable of defending it stoutly against the English. It was in Scotland, or rather a good part of the most densely populated and prosperous area of it, that the influence of England—in law, institutions, tenurial custom, burghal development, coinage, trade patterns, language, and so forth—was arguably

[107] Cf. Michael Mann, *The Sources of Social Power*, I (Cambridge, 1986), 7.

[108] The Dublin feast: Gerald of Wales, *Expugnatio Hibernica*, 96–7; coins at Llanfaes: above, n. 81.

[109] Ranulf Higden, *Polychronicon*, I, 411.

[110] Robert Bartlett, *The Making of Europe. Conquest, Colonization and Cultural Change 950–1350* (1993), ch. 11.

most profound. In Wales and Ireland the impact of Anglicization—for all its striking achievements—was by 1300 still essentially limited and external, as it were, to native society and culture. Was this due to the political, social, and cultural resilience—or, if one prefers, backwardness—of the Welsh and Irish? Or was it due to the exclusiveness of the English both as colonial communities and as a people which was only able to assimilate, or even to come to an accommodation with, these other peoples on its own terms, political, social, and cultural? Was it 'the united kingdom' of the English which was the greatest impediment on the road to the creation of a unitary British Isles?[111]

[111] This is an echo of the title of James Campbell's essay, 'The United Kingdom of England', in *Uniting the Kingdom?*, ed. Grant and Stringer, 31–48.

7

THE EBB TIDE OF THE ENGLISH EMPIRE, 1304–1343

Edward I spent Christmas 1304 in Lincoln *en route* from Scotland to Westminster. It was a welcome break from the rigours of an exhausting reign. It was also a victor's Christmas.[1] The submissions of the leaders of the Scottish political community in spring 1304 and the subsequent surrender of Stirling castle in July seemed at long last to herald the final capitulation of the Scots.[2] So confident indeed was Edward that this was so that he ordered the exchequer and the bench, which had been transferred to York in 1298, to return to Westminster; it required twenty-seven carts to carry the accumulated records of the English bureaucracy back to its headquarters.[3] During the Christmas festivities at Lincoln, Edward showed unusual magnanimity in distributing largesse and compliments to his magnates and knights. They no doubt reciprocated, for, as the Westminster chronicler put it, Edward was indeed 'the most victorious of kings', the author of 'a triumphant peace', and 'king and lord of two kingdoms' (England and Scotland). When the royal party eventually reached Westminster a special service was held in the abbey on 25 March to give thanks to God and St Edward for the victories over the Scots.[4] Thanks and triumphalism no doubt marched hand in hand on that occasion, as on many such subsequent occasions.

As 1305 unfolded Edward had good reason to persuade himself that his power and authority within the British Isles were more ample and secure than ever. In the Lent parliament at Westminster teams of auditors sifted through some 135 petitions from Scotland and over 40 from Ireland, while the Prince

[1] For the expenses of the royal household at Lincoln 1304 (totalling £612 for a week, whereas £150–£160 was the norm), PRO E 101/368/3.

[2] G. W. S. Barrow, *Robert Bruce*, 129–34; Fiona Watson, 'Settling the Stalemate: Edward I's Peace in Scotland, 1303–5', *Thirteenth Century England* 6 (1997), 127–43; and eadem, *Under the Hammer. Edward I and Scotland 1286–1307* (East Linton, 1998). Note the comment of the Kilkenny Chronicle ('The Kilkenny Chronicle in Cotton MS Vespasian B XI', ed. Robin Flower, *Analecta Hibernica* 2 (1931), 330–40) at *s.a.* 1304: 'Scocia plena est conquista.'

[3] *Chronicles of the Reigns of Edward I and Edward II*, ed. W. Stubbs (R.S., 1882–3), I, 134.

[4] *Flores Historiarum*, ed. H. R. Luard (R.S., 1890), III, 120–1, 320–1. In another paean of praise, after his death, Edward was considered to have surpassed Brutus, Arthur, Edgar, and Richard I (*Chronicles of Edward I and II*, II, 3–21, esp. p. 15).

of Wales's council attended to over 70 individual and communal petitions from North Wales.[5] There could be no more striking evidence that Scotland and Wales, as well as the lordship of Ireland, were now beholden to the grace and favour of the king of England and his eldest son, and were learning the administrative processes which tapped that grace and favour. At the same parliament Scottish representatives were present to give Edward advice on proposals for the future government of the land—as he now normally called it—of Scotland. During the summer further news confirmed the victory in Scotland as apparently definitive: on 3 August a group of Scots captured William Wallace and turned him over to the English; three weeks later he was paraded through the streets of London on his way to a summary trial and a ghoulish death. When the second parliament of the year assembled at Westminster on 15 September, Edward invited a group of English and Scottish magnates to dinner and took counsel with the Scottish representatives on the Ordinance which he now issued for the governance of their country.[6] The omens for the establishment of a high kingship of the British Isles seemed altogether promising: Edward's justices were holding sessions at Ardfert and Tralee in the far south-west of Ireland; and his officers were collecting a handsome income from the recently conquered districts of north and west Wales.[7] This was certainly no unitary British state: Scotland retained a governmental framework of its own; English Ireland had, at least outwardly, a pattern of institutions, including a parliament, which consciously mimicked those of England but were separate from them; while Wales was an anomalous and incongruous assemblage of quasi-independent Marcher lordships on the one hand and recently created royal counties on the other. It was a ramshackle empire maybe, as most empires are; but one which was firmly England-dominated and England-centred. No wonder that contemporaries felt that comparisons between Edward I and Arthur were in order.

Triumphs in politics are rarely what they seem. So it proved to be on this occasion. Within ten years, the islanders were very far from being 'joined together' or 'united' as English enthusiasts had predicted in the later years of Edward I.[8] On the contrary, the crushing defeat of Bannockburn, 24 June

[5] *Memoranda de Parliamento, 1305*, ed. F. W. Maitland (R.S., 1893), 168–255; *Record of Caernarvon*, ed. H. Ellis (1838), 212–25.

[6] PRO E 101/365/10 f.29v; 368/3; *Anglo-Scottish Relations*, ed. Stones, 240–59.

[7] Ireland: Orpen, *Ireland under the Normans*, IV, 49. (This was the last royal assize to be held in Kerry for three centuries.) Note the comment of Katharine Simms (*Law and Disorder in Thirteenth-Century Ireland*, ed. J. Lydon, at p. 66) that the 'short spell just before and after AD 1300 . . . marks the fullest geographical extent of English authority [in Ireland]'. Wales: E. A. Lewis, 'Account Roll of the Chamberlain of the Principality of North Wales 1304–5', *Bulletin of the Board of Celtic Studies* I (1921–3), 256–75; idem, 'Account Roll of the Chamberlain of West Wales 1301–3', ibid., 2 (1923–5), 49–86.

[8] See above, ch. 2, n. 37.

1314, inaugurated a period of over four years when English power in the British Isles was challenged in a fashion which had not been witnessed since the reign of Stephen, if even then. The news in the dreadful summer of 1315, for example, was dire: Robert Bruce was laying siege to Carlisle and Scottish forces were bringing pressure to bear on Berwick; Edward Bruce was simultaneously laying siege to the great Ulster fortress of Carrickfergus and before the autumn was out had burnt Louth and Dundalk; and there were dark suspicions that the earl of Ulster connived at the Scottish raids.[9] The castles of west and north Wales were provisioned with troops and supplies, and with reason—for in September a Scottish pirate sailed into Holyhead, and rumours were rife of deep unease among the volatile Welsh.[10] And so the story of alarms and setbacks continued for the next three years, including as they did a serious revolt in south Wales early in 1316, the capture of the Isle of Man by the Scots in October 1317, and devastating raids by the Bruces throughout eastern Ireland, reaching the very outskirts of Dublin, at the very same time that one-fifth of the kingdom of England lay open to forays from the Scots.[11] The cumulative effect seemed to be a collective loss of will and nerve on the part of the English; such sentiments were further fanned by talk of treachery in high places, both in Ireland and in Wales.[12] Furthermore the English in the British Isles seemed now, for the first time, to be on the ropes ideologically as well as militarily. A propaganda war—much of it orchestrated by the Scots, but by no means confined to them—peddled virulent anti-English sentiment, appealed loftily to concepts of freedom and liberty, and traded on the common bonds of descent between the Scots, the Irish, and the Welsh. It was an eloquently argued ideological and historical assault on the English domination of the British Isles.[13] Some of the ambitions fostered during these heady

[9] C. McNamee, *The Wars of the Bruces. Scotland, England and Ireland, 1306–1328* (East Linton, 1997), chs. 2–5; *NHI*, II, 282–94 (with full references to other excellent discussions of the Bruces in Ireland).

[10] J. B. Smith, 'Edward II and the Allegiance of Wales', *Welsh History Review* 8 (1976–7), 139–71; idem, 'The Rebellion of Llywelyn Bren', in *Glamorgan County History*, II, 72–87; *Calendar of Ancient Correspondence concerning Wales*, 253–4.

[11] McNamee, *The Wars of the Bruces*, provides a good recent account of the interlocking spheres of conflict and tension in the northern and western British Isles across these years. See also S. Duffy, 'The Bruce Brothers and the Irish Sea World, 1306–29', *Cambridge Medieval Celtic Studies* 21 (1991), 55–86.

[12] Gruffudd Llwyd, the most prominent Welsh leader in north Wales, was arrested in December 1316; the earl of Ulster was arrested and imprisoned in February 1317.

[13] Among the key documents are the letters proposing an alliance between the Scots and the Irish based on common descent and customs (*RRS*, V, no. 564); the so-called Remonstrance of the Irish to the Pope *c.*1317 (the most recent version of the text is in Walter Bower, *Scotichronicon*, ed. D. E. R. Watt et al. (Aberdeen, 1987–96), VI, 384–403, 465–81); the letters exchanged between Gruffudd Llwyd and Edward Bruce (published in J. B. Smith, 'Gruffydd Llwyd and the Celtic Alliance', *Bulletin of the Board of Celtic Studies* 26 (1974–6), 463–78); and the Declaration of Arbroath 1320 (for which see A. A. M. Duncan, *The Nation of Scots and the Declaration of Arbroath* (1970)).

years—notably Edward Bruce's extraordinary dream of establishing a western kingship embracing Ireland, the Western Isles,[14] and Wales—may have been risible;[15] but it must have become increasingly clear to hard-headed political realists that the map of political power in the British Isles was undergoing a fundamental reassessment and that it was the limits, as much as the extent, of English power which were now the key issue.

Coming to terms with changed political realities and with the retreat from empire is never easy; so it proved to be on this occasion. Some hard-headed realists, no doubt driven by experience and political expediency, had already concluded that English domination of the whole of the British Isles was no longer feasible, and in particular that any attempt to reduce Scotland was doomed to failure. It was such a realization that drove Andrew Harclay in December 1322 to enter into secret negotiations with the Scots, based on the premiss that 'both kingdoms prospered while each had a king of its own nation and was maintained separately, with its own laws and customs.'[16] The negotiations cost Harclay his head; but, as is the wont of governments, Edward's ministers came to the same conclusion a few months later in the thirteen-year truce with the Scots agreed on 23 May 1323.[17] The government of Roger Mortimer and Isabella went considerably further in the Treaty of Edinburgh–Northampton of March 1328. It was to be 'a final peace and settlement', acknowledging Robert Bruce's title as king of Scotland and recognizing the independence of his kingdom;[18] it was to be sealed by the marriage of his heir, David, to the sister of the young Edward III at Berwick.[19] It also—and very significantly from our point of view—formally divided the British Isles into two major zones of power, designating Ireland (and of course, though not by name, Wales) as belonging to the English zone, and the Western Isles and the Isle of Man as within the Scottish

[14] According to the *Annals of Connacht*, *s.a.* 1318, among those supporting Edward Bruce in 1318 were 'the king of Hebrides and the king of Argyll and their Scots'. See also S. Duffy, 'The "Continuation" of Nicholas Trevet: A New Source for the Bruce Invasion', *Proceedings of the Royal Irish Academy*, 91 (1991), C, 303–15.

[15] A. A. M. Duncan, 'The Scots' Invasion of Ireland, 1315', in *The British Isles 1100–1500*, ed. R. R. Davies, 100–18.

[16] *Anglo-Scottish Relations*, 310–11. For an excellent full account of the conspiracy and fall of Andrew Harclay, see Henry Summerson, *Medieval Carlisle*, I, 230–56.

[17] The full terms of the truce of 1323 are published in *Foedera*, II, i, 521, and in *RRS*, V, no. 282. It was concluded by Edward II 'on behalf of our lands (*terres*) of England, Wales, Gascony and Ireland . . . and Sir Robert Bruce, his subjects, followers and supporters and his land (*terre*) of Scotland'.

[18] *Anglo-Scottish Relations*, 322–41. Scotland was to be 'separate in all things from the kingdom of England . . . entire, quit and free of any subjection, servitude, claim or demand'.

[19] The account in *Chartulary of St Mary's Dublin*, II, 367, of the marriage at Berwick and of King Robert, the earl of Ulster, and many Scottish magnates subsequently crossing together 'peacefully' to Ulster is noteworthy. For discussion, see R. Frame, *English Lordship in Ireland 1318–61* (Oxford, 1982), 152, 184–5.

orbit.[20] Neither contemporaries nor historians have taken a kindly view of the Treaty of Northampton: it has been almost universally condemned as a treacherous peace, *turpis pax*, and as an example of the extraordinary lengths to which Mortimer was willing to go in order to buy external peace so that he could bolster his illegal and unpopular regime in England. All that may be true; but it may be as well to remember that Roger Mortimer—a holder of vast estates in both Wales and Ireland, and with extensive military and governmental experience in both—may have estimated more realistically than did most of his English-based contemporaries the limitations of English power in the outer zones of the British Isles and the need to come to terms with those limitations.[21]

Be that as it may, Roger Mortimer was ousted from power in October 1330. For a while in the 1330s it looked as if Edward III was to succeed in reconstituting the British empire which his grandfather had so tantalizingly glimpsed in 1305. He planned a major expedition to Ireland in 1331–2 and took bold initiatives with respect both to the Anglo-Irish magnates and to the native Irish.[22] In Scotland Edward's successes were truly remarkable. After a series of military hammer blows, the country was virtually in his grip by 1335: his puppet ruler had been installed; King David II had fled to France; and a large swathe of southern Scotland, including Edinburgh, had been ceded to the English.[23] The events of the 1330s in Scotland are indeed a reminder, if one were needed, of how much the shape of the British Isles was determined by what is often called, pejoratively, *histoire événementielle*.

Yet by 1343 one might conclude—without resorting unduly to the historian's philosopher's stone, hindsight—that the English empire of the British Isles had indeed overextended itself. What, one may well ask, is the significance of 1343? Apart from the fact of the pleasing symmetry of its being exactly two centuries and a half after the *terminus a quo* of this book, 1093, and apart also from the fact that on 12 May 1343 the king's eldest son, Edward, was created prince of Wales, the precise year has no particular significance. But around that time the signs of the changing character and contraction of

[20] Cf. the comments of Frame, *English Lordship*, 138–42, 148–52 (for the 're-emergence of a largely autonomous north-west world').

[21] For Roger Mortimer's policies etc. in Wales, see, briefly, Davies, *Conquest*, 405–7, 410 and in Ireland, Frame, *English Lordship*, ch. 5.

[22] Frame, *English Lordship*, ch. 6. The initiatives included the major ordinances of 1331, the offer of English law to all free Irishmen, the arrest of the earl of Desmond, and the execution of William Birmingham (July 1332).

[23] R. Nicholson, *Edward III and the Scots, 1327–35* (Oxford, 1965). For a recent excellent contribution to our understanding of the situation and possibilities in Scotland in the 1330s, see Bruce Webster, 'Scotland without a King, 1329–41', in *Medieval Scotland*, ed. Grant and Stringer, 223–39.

English power in the British Isles were becoming ever more evident: the story of the advance of English power in the British Isles since the late eleventh century was coming, at least temporarily, to a close. In Ireland the crisis in relations between the king of England and the leaders of the English community there in 1341–2 was an important chapter in the emergence of an Anglo-Irish sense of identity and with it a weakening, ultimately, of the bonds with England.[24] Even more important was the awareness that the tide of power had turned within the island: it was in 1342 that the English community there declared that 'the third part and more of your land of Ireland, which was conquered in the time of your progenitors, is now come into the hands of your Irish enemies.'[25] Alarmist exaggerations maybe; but the overall conclusion of modern historians concurs. 'By the middle of the fourteenth century,' says Robin Frame, 'the dominance of English law and English administrative forms [in Ireland] had ceased to be a half-truth and was on the way to becoming an illusion.'[26]

As to Scotland, what is remarkable is the speed of its recovery from the débâcle of the early and mid-1330s. King David II returned from France to resume his throne in June 1341; during the course of 1341–2 the key centres of Edinburgh, Roxburgh, and Stirling were recovered; and by 1343 even John Macdonald of the Isles had made peace with the Bruce dynasty, thereby accepting in effect that the attempt to install an English-supported Balliol candidate had failed.[27] Scotland was to suffer ignominious defeats in the future—notably the capture of its king in 1346—but it became increasingly clear that even in the most favourable circumstances for the English (as in 1357 and 1363) the prospect of a union of Scotland and England, let alone the subjection of the former to the latter, was no longer a practical proposition. It would only remain for John of Fordun (d.*c.*1387) to provide the first sustained history of the Scots as a people and its kingdom, built on the assumption of their total separateness, historically, from the rest of Britain.[28]

[24] Frame, *English Lordship*, ch. 7. The statement made in 1341 is symptomatic: 'never has there been such a notable and public division between the English born in England and the English born in Ireland', *Chartulary of St Mary's Dublin*, II, 383.

[25] Berry, *Early Statutes*, 232. For Ireland as a 'land of war', see Frame, *English Lordship*, 1, 328–9; idem, 'War and Peace in the Medieval Lordship of Ireland', in *The English in Medieval Ireland*, ed. Lydon, 118–41, reprinted in Frame, *Ireland and Britain 1170–1450*, ch. 12.

[26] R. Frame, 'English Officials and Irish Chiefs in the Fourteenth Century'. *English Historical Review* 90 (1975), 748–77 at p. 748 (reprinted in idem, *Ireland and Britain*, ch. 14). G. H. Orpen's viewpoint and approach (*Ireland under the Normans*, IV, 249) were very different; but he likewise chose to see the murder of the earl of Ulster in 1333 as the closing of the era of *pax normannica*.

[27] R. Nicolson, *Scotland in the Later Middle Ages*, 139–44; *A New Historical Atlas of Scotland to 1707*, 106–7.

[28] R. James Goldstein, *The Matter of Scotland*, ch. 4.

Overshadowing all these developments, and also profoundly influencing them, was the opening of hostilities between England and France in 1337 and Edward's assumption of the title of king of France in January 1340. A fundamental reorientation in England's territorial and political ambitions was taking place. Such reorientations, it may be argued, are clearer in hindsight than they are to the contemporary eye. Yet even contemporaries were aware that the Arthurian dream of a single monarchy of the British Isles was disappearing over the horizon of realities by the mid-fourteenth century. When Robert Manning composed his massive 'story of England' in the vernacular in the 1330s he was faced with a dilemma. All of Britain (England, Scotland, and Wales), he remarked, was once one and was called Albion. What is more, Merlin had foretold that this tripartite kingdom would again be reunited. But, added Robert despondently, 'I reply that it isn't so; they are divided. What he [Merlin] had prophesied has very remarkably not come to pass.'[29] It is as eloquent a comment as any that the dream of a single Britain had been, but was no more.

If Robert Manning, writing in the 1330s, could sense that the dreams remained unrealized, the historian can perhaps see even more clearly that a fundamental shift was happening in the story of the English domination of the British Isles in the first half of the fourteenth century. English expansion into Wales and Ireland had been substantially driven by aristocratic ambition and acquisitiveness, often underwritten by royal licence and patronage. From the middle of the thirteenth century, if not earlier, the momentum of that aristocratic drive seemed to be faltering, not least perhaps because the rich and easy pickings had already been garnered and shared out. What now remained to be done was to defend and, if possible, consolidate existing positions (as the Clare earls of Gloucester did so dramatically in Glamorgan and Gwent) or snatch up and build upon acts of royal largesse (as Lacy, Grey, Warenne, Mortimer, and others did in north-east Wales in the wake of the Edwardian conquest or Thomas de Clare in south-western Ireland). Indeed there were now indications that some magnates no longer had the appetite for the challenges which they met in the western British Isles. This was occasionally true of Wales: so it was that we hear of the surrender of a border manor to the king because its owner was 'wearied with war' or of another because its lord 'could not hold his own against the Welsh'.[30] But it was in Ireland that

[29] Robert Manning of Brunne, *The Story of England*, ed. F. J. Furnivall (R.S., 1887), I, ll. 1939–42; *Peter Langtoft's Chronicle*, ed. T. Hearne, 2 vols. (Oxford, 1725), II, 282. For comment, Thorlac Turville-Petre, *England the Nation. Language, Literature and National Identity, 1290–1340* (Oxford, 1996), 15–16.

[30] *Calendar of Inquisitions Post Mortem*, V, no. 747; *Calendar of Inquisitions Miscellaneous*, I, no. 1089.

the withdrawal symptoms were most alarming. Among the families which quit the scene, more or less voluntarily, between 1280 and 1306 were Marsh, Vescy, Pipard, Mohun, and Bigod. Others would follow suit in the fourteenth century; and even among those who kept their estates on either side of the Irish Sea, absenteeism now became a disturbing and much-deplored feature.[31] The profile of the English aristocracy in Ireland was changing significantly during this period, and with it the relationship between England and English Ireland.[32]

Even more significant was the fact that the great wave of English colonization into the outer zones of the British Isles had now long since exhausted itself. A few late ripples there certainly were (as in north-east Wales and in south-west Ireland), but in most of the British Isles the heroic and transformative stage of English colonization lay well in the past. It may well have passed its effective peak in south Wales by the mid-twelfth century, and in Scotland (where it did not get under way until the 1120s) by the end of the reign of William the Lion (1214). In Ireland English migration was in full flood in the late twelfth and early thirteenth centuries. There would be later notable gains, especially in the west and north-west; but historians have concluded of late that 'those parts of Ireland that were to be held securely in the late middle ages were probably already in English hands by the 1220s.'[33] The colonists, as was argued in an earlier chapter, were the agents *par excellence* of the process of Anglicization, broadly interpreted. In cultural, economic, and ultimately political terms it was they—not military expeditions nor castles nor governmental decrees nor royal writs—who had the capacity to bring parts of the outer zones of the British Isles effectively into the orbit of sustained English power and influence. By the later thirteenth century they were visibly faltering in that role, especially in Ireland. It may be that the demographic upswing, which had been as crucial to the English diaspora in the British Isles as to similar migration movements elsewhere in Europe, had now lost its momentum. Nor was it just the case that the stream of colonization had been reduced to a trickle; it was now fully in retreat. Contemporary inquisitions and historical comments from areas such as counties Tipperary, Kilkenny, and Kildare make it abundantly clear that by the 1340s, districts which had once

[31] Otway-Ruthven, *Medieval Ireland*, 212; *Law and Disorder in Thirteenth-century Ireland*, ed. J. F. Lydon, 46. Absenteeism: Frame, *English Lordship*, ch. 2.

[32] See esp. Frame, *English Lordship*, 52–3, 334; idem, '"Les Engleys nées en Irlande": The English Political Identity in Medieval Ireland', *Transactions of the Royal Historical Society*, 6th ser., 3 (1993), 83–103, reprinted in idem, *Ireland and Britain 1170–1450*, ch. 8.

[33] Robin Frame, 'King Henry III and Ireland: The Shaping of a Peripheral Lordship', *Thirteenth Century England* 4 (1992), 179–202 at p. 179 (reprinted in idem, *Ireland and Britain*, ch. 3).

been English settlements were now once more in native Irish hands.[34] The frontiers of English-controlled Ireland were contracting, sometimes very rapidly, at the very time that the English military and political pretensions in Scotland were collapsing.

As a consequence, English economic and cultural dominance of the British Isles was also in retreat. It had been a feature of the era of English expansion that the areas of the British Isles within the zone of English influence and power had, in some measure, been integrated into the cultural and economic orbits, and also into the political stratagems, of the English state and its rulers and agents. One vignette may speak for scores of others as an example of the integrative capacities of the English-dominated world within the British Isles (and indeed beyond) in the twelfth and thirteenth centuries: large supplies of corn and other provisions were exported from the English-settled estates of Roger Bigod, earl of Norfolk (d.1306), in the Barrow valley via the port of New Ross to supply Bigod's household and Edward I's armies in north Wales (just as later they would supply English armies in Scotland and Gascony).[35] South-eastern Ireland had indeed been one of the major granaries of the English world for much of the thirteenth century. That increasingly ceased to be so in the early fourteenth century; indeed, in later years Ireland become an importer of grain. There was also a sharp fall—perhaps of the order of 75 per cent—in the exports of wool, woolfells, and hides from Ireland between the 1280s and the 1340s. The explanations for these apparently dramatic changes in the pattern of trade are doubtless many and varied; but it is difficult to deny that they were transforming the scale and texture of relationships, political as well as economic, within the British Isles.

Coinage seems to reflect the same story of the weakening of economic bonds. In Ireland, Edward I initiated a recoinage in the early 1280s, shortly after his great English recoinage and deeply imitative of it. But subsequent efforts at recoinages were either feeble or unsuccessful, and there were bitter complaints of the lack of an Irish mint. To no avail: no coins seem to have been struck in English Ireland between the late 1330s and the 1430s.[36] As for Scotland, the closeness of its economic relationships with England had been demonstrated by the fact that its coinage during the twelfth and thirteenth

[34] For example, the English settlement at Dunamase, Co. Kildare, declined dramatically (A. J. Otway-Ruthven, 'The Medieval County of Kildare', *Irish Historical Studies* 11 (1959), 181–99, esp. p. 184). Likewise the 1338 inquisition on Moyaliff, Co. Tipperary, which stated that 'no English could now hold the land . . . or hold pleas, (idem, 'The Character of the Norman Settlement in Ireland', *Historical Studies* 5 (1965), 75–84 at p. 81).

[35] *CDI*, II, no. 2009. Edward I dealt with a petition about waste land and settlement in Connacht when he was at Rhuddlan in 1282: ibid., no. 1986.

[36] *NHI*, II, 484–7, 509–14, 820–2.

centuries had been interchangeable with that of England and had the same silver content; indeed, the coins actually in circulation in thirteenth-century Scotland were mostly English. It was inevitable that sooner or later part of the price that would have to be paid for the calamitous breakdown in Anglo-Scottish relations from the 1290s would be the dissolution of this common monetary zone. So it was that from the 1360s England and Scotland went their own monetary ways.[37] Such changes in monetary and commercial patterns—whatever the multiple reasons which underlay them—have more than an economic significance; they reflected, and promoted, profound reorientations in the patterns of relationships and power within the British Isles.

The same seems to be true in other spheres of life. In cultural terms the advance of English as a spoken language and the seductive appeal of Anglo-Norman cultural norms had been among the distinctive features of the growing English dominance in the British Isles in the twelfth and thirteenth centuries. But now that English power was in retreat and English colonies on the defensive, the cultural pendulum began to swing in the other direction. In Scotland the spread of the English language at the expense of Gaelic came to an end; indeed some Anglo-Norman families—including the most famous of all, the Bruces—may well have borrowed Gaelic traditions and language. The linguistic frontier between the two languages remained largely unchanged for the next four centuries.[38] In Wales and Ireland, it was not merely a case of establishing linguistic boundaries but of the advance of the vernacular languages at the expense of English. Even the descendants of colonial settlers were becoming at least bilingual and often more comfortable in the native language. 'Men of the English race in that land,' so a petition about Ireland averred in the mid-fourteenth century, 'study and speak the Irish language and foster their children among the Irish . . . so that our country dwellers of the English stock for the most part are becoming Irish in language.'[39] Nor does such a comment come as a surprise when we read, for example, of the death of John Bermingham, earl of Louth and descendant of a settler Anglo-Norman family, in Louth in 1329: it was by his Gaelic name, Sir Seon MacFeorais, that his death was recorded in the native annals, and it was equally noteworthy that with him fell his troupe of Irish minstrels, 'the king of music making' and twenty of his pupils.[40] John inhabited two cultural worlds and the drawing

[37] See above, p. 162; R. Nicholson, *Scotland in the Later Middle Ages*, 175–6.

[38] G. W. S. Barrow, *Kingdom of the Scots*, 363; idem, *Bruce*, 26; Nicholson, *Scotland*, 73, 274–5; *Atlas of Scottish History to 1707* (1996), 426–9.

[39] *Historical Mss. Commission. Tenth Report*, Appendix V, 260–1.

[40] *Annals of Connacht*, *s.a.*; *The Annals of Ireland by Friar John Clyn*, ed. R. Butler (Dublin, 1849), *s.a.* For the episode, J. Lydon, 'The Braganstown Massacre, 1329', *Louth Archaeological Society Journal* 19 (1977), 5–16.

power of the Gaelic one was becoming ever stronger. There were many like him. Gerald fitz Maurice (d.1398) was earl of Desmond and briefly justiciar of Ireland, but it is as Gearóid Iarla, Gaelic poet and patron of poets, that he is better known.[41] There is no parallel in Wales to Gerald fitz Maurice; but it is as well to recall that the poet, Iolo Goch, could write odes in honour of Edward III and of Roger Mortimer, earl of March (d.1398), and that Sir David Hanmer, one of the chief justices of the King's Bench in England, was both the father-in-law of Owain Glyn Dŵr and the subject of an affectionate ode by one of the masters of Welsh medieval verse.[42]

This handful of examples directs us to the shifting, multilayered, and complex cultural worlds of the British Isles in the fourteenth century. It is a century which has very properly been regarded as 'the age of the triumph of English'. So it was, especially by its closing decades, in England. But elsewhere in the British Isles it was the age of the confident flourishing of native languages and literature. In both Wales and Ireland there can be little doubt that the linguistic tide turned during the course of the century, and that the indigenous languages were making substantial gains at the expense of, or at least alongside, English, the premier language of the governing elite.[43] The situation was different in Scotland, but even there the advance of Scots was used to bolster separateness, as the English language 'advanced rapidly up the social scale . . . and began to become standardised as a dialect distinct from that of northern England'.[44] As to literature, it is as well to recall that it was not only in England that one was on the threshold of a 'golden age': in Wales it was the era of Dafydd ap Gwilym (fl.1320–50), the greatest of all Welsh poets; in Scotland, of John Barbour's masterpiece, as literature and history, in Scots, *The Bruce*; in Ireland, of the production of some of the greatest treasures of Gaelic literature, such as the Yellow Book of Lecan. Whatever the dominance of England and the English, it was clear that they had still to share the cultural stage in the British Isles with other vigorous and self-confident language and cultural communities.

[41] *NHI*, II, 315, 697–8.

[42] Iolo Goch: *Gwaith Iolo Goch*, ed. D. R. Johnston (Cardiff, 1988), nos. 1 and 20; idem, 'Iolo Goch and the English: Welsh Poetry and Politics in the Fourteenth Century', *Cambridge Medieval Celtic Studies* 12 (1986), 73–98; G. A. Williams, 'Cywydd Iolo Goch i Rosier Mortimer: Cefndir a Chyd-destun', *Llên Cymru* 22 (1999), 57–79. Sir David Hanmer: R. R. Davies, *The Revolt of Owain Glyn Dŵr* (Oxford, 1995), 137–8.

[43] For Wales, see especially Llinos Smith, 'The Welsh Language before 1536', in *The Welsh Language before the Industrial Revolution*, ed. G. H. Jenkins (Cardiff, 1997), 15–48.

[44] Nicholson, *Scotland in the Later Middle Ages*, 274; Hector L. MacQueen, 'Linguistic Communities in Medieval Scots Law', in *Communities and Courts in Britain 1150–1900*, ed. C. Brooks and M. Lobban (1997), 13–23.

Even in the visual arts, the cultural leadership of England, which once had appeared to be beyond question in shaping taste and practice in the outer part of the British Isles (albeit often on northern European models), now seemed increasingly to be challenged, or at least to lose much of its appeal. 'The Wars of Independence,' so it has been observed of Scotland, 'were to result in the severance of the artistic ties with England, so that the later thirteenth century was arguably the last period until the eighteenth century when the architectural courses of the two countries [sc. Scotland and England] ran essentially in parallel.'[45] Observers of architectural developments in Ireland have come to much the same conclusion. From about the mid-thirteenth century building work in English Ireland becomes 'more introspective and archaic', and by 1350 an age of 'isolation' had dawned in which local craftsmen increasingly placed their own, local stamp on their work.[46] The anxiety, or ability, to keep up, or even in touch with the English world, was no more.

This sense of a loosening of ties with the English world can be noted in other directions, more especially in Ireland, far less so in Wales. One of the manifestations of the drawing power of England in the thirteenth century had been the anxiety of individuals and communities living on the edges of English Ireland to secure the privileges of English law. That ambition continued, and indeed grew, in Wales in the later Middle Ages; but in Ireland there was a sharp decline in such requests during the reign of Edward III.[47] Even before then, and equally significantly, the number of cases from Ireland brought before the court of the King's Bench declined sharply from about 1326.[48] Furthermore, Ireland, which had been a huge source of opportunities, supplies, troops, and money for the English for well over a century, gradually ceased to be so. However we interpret the figures, the average annual revenue payable to the Irish exchequer collapsed from the late thirteenth century onwards,[49] not least because of the ruthless way in which the country (as

[45] Richard Fawcett, 'Ecclesiastical Architecture in the Second Half of the Thirteenth Century', in *Scotland in the Reign of Alexander III 1249–1286*, ed. N. H. Reid (Edinburgh, 1990), 148–77 at p. 176.

[46] Roger Stalley, 'Irish Gothic and English Fashion', in *The English in Medieval Ireland*, ed. Lydon, 65–87 at pp. 77, 79; for comparisons with Scotland, ibid, p. 86. For similar general comments, see Edwin C. Rae in *NHI*, II, 762, and at a local level C. A. Empey, in *Kilkenny: History and Society*, eds. Nolan and Whelan, esp. p. 82 ('late gothic in Ireland developed its own distinctly provincial style, exhibiting less and less contact with England and the continent').

[47] Wales: J. B. Smith in *Welsh History Review* 3 (1966–7), 145–71; Davies, *Lordship and Society in the March of Wales*, 452–5; Ireland: B. Murphy, 'The status of the native Irish after 1331', *Irish Jurist* 2 (1967), 116–38. For letters of denization for Welshmen, see *Calendar of Ancient Petitions relating to Wales*, nos. 1062, 1222, 1318, 4475–6, 4630, 4660, 6186, etc.

[48] *NHI*, II, 296.

[49] H. G. Richardson and G. O. Sayles, 'Irish Revenue, 1278–1384', *Proceedings of the Royal Irish Academy*, 62 (1962), C, 87–100; Frame, *English Lordship*, 240–1; *NHI*, II, 189, 366.

contemporaries recognized) had been exploited by Edward I for his wars in Wales, Scotland, and Gascony.[50] It was a sign of changed circumstances that the last request for provisions from Ireland was apparently made in 1323 and that Ireland made virtually no contribution to Edward III's forces in his French wars.[51] The balance of power and opportunities within the western orbit of the British Isles was changing fundamentally.

How, then, may one characterize the nature of power in the British Isles in 1343? England and the English remained, of course, the dominant seat of power; but dreams of a new Arthurian empire of the British Isles and of an eirenic unity among its peoples—dreams which had exercised excitable peoples and ambitious politicians in the later years of Edward I—were no more. With them largely disappeared notions of what has been called a 'British informal empire', built, in some measure, around 'a single political dynamic'.[52] The consequences were far-reaching, not only for England itself, but for future patterns of loyalty and identity within the British Isles as a whole. The failure to establish a 'British informal empire' under English tutelage would prompt future generations to think increasingly in terms of formal incorporation and union—in short, of the conversion of 'the united kingdom of England' in the fullness of time into 'the United Kingdom of Great Britain and Ireland'. In the meantime, however, it was necessary to come to terms—in substance and in vocabulary—with the fact that the *regnum Anglorum* and the *orbis Britanniae* were to remain distinct, even opposed, concepts. That was the world of the later Middle Ages—in the words of one historian, 'a time of disengagement and divergence instead of convergence'.[53]

Scotland remained, of course, the clearest reminder of the limits of English power and achievement. There is no reason to believe that the pretensions and ambitions of the English monarchy, aristocracy, and Church towards Scotland in the two centuries after 1093 were, for the most part, other than those of a benevolent, if occasionally overbearing, senior partner. On the contrary, relationships between the two societies had generally been easy-going and

[50] For a summary, *NHI*, II, 195–204 (and the literature cited there, including the remarkable letter of 1311 at pp. 201–2), and *Law and Disorder in Thirteenth-Century Ireland*, ed. J. Lydon, 11–13.

[51] M. D. O'Sullivan, *Italian Merchant Bankers in Ireland in the Thirteenth Century* (Dublin, 1962), 122; Frame, *English Lordship*, 153–6.

[52] Robin Frame, 'Aristocracies and the Political Configuration of the British Isles', in *The British Isles 1100–1500*, ed. Davies, 142–59 at pp. 151–2 (reprinted in idem, *Ireland and Britain*, ch. 9). See also R. R. Davies, 'In Praise of British History', in ibid., 9–26, and idem, 'The English State and the "Celtic" Peoples 1100–1400', *Journal of Historical Sociology* 6 (1993), 1–15.

[53] Alexander Grant, 'Scottish Foundations: Late Medieval Contributions', in *Uniting the Kingdom?*, ed. Grant and Stringer, 97–108 at p. 101.

constructive. The rich texture of bonds—political, social, cultural, economic, and religious—between the two kingdoms, especially at the higher levels of lay and ecclesiastical society, seemed to be paving the road for even further cooperation and exchange. When arrangements were made in 1290 for the marriage of the heir of England and the heiress of Scotland, the dynastic union so created clearly opened up the opportunities for an effective and organic yoking together of the two countries, however careful contemporaries might be to show respect for the separate identities of both. Yet all such prospects were irretrievably shattered in the decade 1296–1306; at the very best, they could be repaired only briefly and unconvincingly thereafter. Where there had once been creative cooperation, there was now a propaganda and mythology of mistrust and hate, a militarized border, and an apparently endless round of campaigns, raids, and recriminations. Ethnic and political identities hardened into uncompromising postures on either side. So it was that the Scots expelled canons from Dryburgh and Jedburgh in the early fourteenth century 'because they were English by birth';[54] so it was, revealingly, that a Scottish woman living in Penrith could be cleared of a charge of treachery (for warning her fellow Scots of an imminent attack by an English raiding party) because her premier loyalty lay to her native Scotland.[55] The national shutters had come down firmly; they were not to be lifted for centuries. So long as this was so, the prospect of a single Britain remained a pipe dream.

The prospect in Wales in this respect seemed altogether more promising. The country had been conquered and settled; the title 'prince of Wales' had been absorbed into English royal nomenclature, either for the king himself or for his heir apparent; and the territorial, military, financial, and ecclesiastical resources of the country had been firmly tied to the apron-strings of the English state and its ruling elites. Even the native Welsh themselves seemed increasingly to have come to terms with their predicament. Yet periodic alarms—as in 1315–16, 1327, and the late 1330s—indicated that a veneer of stability concealed deep-lying disaffection and resentment.[56] The Black Prince may have been created prince of Wales in 1343 and received individual and communal oaths of fealty from his Welsh subjects; but within two years he was being warned that 'the Welsh have never been so disposed . . . to rise against their liege lord and to conquer the land from

[54] *Calendar of Documents relating to Scotland*, III, no. 509. For early examples of the confiscation of the properties of Scots in Northumberland, ibid., II, nos. 736, 1131.

[55] Henry Summerson, 'Responses to War: Carlisle and the West March in the Late Fourteenth Century', in *War and Border Societies in the Middle Ages*, ed. A. Goodman and A. Tuck (1992), 155–77 at pp. 170–1. See also C. J. Neville, *Violence, Custom and Law: The Anglo-Scottish Border in the Later Middle Ages* (Edinburgh, 1998).

[56] See, briefly, Davies, *Conquest*, 387–8, 436–7.

him.'[57] Furthermore there was little attempt to integrate Wales politically, administratively, or judicially into the framework of the English state. Some moves in that direction—such as the tax levied on the whole country (Principality and March) in 1292, or the showdown with several leading Marcher lords in the 1290s, or the summoning of representatives from royal lands in Wales (but not from the Marcher lordships) to the English parliaments of 1322 and 1327—were not followed through.[58] Instead, Wales remained in a historical time-warp. Its Marcher lordships, old and new, survived as an anomalous memento of a past seignorial age, while the recently created royal counties of the north and west were treated as colonial annexes under the regional rule of an English higher officialdom.[59] So long as that was the case, neither Wales nor the Welsh could qualify for membership of the English body politic.

The position in Ireland was in some respects more favourable than that in Wales, in as much as the institutions and habits of English governance had been introduced, both centrally and locally, into great swathes of the country and had been underpinned by a very substantial and cohesive English settler population. To that extent, English Ireland was indeed, in Maitland's phrase, a little England beyond the sea. But in reality such an image was a dangerous illusion, and ever more so with the passage of decades. Contemporaries knew it: 'within the last forty years,' so they bewailed in 1317–19, 'the English [in Ireland] had lost three parts and more of what they had conquered and that before the advent of the Scots' (that is, the invasions of Edward Bruce, 1315–18).[60] It might have been a hysterical comment; but neither its chronology nor its broad substance could be challenged. From the 1270s the pendulum of power began to swing away from the English in Ireland: the greatly overextended zone of English lordship in areas such as Ulster or the south-west or the midlands gradually slipped out of effective English control.[61] In a fluid and highly localized world such as that of medieval Ireland, it is

[57] D. L. Evans, 'Some Notes on the Principality of Wales in the time of the Black Prince', *Transactions of the Cymmrodorion Society* (1925–6), 25–110; oaths of fealty: 'Original Documents', supplement volume to *Archaeologia Cambrensis*, 1877, cxlviii–clxxv; 1345 quotation: *Calendar of Ancient Correspondence concerning Wales*, 230.

[58] 1292 tax: *The Merioneth Lay Subsidy Roll 1292–3*, ed. K. Williams-Jones (Cardiff, 1976); showdown with Marcher lords: Davies, *Lordship and Society*, 257–69; Welsh representatives in parliament: Natalie Fryde, 'Councils and Consent in Medieval Wales c.1200–1327', *Album François Dumont* (Brussels, 1977), 43–60.

[59] See generally R. R. Davies, 'Colonial Wales', *Past and Present* 65 (1974), 3–23.

[60] *Documents on the Affairs of Ireland before the King's Council*, ed. G. O. Sayles, 99–101.

[61] This is a theme which has been much explored in Irish historiography, central and local. For recent general comments, see, *inter alia*, R. Frame in *Colony and Frontier in Medieval Ireland*, ed. T. B. Barry et al., 158–60; Cormac O Cleirigh and Katharine Simms in *Law and Disorder in Thirteenth-Century Ireland*, 30–1, 82.

not easy—nor was it for contemporaries—to grasp the general situation or to calibrate the level of violence and retreat; but the intensity of atrocities and the memory of those atrocities (such as the murder of the Macmurroughs in 1282 and the O'Connors in 1305), the launching of frequent military expeditions by the justiciar, the growing distinction between the 'land of peace' and the 'land of war', and the first official legislation (1297) on the issue of degeneracy all indicated that the English in Ireland were now very much on the defensive.[62]

Arguably even more worrying was the fact that in large parts, though by no means all, of what might still outwardly be classified as English Ireland, a society was emerging which was increasingly taking on the colour and conventions of its local habitat, and in the process becoming less recognizably English in its cultural and political norms and ever more so as more and more major English families either sold up their estates in Ireland or became absentees. Ties with England, socially and governmentally, were still important for the resident greater aristocracy—men such as the earls of Kildare, Ormond, and Desmond; but the regional power structures which they were now creating (and had no option but to create if they and their communities were to survive) and the conventions and habits by which they ruled in them approximated ever more closely to those of some of their Gaelic neighbours and proportionately distanced them from 'true' English practice. It was a feuding, militarized, tribute-gathering, faction-ridden society; the mismatch between the rhetoric and models of the Dublin government (often staffed by men brought in from England) and the realities of power in much of English Ireland was greater than ever. As this process accelerated it was inevitable that the English community in Ireland should—like so many other colonial communities—come to feel neglected, misunderstood, and unappreciated by the mother country which was now so France-oriented in its ambitions. It was out of such sentiments that the Anglo-Irish community increasingly forged its own identity and bolstered it with historical memories.[63]

Wherever one looks in the British Isles in the mid-fourteenth century, the theme seems to be one of disaggregation and dissolution rather than the unity which ideologues and dreamers had occasionally glimpsed in the mid- and late thirteenth century. That was true not only, self-evidently, of Scotland but even of those areas beyond England which were apparently to a greater or lesser degree within the orbit of English power. The language is one of separation,

[62] See esp. R. Frame, *Ireland and England*, chs. 11–15; Cormac O Cleirigh, Séan Duffy, and Brendan Smith in *Law and Disorder*.

[63] See, generally, the fundamental studies of Robin Frame, *English Lordship*, and idem, *Ireland and England*.

not of integration: in Wales, of Welshries and Englishries and all the tired paraphernalia of administrative and judicial ethnic distinctions; in Ireland, of faithful and not so faithful English, and of 'wild Irish, our enemies', of marches and lands of war and lands of peace, of English born in Ireland and English born in England, of 'a middle nation', and so forth. It is the language of categorization and even exclusion, not of easy relationships and integration. Likewise, the tissue of bonds which had apparently so effectively woven such large parts of the English-controlled and English-dominated districts of the British Isles together in the twelfth and thirteenth centuries often became frayed or snapped as the fourteenth century progressed. In particular, the aristocratic, tenurial, and ecclesiastical links which had, to a greater or lesser degree, bound England, southern and eastern Scotland, coastal south Wales, and much of English Ireland together in a world of common concerns, norms, and even cultural orbits became increasingly less secure. So it is that there is a detectable switch, as one Irish historian has put it, 'in the cultural gravity [of English Ireland] from the more international society of the thirteenth century to the more regional influences of an increasingly self-contained society in the fifteenth century'.[64]

As this happened, any prospect which might once have been periodically entertained of an integrated British Isles, or even indeed a well-knit English or Anglicized world within the British Isles, grew dimmer. The British Isles were to be a world of separate countries and separate peoples. Political structures and political aspirations determined that it should be so. Most obviously was that true of Scotland. By the later thirteenth century Scotland was a remarkably resilient and, on its own terms, politically cohesive kingdom, underpinned by a 'community of the realm' whose credentials were to be tried and honed by the rigours of a prolonged 'war of independence'. Neither Wales nor Ireland had ever enjoyed the 'regnal solidarity' that now characterized Scotland, as it had long since characterized England. By 1300 Wales had been thoroughly conquered by a combination of baronial enterprise and English royal power. As for Ireland, much of the country, and particularly its more fertile and economically prosperous districts, lay within the ambit of English rule. Yet neither in Wales nor in Ireland had native political mythology, aspiration, and dreams been eliminated; the prospect of deliverance from English power was a profound undercurrent within both societies. It was a reminder that countries are made in the hearts and minds of men and women as much as in the institutions of power. By that token the Welsh and the Irish remained

[64] C. A. Empey, 'County Kilkenny in the Anglo-Norman Period', in *Kilkenny: History and Society*, at p. 91.

peoples and Wales and Ireland remained countries. Neither conquest nor political annexation could of themselves change that situation.

Nor was it merely a matter of identities and mythologies, crucial as those are in creating and sustaining countries and peoples. Incompatibilities in political, cultural, social, and even economic norms between England and the Anglicized British Isles on the one part and the native societies of the northern and western parts of the British Isles on the other thwarted, or at least greatly impeded, the pace of progress towards political and social integration, or even towards an acceptable *modus vivendi*. Power—be it military, political, or economic power—cannot of itself necessarily command loyalty, least of all if it is not able to work with the grain of entrenched traditions and to win the respect of indigenous societies.

The medieval kingdoms of England and Scotland present an instructive contrast with each other in this respect. Both were expansionist and acquisitive kingdoms in the twelfth and thirteenth centuries; both were bringing their northern and western outer zones within the reach of their military and political power (by external conquest and settlement in the case of England, by internal integration in Scotland, at least in our sense of the word 'Scotland'); both did so from a platform of vastly superior economic wealth and development, whether in southern and midland England or in southern and eastern Scotland. But the character of this 'state-building' process had very different outcomes. In Scotland—not least because of the geographical character of the country, the profound cultural chasm in its society, and the limited reach of the political and institutional power of its royal government—there was a flexible and inclusive dimension to its progress towards political integration. What is more, all the peoples within the loose ambit of the authority of the kingdom were now, at least formally, ethnically one; they were Scots. The story of England's expansion was different. It did, it is true, effectively absorb what we know as the north of England beyond Ribble and Tees into its political and institutional structures and into its orbit of loyalties.[65] But English expansion into Wales and Ireland was a colonizing, 'external', and annexing process. It ensconced the English settler population in Wales and Ireland as distinct English communities; it did not absorb the native Welsh or Irish, especially their elites, into its own political and institutional structures; it accepted and indeed institutionalized a duality of peoples—English and Welsh, English and Irish—into its governance of, and assumptions about, those parts of the British Isles which were under English rule (more or less) but were not

[65] See, especially, Keith Stringer, 'Identities in Thirteenth-Century England: Frontier Society in the Far North', in *Social and Political Identities in Western History*, ed. C. Bjørn, A. Grant, and K. J. Stringer (Copenhagen, 194), 28–66.

of England. As English power ebbed and as English colonization came to an end, the tensions inherent in such a situation were more likely to become transparent. Successful power often appears to be its own justification; it is when the momentum of that power falters that some of its contradictions became evident. To say as much is not to indulge in judgements, historical or otherwise. It is to acknowledge that the lineage of 'the Welsh question' and more particularly 'the Irish question' in the history of the British Isles may need to be traced, in part, to England itself and to the way it engaged with Wales and Ireland, and with the Welsh and the Irish, in the twelfth and thirteenth centuries.

EPILOGUE
THE BRITISH ISLES AND THE IDENTITY OF ENGLAND

This book has been concerned to trace and analyse the advance of English power in the British Isles in the twelfth and thirteenth centuries, and also to investigate some of the constraints on this advance. The scale of the advance can be truly appreciated only by taking an overview of the British Isles as a whole and by acknowledging the multifaceted character of the advance. By 1300 or thereabouts English power was present in the furthest reaches of the British Isles, not only in terms of political annexation, military control, and the instruments of English governmental rule, but also in colonies of English settlers in town and country alike, complex economic and commercial networks, the universal circulation of English coinage, the ubiquitousness of English law and judicial mechanisms (be it through borrowing or external imposition), and the dominance of English cultural and even social norms. English power was, of course, in no way utter or complete; it was often imitative and indirect in its impact, even where it was successful. But we are more likely to underrate it, and to underrate what it had achieved across two critical centuries, than we are to overestimate it. When we recall, for example, that English castles of awesome power were built in the late thirteenth century in Ballymote (modern Co. Sligo) or at Harlech on the distant coast of the new-fangled shire of Merioneth in north-west Wales, or that English royal justices were holding their sessions at Ardfert and Tralee in County Kerry, or that Edward I's officials in Wales could be commanded to levy a debt contracted in Ireland, or that the king's council at Westminster was vetting petitions on the customs of Galloway or a theft in Carlow, or that English was the main language in Beaumaris (Co. Anglesey) or in the town of Kilkenny in Ireland, or in Aberdeen and Elgin in Scotland, we are catching a glimpse, however impressionistic it might be, of the scale and intensity of the domination of England and the English within the British Isles by 1300.[1] It was very different from the world of 1093.

[1] Ballymote and Harlech: *NHI*, II, 219–20; sessions in county Kerry: Orpen, *Ireland under the Normans*, IV, 249; instruction to officials in Wales re. Ireland: *Calendar of Justiciary Rolls of Ireland 1295–1303*, 314; petitions from Galloway and Carlow: *Memoranda de parliamento*, ed. F. W. Maitland, 171, 235.

The scale of the transformation can hardly be doubted. And yet the British Isles by the end of this process was apparently no nearer to being an effectively integrated unit in formal terms by 1300 than in 1100. Indeed, arguably it was now more securely a world of four countries and four peoples—though countries and peoples by no means exactly coincided—than it was at the beginning of the process.[2] This is not an issue which excites comment from historians, because they take the division of the British Isles into four countries (and four peoples) as a given. Yet countries and peoples are artefacts of time; there is no inevitability about them or about their survival. Indeed, the map of the countries and the peoples of the British Isles had been dramatically redrawn, several times, in the past. 'England' and 'the English' themselves were the recent creations of such a process. And in the very centuries covered by this book the country we know as Scotland, and the Scots as a people, were emerging from such a process. Why, then, did England, which in terms of military power, political cohesion, and economic development was so far ahead of other parts of the British Isles, not convert its undoubted, if incomplete and fitful, domination of much of these islands into a more sustained and integrative hegemony during the twelfth and thirteenth centuries? Why did the prospect that 'all the islanders' might be 'joined together' or 'united', as one contemporary author expressed it, remain no more than a poetic reverie?[3]

One might dismiss the question as one of those *questions mal posées* with which our historiographies are so abundantly littered. After all, any notion of a unitary or uniform authority over the British Isles can rarely, if ever, have figured on the agenda of a kingship and aristocracy whose ambitions and aspirations, culturally and socially as well as politically and militarily, were northern European rather than specifically British. Theirs was a world whose epicentres lay in midland and southern England and northern France; the outer parts of the British Isles intruded themselves on their consciousness and ambitions only very spasmodically. When the English political nation engaged with these outer zones of the British Isles it generally did so reactively and for short spells; for the majority of the political nation they were at best a diversion and an irritant, not a major preoccupation. Given that this was so, a series of well-behaved and amenable protectorates, satellites, and colonial annexes around the periphery of the English kingdom was, perhaps, the best that the English kings and their magnates wanted or could hope for.

Moreover, kings and magnates were shrewd judges of the possible and the profitable. Gerald of Wales, in the fashion of armchair critics in all

[2] Davies, 'The Peoples of Britain and Ireland. 1. Identities', *Transactions of the Royal Historical Society*, 6th ser., 4 (1994), 1–20, esp. pp. 16–19.

[3] Peter Langtoft, as quoted above, p. 43.

generations, might work out a blueprint for the complete conquest of Wales and Ireland; and the author of the fifteenth-century *Libelle of Englische Policye* might advocate that if the king of England directed to Ireland the resources that he was pouring into the French wars, he could complete the conquest of the country in one year.[4] But not only did such formulae simplify hopelessly the complexity and unpredictability of the situation, they also made highly questionable assumptions about the economic worthwhileness and sustainability of such an exercise and the priority to be given to it. Much of western Britain and Ireland offered poor economic returns in terms of what we may call, by way of shorthand, English-type exploitation.

This suggests that, in seeking to answer the question regarding the limits and character of English expansion in the British Isles, we ought to attend as much to the economic and social context in which it could, and did, operate as to the political stratagems and military power which informed it. English advance was ultimately sustainable in depth and over a long period only in conditions which were sufficiently attractive for intensive colonization and for the replication of conditions in which an English-type society and economy could flourish—be it by assimilating itself to an existing, and not hugely dissimilar, social and economic matrix (as in parts of Scotland) or by formally keeping itself to itself (as happened to a considerable degree in Wales and Ireland). Beyond this zone of compatible custom and conditions, assimilation was not, in the short or medium term, possible or contemplated. The incompatibilities of economic practice, social custom, and political norms were simply too great. The limits of English advance were thereby the limits of Englishness itself, as a social, economic, and cultural construct, and as a gamut of social experience and behaviour which was apparently broadly comparable with that of England itself.[5]

The same may be said to be broadly true with regard to what we may term English political mythology and loyalty. By 1300 or so the zone of ultimate English overlordship could be claimed, at least theoretically, to extend to the four corners of the British Isles. Yet the area of English political culture and mythology was very much smaller. It included much of English Ireland, where English-type institutions, including political institutions, had been deeply embedded, and where sentimental and practical ties with mainland England were still self-consciously cultivated. It also included the substantial English communities in Wales, especially south Wales; they might lack the formal

[4] Gerald of Wales, Description of Wales, II, chs. 8–9 (*Opera*, VI, 218–25); idem, *Expugnatio Hibernica*, 248–9; *The Libelle of Englyshe Polycye*, ed. G. Warner (Oxford, 1926), 34–40.

[5] See above, Chs. 4–5.

English institutional structures of English Ireland, but they were fiercely proud of their Englishness.

Yet once one has mentioned these two English communities beyond England one has in fact reached the outer limits of the zone of true English political loyalty and culture. Scotland was now self-evidently not part of that zone, however much Scottish institutions and habits may have aped those of England. When a formal association between England and Scotland was contemplated—as in the Treaty of Birgham (1290)—it was designed solely as a dynastic union, fully preserving the individuality of both countries. Even in 1305—when Scotland was kingless and apparently finally conquered—there was no talk of an integrative union with, or a political assimilation into, England. As for the native Welsh and Irish—and thereby in effect large parts of their respective countries—they lay fairly firmly outside the zone of English political culture and ideology. Occasional feelers might be put out to their political leaders; and opportunities for service, mainly military service, might be opened up to them. But for the most part they were regarded as culturally too backward and politically too immature to be admitted on a regular basis into the ambit of an England-centred political culture. Instead they cultivated their own political mythologies and aspirations and could deploy them on occasion to promote their sense of oppression, disinheritance, and exclusion. The British Isles in 1300 may have been a world dominated by the power of England and the English; but it remained a world of plural political mythologies and loyalties, a world of at least four peoples and four countries.

How then in these centuries of the momentous advance of English power in the British Isles did England and the English interpret and construct their relationship with the other peoples, societies, and countries of the British Isles? At ground level, in the myriad societies across the face of the British Isles where English colonists and native communities lived cheek by jowl with each other, the story was very considerably, and more so over time, one of mutual accommodation and acculturation. But that was not the whole story, nor in many respects the most important part of the story. The English had come in as colonists and, often, as conquerors. They constructed the world of their power and relationships in terms of the metaphors, categories, and classifications which they had brought with them. They did so because such a construction defined their status, power, and privilege. In short, it was a state of mind. It was, furthermore, a state of mind that was bolstered by reference, conscious or unconscious, to the norms of Englishness in England itself, be it by collective memory or by the language and assumptions of English governmental command. That is why, ultimately, any explanation of the format of relationship which England constructed, or did not construct, with the rest of the British Isles in these momentous centuries must look towards England itself. Indeed, the character of the medieval English state—to borrow, with whatever reservations, a term much in vogue currently among historians of medieval England—is best glimpsed, by refraction as it were, through the story of the advance of its power in the British Isles.

It is the precociousness and sophistication of this medieval English state which have been seen as amongst its most distinctive hallmarks. Paradoxically, this early definition of the character of the English polity may itself have impeded its capacity to accommodate other polities, societies, and cultures comfortably and inclusively into its orbit. The closely woven institutional structure of lowland England, the centrality of the king's court to the political process, and the symbiotic relationship of centre and locality were not easily reproduced in a different environment. Shires and writs, commissions of the peace and itinerant justices might be exported and transplanted; but they rarely took effective root other than in areas where there was an English settler population (as in parts of southern and eastern Ireland) or a social and political order which broadly corresponded to that of England (as in eastern and southern Scotland). Even where the transplant was apparently institutionally successful, it increasingly had to make compromises with its host societies. The inflexibility of the English institutional paradigm became more marked with the passage of time, as bureaucratic and judicial habits became more professional and centralist in their assumptions, and as the written formulae of the law and governance restricted the sphere of freedom of action to allow for local circumstances. The contrast between the Anglo-Norman penetration of Wales in the twelfth century and English rule in Ireland in the thirteenth century is instructive in this respect:[6] in the former a pluralist and accommodating approach allowed the development of the hybrid and eclectic institutions of the March; in the latter the law and governmental practice of England, and a very royal England at that, were considered the only acceptable norm.[7] One has only to consider the ordinances issued by Edward III for Ireland in 1336 (and parallel ones for North Wales in 1337–9) to recognize that the English administrative mind could entertain no real alternative to English governmental and legal practice. As Robin Frame has put it, 'Ireland ought,

[6] A. J. Otway-Ruthven, 'The Constitutional Position of the Great Lordships of South Wales', *Transactions of the Royal Historical Society*, 5th ser., 8 (1958), 1–20; R. R. Davies, 'The Law of the March', *Welsh History Review* 5 (1970–1), 1–30; idem, 'Kings, Lords and Liberties in the March of Wales 1066–1272', *Transactions of the Royal Historical Society*, 5th ser., 29 (1979), 41–61.

[7] For an example of this mentality, see *Calendar of Patent Rolls 1232–47*, 488: 'Inasmuch as for the common utility of the land of Ireland and the unity of the king's lands, the king wills . . . that all laws and customs which are kept in the realm of England be kept in Ireland . . . and that all the writs of common right which run in England shall likewise run in Ireland.'

in short, to be like England.' A multiple kingdom can scarcely be built on such foundations.[8]

Nor could it be built on the basis of an ethnically conceived polity. England was shaped in the later ninth and the tenth centuries as the country of the English, the *Angelcynn*.[9] Its king was titled simply king of the English, *rex Anglorum*. Those who designated themselves as English or allowed others so to designate them were the sole privileged members of his polity. Those who were not so designated could either be assimilated (as were the Danes in England by and large during the tenth and eleventh centuries) or be excluded. England, like most other countries, was defined in part by otherness. The difference in its case was that otherness was developed at a remarkably early age and was aligned with a particular legal, ethnic, institutional, and territorial formation. England had in effect closed its definition of itself at a remarkably early date. Even the grand imperial titles of its tenth-century kings made this evident: they drew a distinction between rule over the English and that over the other peoples within the *orbis Britanniae*. Thus Aethelred described himself as 'king of the English and governor of the other adjacent lands roundabout': the grand pan-British pretensions cannot conceal the primacy and apartness of the English in this formulation.[10] The advent of Scandinavian, Norman, and Angevin dynasties and their aristocracies did not, at least in the long run, override this sense of the essential Englishness of the polity and the country; on the contrary, they were absorbed into, or grafted upon, this ideology. Nowhere was this more clear than in the writings of the remarkable group of historians—William of Malmesbury, Henry of Huntingdon, and Geffrei Gaimar in particular—of the early twelfth century. What they celebrated uniformly was the history of the English, 'our people', and of 'our dear country' as they referred to it.[11]

The challenge to the reach and authority of this robust Englishness came during the centuries covered by this book, as the English came to colonize and dominate large parts of the British Isles beyond England. The response to this

[8] Ireland: *Affairs of Ireland before King's Council*, no. 192; for discussion, Frame, *English Lordship*, 232–5; Wales: *Calendar of Close Rolls 1339–41*, 249–54; W. H. Waters, *The Edwardian Settlement of North Wales* (Cardiff, 1935), 72–5, 81–4.

[9] See, most recently, Sarah Foot, 'The Making of *Angelcynn*: English Identity before the Norman Conquest', *Transactions of the Royal Historical Society*, 6th ser., 6 (1996), 25–49. A. P. Smyth, 'The Emergence of English Identity, 700–1000' and Timothy Reuter, 'The Making of England and Germany, 850–1050: Points of Comparison and Difference', in *Medieval Europeans. Studies in Ethnic Identity and National Perspectives in Medieval Europe*, ed. A. P. Smyth (1998), 24–71.

[10] *English Historical Documents, I, 500–c.1042*, ed. D. Whitelock (2nd edn., 1979), 569. See in general E. John, *Orbis Britanniae and Other Essays* (Leicester, 1966), esp. pp. 48–63.

[11] Rees Davies, *The Matter of Britain and the Matter of England* (Oxford, 1996).

challenge could very broadly take three forms. In those areas—lowland south Wales and parts of southern and eastern Ireland—where English colonization transformed the social fabric, the immigrant communities vociferously and consistently proclaimed their Englishness and apartness from native societies and polities: they were in effect English colonies beyond England, proud of what they sometimes called their exiled status. In lowland Scotland, on the other hand, they gradually, and sometimes rapidly, assimilated themselves and were assimilated into an existing society and polity with which they could identify and which indeed they did much to transform in their own image. Where neither of these two conditions prevailed—in other words, where the English colonization was limited in its impact and where there was no comparable pre-existing polity which could become an alternative focus of English-type loyalty (as in Scotland)—then English domination and ambitions over the non-English or non-Anglicized zones of the British Isles took the form of a loose annexation of native societies. There was no attempt at union or incorporation, nor much at integration beyond the special permission given to individual Welshmen and Irishmen to enjoy the status of honorary Englishmen, notably in respect of law and the tenure and inheritance of land.[12] These areas—the native districts of Wales and Ireland and their inhabitants—were (to borrow a Scotticism) outwith the English state and outwith Englishness. Such an attitude was not of itself discriminatory; rather it was an acceptance of the plurality of the peoples of these islands and thereby of the differences between them. It was, however, no basis on which to build a united kingdom.

Furthermore, it was a cast of mind in which the opportunities for inclusiveness, social or political, were extremely limited, and in which the chances that categorization might be transformed into discrimination were high. During the course of the thirteenth and fourteenth centuries, to some extent in Wales and to a far greater extent in Ireland, that is precisely what happened.[13] In both countries the ethnic divide between the English and the natives was institutionalized in law, administration, justice, and so forth: in the creation of Welshries and Englishries; in the designation (as in the see of Armagh) of areas as 'inter Anglicos' and other areas as 'inter Hibernicos'; in the distinction

[12] One of the earliest grants of the privilege to enjoy English law and liberty is recorded in Ireland in 1215: *CDI*, I, no. 659 (but see *Calendar of Justiciary Rolls, Ireland 1297–1303*, 271, for a reference to an even earlier grant by William Marshal). For the much later evidence from Wales, Davies, *Lordship and Society*, 449–56.

[13] Ethnic categorization could occasionally be overridden by evidence of political loyalty. In March 1253 two Irishmen were allowed to claim their lands as if they were English, 'notwithstanding that they are Irish' (*licet Hibernienses sint*), because they and their ancestors had supported the English against the Irish (*cum Anglicis contra Hibernienses*) since the conquest: *Close Rolls 1251–3*, 458–9.

between English, mere Irish, and wild Irish. When the Statute of 1297 assumed that 'the killing of Englishmen and Irishmen requires different modes of punishment'; or when a litigant argued that a Welshman could not essoin in a case against an Englishman; or when the chapter of St Patrick's, Dublin, confirmed the ancient custom that Irishmen 'by race (*natione*) or manners or blood' should be excluded from all appointments; or when the burgesses of Conway as late as Henry VIII's reign delivered themselves of the opinion that 'it is no more meet for a Welshman to bear any office in Wales . . . than it is for a Frenchman to be officer in Calais,' then we can see that the fact that Englishness was an ethnic construct brought with it a heavy price in terms of the relationships of peoples within the ambit of English power but outside the borders of the English state and the English colonies.[14] It was the pope who in 1256 took it upon himself to remind the English rulers in Ireland that 'nature has made the Irish and the English equal and they should both be treated by the same law.' But Englishness was too deeply rooted to surrender to such papal *obiter dicta*.[15] The neurotic legislation against degeneracy which starts in 1297 makes that abundantly clear: its purpose was to bolster the identity and purity of the English *gens* in Ireland and thereby, as it were, to fortify an outer barbican of Englishness. A common British identity could not be forged when the drawbridge of ethnic Englishness was being lifted into position.

Another reason why it proved difficult to create or even consider a single British identity lay in the social fabric of the early English polity itself and the assumptions it made. The format and institutions of the English kingdom were grounded in a particular social and economic formation and its relationship to patterns of power. The symbiosis of state and society (and indeed economy) was a critical one.[16] Indeed, one might go further: institutions, state formation, and the conscious policies of kings have been given a prominent

[14] 1297 statute: *Law and Disorder in Thirteenth-Century Ireland*; Welsh and English: *Calendar of Ancient Petitions relating to Wales*, no. 7249; PRO Court Rolls 216/14 m.6 ('Et mos patrie istius est quod anglicus non debet esse ad legem contra wallicum'); St Patrick's, Dublin: *Dignitas Decani*, ed. N. B. White, no. 53; burgesses of Conway: quoted in P. R. Roberts, 'The Welsh Language, English Law and Tudor Legislation', *Transactions of the Cymmrodorion Society* (1989), 19–75 at p. 21.

[15] *Affairs of Ireland before the King's Council*, 3. Cf. the plea on behalf of the Irish in 1277 'to be treated as the English are treated, alive and dead, in body and in real and personal property': A. J. Otway-Ruthven, 'The Request of the Irish for English Law, 1277–80', *Irish Historical Studies* 6 (1948–9), 261–70 at p. 267. As Robin Frame has pointed out (*Ireland and Britain 1170–1450*, p. 139), 'the proliferation of county courts [in Ireland] multiplied the points of exclusion at local level.'

[16] For suggestive comments on this issue, see James Given, *State and Society in Medieval Europe. Gwynedd and Languedoc under outside rule* (1990), and K. J. Stringer, 'Social and Political Communities in European History', in *Nations, Nationalism and Patriotism in the European Past*, ed. C. Bjørn et al. (Copenhagen, 1994), 9–34.

place in the historiography of England; but the social and economic matrix—the existence of a well-entrenched gentry class, the rapid circulation of money and goods, a configuration of power which allowed a close liaison between kingship and the locality, to name but three of the crucial factors—was arguably quite as important in the making, and determining the distinctive identity, of the English state.[17] Where that matrix was lacking, the limits of effective English-style rulership were reached—most obviously in those parts (increasing in size) of Ireland which lay beyond effective and detailed English control, to a lesser extent in areas such as north Wales, where the veneer of English-imported institutions barely concealed the continuing strength of native power structures and relationships.[18] This meant that the need for a growing measure of convergence between the outer parts of the British Isles and the English polity—in social customs and structure, economic attitudes and practices, laws, land tenure, civic notions, and, preferably, language—was a *sine qua non* if English institutions were to be effectively exported into native Wales and Ireland and if those areas were to be admitted eventually into a broader-based polity. It was the gradual adoption and promotion of such cultural and socio-economic customs which eventually encouraged Tudor legislators to incorporate Wales institutionally and politically into the English polity in Henry VIII's reign and even to hope that a similar 'Welsh policy' (as it has been called) might eventually work in Ireland.[19]

In the early fourteenth century, however, such aspirations lay very much in the future; in the meantime the English polity and English settlers beyond England found it difficult, indeed well nigh impossible, to come to a meaningful, sustained, and non-discriminatory relationship with the other peoples and parts of the British Isles. We may, finally, identify one other reason why this was so. Nation-states are ultimately mythological constructs: they are defined as much, if not more, by a common assumed identity, mythology, shared cultural values and attitudes, and state ethnicity (however manufactured) as by borders and institutions. So it was with the medieval English state.[20] It had already by the tenth century forged its identity, as the polity of

[17] Cf. the comments, in a different context, of G. L. Harris, 'Political Society and the Growth of Government in late Medieval England', *Past and Present*, no. 138 (1993), 28–57.

[18] For Ireland the work of Robin Frame is fundamental. See in particular his republished essays *Ireland and Britain 1170–1450*, esp. chs. 11 and 14. For Wales as a land of two worlds and two peoples, see Davies, *Revolt of Owain Glyn Dŵr* (Oxford, 1995), ch. 1.

[19] Ciarán Brady, 'Comparable Histories? Tudor Reform in Wales and Ireland', in *Conquest and Union. Fashioning a British state, 1485–1725*, ed. S. G. Ellis and S. Barber (1995), 64–86.

[20] See in general Patrick Wormald, 'Bede, the *Bretwaldas* and the Origins of the *gens Anglorum*', in *Ideal and Reality in Frankish and Anglo-Saxon Society*, ed. Wormald et al., 99–129; idem, '*Engla Lond*: The Making of an Allegiance', *Journal of Historical Sociology* 7 (1994), 1–24 (now republished in idem, *Legal Culture in the Early Medieval West: Law as Text, Image and Experience* (1999), ch. 14; Sarah Foot, 'The Making of *Angelcynn*' (as cited above, n. 11).

the *gens Anglorum*, the *Angelcynn*, and had bedecked itself with an ethnic and salvational pedigree, the one proclaimed in the centrality it gave to the *adventus Saxonum* in its construction of the past, the other in its cultivation of itself as the new Israel.[21] Its cultic unifying figure was quite simply the king of the English, *rex Anglorum*. Its law was likewise, and ever more so a specifically English law, *lex anglicana* and, as Patrick Wormald has said, 'an essential ingredient in the personality of the English state';[22] it was in terms of law that the distinctions between English, Scots, Irish, and Welsh were increasingly and sharply defined as the thirteenth and fourteenth centuries progressed.[23] Increasingly the English language—whether narrowly or widely used as a term—likewise became part of English identity; only those who spoke it were English—'as evreich Inglische, Inglische can', as a poet was later to put it.[24] Parts of this all-encompassing self-identity kit of Englishness had already been substantially assembled by 1093; two and a half centuries later it was even more elaborate and more firmly entrenched both in mind-set and institutions. It was the tool-box of English identity and had centuries of service ahead of it.

Such an early and well-defined identity, with its accompanying comforting mythology and its cultural border guards (to borrow the phrase of the anthropologists), precluded the necessity, or indeed the desirability, of making accommodations—whether political, institutional, cultural (in the broadest sense of that word) or mythological—with the non-English polities, cultures, and societies of the British Isles, other than reluctantly and on its own terms. In the case of Scotland, the one other polity in the British Isles with the critical mass and social and political cohesion which enabled it to challenge the imperial claims of the English state, the ultimate consequence was the Wars of Independence, and with it the full articulation of its own mythology which—in the Declaration of Arbroath (1320) and the writings of Fordun and Barbour, to name only the most prominent items—was not only a triumphant vindication of the almost aboriginal independence of Scotland but also, by implication, an outright challenge to English claims to the super-overlordship

[21] N. Howe, *Migration and Mythmaking in Anglo-Saxon England* (1989); R. W. Hanning, *The Vision of History in Early Britain: from Gildas to Geoffrey of Monmouth* (1966).

[22] P. Wormald, '*Quadripartitus*', in *Law and Government in Medieval England and Normandy: Essays in Honour of James Holt*, ed. G. Garnett and J. Hudson (Cambridge, 1994), 111–72 at p. 147 (now republished in idem, *Legal Culture* (as cited above, n. 20), ch. 4).

[23] See R. R. Davies, 'Law and National Identity in Thirteenth-Century Wales', in *Welsh Society and Nationhood. Historical Essays presented to Glanmor Williams*, ed. R. R. Davies et al. (Cardiff, 1984), 51–70; idem, 'The Peoples of Britain and Ireland 1100–1400. 3. Laws and Customs', *Transactions of the Royal Historical Society*, 6th ser., 6 (1996), 1–23.

[24] Quoted in T. Turville-Petre, 'Politics and Poetry in the Early Fourteenth Century: The Case of Robert Manning's Chronicle', *Review of English Studies*, new ser., 39 (1988), 1–28 at p. 27. See generally R. R. Davies, 'The Peoples of Britain and Ireland 1100–1400. 4. Language and Historical Mythology', *Transactions of the Royal Historical Society*, 6th ser., 7 (1997), 1–24.

of Britain.[25] In Wales and Ireland the response to the undoubtedly pre-eminent power of the English on the one hand and the closed interpretation of English self-identity on the other was varied. It included the often desperately expressed anxiety of the leaders of native society to be embraced within the social and political ambit of the king of England's court and patronage;[26] they enjoyed some success, but only of a very limited and occasional kind. They and their followers might serve in large numbers in English armies, but they rarely secured a sustained entrée into the higher echelons of English social and political life. Rather did they increasingly feel excluded, 'exiles in their own country', as one Welsh nobleman put it.[27] What is more, the sense of exclusion fed their own mythologies of identity and their own counter-mythologies of oppression and treachery.[28] Llywelyn ap Gruffudd's touching statement of December 1282, the Irish Remonstrance of *c.*1317, the Declaration of Arbroath, and the remarkable sheaf of 'pan-Celtic' correspondence elicited by the ambitions of Robert and Edward Bruce in the 1310s and the 1320s, are all of them eloquent testimonies to the individual identities and, in a small degree, to the shared sense of oppression of the non-English peoples of the British Isles.[29] But they are also a comment on the price that had to be paid in the British Isles for an English identity and power which had defined itself in such an exclusive fashion.

So we return to the paradox which has been at the heart of this book. The very early institutional maturity and self-definition of the English state and the tight weave of its power structures, ethnic self-profile, and historical mythology gave it a remarkable resilience and cohesion. It was much the earliest as it was the most enduring of European nation states.[30] By the same token it was disabled from reaching out effectively and constructively to the other peoples and power centres of the British Isles, except possibly on its

[25] See generally R. J. Goldstein, *The Matter of Scotland. Historical Narrative in Medieval Scotland* (1993), and the works cited above, Ch. 2, n. 48.

[26] For this theme see R. R. Davies, 'Lordship or Colony?', in *The English in Medieval Ireland*, ed. J. Lydon, 142–60.

[27] B. F. Roberts, 'Un o lawysgrifau Hopcyn ap Tomos o Ynys Dawy', *Bulletin of the Board of Celtic Studies* 22 (1966–8), 223–8. For Hopcyn, see briefly R. R. Davies, *The Revolt of Owain Glyn Dŵr*, 55.

[28] As the *Annals of Innisfallen* (ed. S. Mac Airt, Dublin, 1951, *s.a.*) remarked, in the wake of the massacre of the O'Connors by Piers de Bermingham at a banquet in 1305: 'And woe to the Guedel who puts trust in the king's peace or in foreigners after that.'

[29] Llywelyn ap Gruffudd's declaration: *Registrum Johannes Pecham*, II, 471; Irish Remonstrance: Walter Bower, *Scotichronicon*, ed. D. E. R. Watt, vol. 6, 384–403, 465–81; Declaration of Arbroath: A. A. M. Duncan, *The Nation of Scots and the Declaration of Arbroath*; the 'pan Celtic' correspondence: J. B. Smith, 'Gruffudd Llwyd' (as cited above, Ch. 7, n. 13).

[30] Cf. Adrian Hastings, *The Construction of Nationhood. Ethnicity, Religion and Nationalism* (Cambridge, 1997), esp. ch. 2.

own terms. What came to be regarded as a cardinal document of the English constitution and of English historical mythology, Magna Carta, illustrates the point. It was a document issued by a monarch who entitled himself, *inter alia*, lord of Ireland as well as king of England, and of whom it could be said that 'there is now no one in Ireland, Scotland and Wales who does not obey the command of the king of England.'[31] Yet it is essentially and exclusively, in its general intent, an *English* document. Its opening clause confirms the status of the English church (*ecclesia anglicana*), and the liberties which it concedes are granted 'to all the free men of our realm', that is, England, and later, in 1217, to the English community in Ireland. No further. And it was as an essentially English document that it entered into the consciousness of later generations. Magna Carta, said Sir Edward Coke, is such a fellow as he will have no master; that fellow was a quintessentially English fellow. William Stubbs's verdict was even more resonant: 'The Great Charter,' he declared, 'is the first public act of the nation, after it has realized its own identity. . . . The English nation had reached that point of conscious unity and identity which made it necessary for it to act as a self-governing and political body, a self-reliant and self-sustained nation.'[32] Such rotund declarations are no part of contemporary historiographical rhetoric; but the essence of Stubbs's case was, surely, correct. Magna Carta was, and came to be regarded as, an affirmation of the political identity of an essentially English body politic.

This thumping affirmation did good service for England, but it left unanswered the status of the rest of the British Isles and England's relationship to it. In particular, it left it unanswered at that very period when English power was advancing, in theoretical claim or practical effect, into all parts of the islands. One solution would have been for England to re-brand itself—as it was to do so in later centuries by acts of political union and by adopting for the composite amalgam so created the title of 'Great Britain' or 'the United Kingdom'. In fact it adopted a course of action which was the direct opposite and was breathtaking in its bravado. It announced that Britain had been replaced by England. This sweeping terminological take-over was heralded in the tenth century when Ealdorman Aethelweard declared that Britain 'is now called England, thereby assuming the name of the victor'. The equation soon became a commonplace assertion.[33]

So was solved, at least terminologically and in English eyes, the question of the relationship of England to Britain, even to the British isles. It was a solution which has done good service ever since. But, of course, it was a

[31] Quoted as above, Ch. 1, n. 39.
[32] W. Stubbs, *Constitutional History of England* (1884–8), I, 532, 637.
[33] See above, Ch. 2, p. 49 and nn. 56–9.

solution which was transparently specious, and it is in defence of the specious that arguments are often most revealing. So it was that Thomas Polton, future bishop of Hereford, blurted out at the Council of Constance in 1417 that it really was crass of educated men such as the French to claim that 'Wales, Ireland and even Scotland are not part of the English nation simply because they do not do what the king of England tells them to do.'[34] Thomas Polton's bout of irascibility had let the cat out of the bag. There clearly was a mismatch between terminology and reality, and between power and truth. The Irish annalist who commemorated Edward I as king of England, Scotland, Wales, and Ireland was nearer the mark. Edward I did not flaunt such titles: he was content to be king of England and lord of Ireland. But the annalist's composite title has a double appropriateness to it. It acknowledged the remarkable power that the English and their king exercised, theoretically and in many respects practically, over the whole of the British Isles. But equally it made clear that the English empire of the British Isles was an aggregation of countries (and, one might add, peoples). It was not a united kingdom, either in pretension or in reality. That was the legacy that the advance of English power in the British Isles in the twelfth and thirteenth centuries had left as a bequest for future generations.

[34] As cited above, Ch. 2, n. 71.

Index

E = England; I = Ireland; S = Scotland; W = Wales